Beyond the Ivory Tower

Derek Bok

BEYOND the IVORY TOWER

Social Responsibilities of the Modern University

Harvard University Press

Cambridge, Massachusetts, and London, England

Library of Congress Cataloging in Publication Data

Bok, Derek Curtis.
    Beyond the ivory tower.

    Includes index.
        1. Education, Higher—United States—Aims and
objectives. 2. Academic freedom—United States.
I. Title.
LB2331.72.B64   378'.01 '0973   81-20278
ISBN 0-674-06899-8 (cloth)   AACR2
ISBN 0-674-06898-X (paper)

FOR MY MOTHER

Contents

Acknowledgments

MANY FRIENDS and colleagues have read and criticized different portions of this book. Rather than single out the specific contributions made by each, let me simply express my appreciation for the help I have received from Harvey Brooks, Clarke Byse, Malcolm Gillis, Stanley Hoffmann, Robert Klitgaard, Helen Ladd, Herman Leonard, Robert Leone, Oliver Oldman, Edwin O. Reischauer, Michael Roemer, Walter Rosenblith, Henry Rosovsky, Daniel Steiner, Michael Walzer, Donald Warwick, and Jerome Wiesner. I am also grateful to Frank Packer, Jay Rosengard, and Scott Tonneslan, who helped me find material on the problems of academic science and technological innovation; to Susan Davis, who performed a similar service on the subject of technical assistance abroad; and especially to David Ogden, who assisted me with the research on several chapters. To Hilary Bok, Burton Dreben, Charles Fried, Gunnar and Alva Myrdal, and Lloyd Weinreb, I owe a particular debt for undertaking to read the entire manuscript.

I am likewise grateful to the publishers for permission to use material from earlier versions of Chapters 2 and 5: "The Federal Government and the University," *The Public Interest*, 58 (Winter 1980), copyright by National Affairs, Inc., and "Can Ethics Be Taught?" *Change*, October 1976. Both have been substantially revised for this book.

I have also benefited beyond all reasonable expectation from the loyal assistance of my office colleagues, Florence Gaylin, Elizabeth Keul, Margaret Murphy, Coye Richards, Janet Sullivan, and Elizabeth Woodward, who have given me extraordinary support. Above all, I am grateful to my wife, Sissela, who has read each chapter more than once and has given me greater help and intellectual stimulation than I could possibly describe in words.

Beyond the Ivory Tower

Introduction

"WHAT IS the justification of the modern American multiversity? History is one answer. Consistency with the surrounding society is another. Beyond that, it has few peers in the preservation and dissemination and examination of the eternal truths; no living peers in the search for new knowledge; and no peers in all history among institutions of higher learning in serving so many of the segments of an advancing civilization."[1] With these words, Clark Kerr, president of the University of California, proclaimed the triumphs of the contemporary university. To be sure, there were tensions, contradictions, even a confusion of purposes in these vast conglomerates of higher learning, and one could hardly accuse President Kerr of ignoring these difficulties. And yet, he left no doubt that the problems he described were those of a successful enterprise in the full flower of its development as a major force in modern society.

President Kerr delivered his remarks in 1963 to an enthusiastic Harvard audience. Before the decade was over, however, the smell of tear gas pervaded the Berkeley campus, and state police had clubbed protesting students on the lawns of Harvard Yard. At Stanford, Michigan, Cornell, Wisconsin, at almost every one of our major universities, students had occupied buildings, conducted mass meetings, and hurled their lists of strident demands at beleaguered presidents and deans.

The leaders of these protests were inclined to describe their

1. Clark Kerr, *The Uses of the University* (Cambridge, Mass.: Harvard University Press, 1963), pp. 44–45.

universities in terms less generous than those of President Kerr. To quote one statement of the period: "For years Columbia Trustees had evicted tenants from their homes, taken land through city deals, and fired workers for trying to form a union. For years they had trained officers for Vietnam who, as ROTC literature indicates, killed Vietnamese peasants in their own country. In secret work for the IDA [Institute for Defense Analysis] and the CIA, in chemical-biological war research for the Department of War, the Trustees implicated their own University in genocide. They had consistently, as the record shows, lied to their own constituents and published CIA books under the guise of independent scholarship. The military colossus, which the Universities themselves helped to build (in 1965 Columbia was getting $15,835,000 in Military Prime Contract awards), had become a clear and present danger to large sectors of our society . . . We lived in an institution that channeled us, marked us, ranked us, failed us, used us, and treated masses of humanity with class contempt."[2]

At one level, of course, we can brush aside such statements as so much inflated rhetoric penned by militant youths intoxicated with their unexpected notoriety. At a deeper level, however, these declamations raise more troubling questions. The authors did not dispute Kerr's claim that the modern university had many uses and offered many services to society. They directed their protests at the ends that universities chose to serve, at the impact of their programs on ordinary people, at their apparent complicity with public programs and national policies that seemed wantonly destructive and inhumane. What these students were questioning, in short, was nothing less than the moral basis of the university and the proper nature of its social responsibilities. It is those questions which I mean to address in the chapters that follow.

This topic would have been scarcely comprehensible a century ago. Before 1900, American universities were small institutions just beginning to assume their modern form. Their principal

2. Paul Rockwell, "The Columbia Statement" (Political Interpretation of the Columbia Strike, Written by Paul Rockwell and Adapted by the Columbia SDS on September 12, 1968), in Emmanuel Wallerstein and Paul Starr, eds., *The University Crisis Reader*, vol. 1 (New York: Random House, 1971), p. 24.

function was to provide a college education that emphasized mental discipline, religious piety, and strict rules governing student behavior. Thus conceived, they remained quiet enclaves, having little direct impact on the outside world and little traffic with the corporations, the banks, and the legislative bodies that were busy transforming America into a modern industrial state. Less than 5 percent of the nation's youth attended college. Neither a professional degree nor even a liberal arts diploma was considered essential to most careers; in fact, the proportion of lawyers and doctors who had attended college declined over much of the nineteenth century. Few universities enrolled more than a thousand students or employed as many as a hundred professors. There were no large endowments, no foundation grants, no federal funding for research. In Wisconsin, President Charles Van Hise would shortly dedicate himself to creating a public land-grant university that could act as an instrument of service throughout the state and a source of expert advice to its legislature. But his vision only foreshadowed changes yet to come and was not widely shared by other institutions.

Despite the placid appearance, however, great changes were actually taking place. Under the leadership of energetic presidents, the American university was evolving from a church-oriented college into a larger, more diverse institution with stronger graduate and professional programs capable of serving the needs of a developing economy. Its purposes were still in dispute. Some saw its mission in highly utilitarian, vocational terms. Others perceived the university as a place in which to pursue research and acquire knowledge for its own sake. Still others stressed the value of academic institutions as vehicles for promoting a liberal culture that might soften the rough edges of a society absorbed in commerce and industry. By 1910, however, these competing visions had somehow joined together in an uneasy coexistence, and universities were beginning to grow at a rapid pace both in size and in public esteem.

During this period of expansion, universities needed strong leaders—tireless men who could plan ambitiously and convince the public of its stake in higher education. But universities were also critically dependent on great benefactors with resources ample enough to construct new buildings or even found entire institutions. In the last decades of the nineteenth century, Ezra Cornell, John D. Rockefeller, Leland Stanford, and other industrialists supplied the capital needed to promote expansion and allow the transformation from college to university to go forward.

In keeping with their important role, businessmen and financiers quickly replaced the clergy as dominant figures on the boards of leading universities. As major contributors, they believed that they should have something to say about the operation of the institution and some control over the kinds of social opinions and philosophies expressed by members of the faculty. Before long, these worldly men began to take exception to the writings and speeches of professors who held controversial views on political and economic issues. Some objected to writings in behalf of antitrust laws; others took offense at speeches and articles advocating strikes and boycotts. In a number of cases, professors who spoke freely on such issues were not only criticized but summarily dismissed.

To powerful trustees, there was nothing odd or questionable about a decision to sack a controversial professor. As George Wharton Pepper observed in 1915 to explain why he did not need to justify firing the radical Scott Nearing from the University of Pennsylvania faculty: "If I am dissatisfied with my secretary, I would suppose that I would be within my rights in terminating his employment."[3]

Although many professors were prepared to accept such interference, others were deeply resentful. Influenced by the example of German universities, the more cosmopolitan faculty members loudly deplored the practice of removing scholars for political reasons. In several instances, ad hoc committees were appointed to investigate such dismissals and published reports attacking the decisions. At Stanford, seven professors actually resigned in 1901 to protest the firing of the economist Edward Ross, who had angered Mrs. Stanford by his speeches on the subject of Chinese immigration. Eventually, under the leadership of John Dewey, E. R. Seligman, and Arthur Lovejoy, faculty members from several in-

3. Walter P. Metzger, "Institutional Neutrality: An Appraisal," in *Neutrality or Partisanship: A Dilemma of Academic Institutions*, Carnegie Bulletin 34 (New York: The Carnegie Foundation for the Advancement of Teaching, 1971), p. 40.

stitutions met in New York to found the American Association of University Professors (AAUP) and to consider how scholars might be suitably protected in their efforts to teach and write. From this initial meeting emerged the celebrated Declaration of 1915, which announced the principal tenets of academic freedom: the right of professors to speak their minds freely as teachers and scholars; the guarantee of tenure, with its protection from dismissal except for incompetence or moral dereliction; and the right of faculty members to have a hearing before being disciplined.

The professors who drafted the Declaration of 1915 regarded the university as a nonpartisan forum detached from the struggles and disputes of the outside world. In their view, while individual professors could express their opinions freely on controversial subjects, academic institutions should observe a strict neutrality toward all political, economic, and social issues. This principle can only be understood against the backdrop of events that gave rise to the AAUP itself. For Arthur Lovejoy and his colleagues, the overriding threat to academic freedom came from conservative trustees and compliant university presidents. Thus the principle of neutrality was conceived as a necessary bulwark to prevent the university administration from establishing official orthodoxies that it might use, directly or indirectly, to inhibit professors from expressing unsettling ideas and unpopular opinions.

In the decades that followed, the idea of academic freedom steadily expanded in scope. In addition to protecting individual professors, the concept gradually came to include a recognition of institutional autonomy in matters of educational policy. Specifically, universities insisted with ever greater success that curricula, admissions policies, and academic standards should be established by the faculty, rather than by outside groups, and should be fashioned for the sole purpose of carrying out the educational aims of the institution.

The notion of neutrality likewise evolved and came to mean something more than simply a shield against intolerant governing boards. As trustees were more understanding of universities and less inclined to impose their views upon the faculty, the need for such protection diminished, and neutrality grew in scope to imply a form of social contract with society at large. Universities insisted on the greatest possible freedom from outside interference with their teaching, research, and educational policies. But neither professors nor administrators could expect to receive such protection unless they were willing to have the university refrain from taking official stands or exerting collective pressure in behalf of its own political objectives. Trustees, alumni, and other outside groups were prepared to tolerate a controversial professor so long as he spoke only for himself. But one could hardly expect the custodians of power to exercise such restraint, let alone continue to provide financial support, if the university itself abandoned its official neutrality and began to press for specific social and ideological goals.

In theory, then, the principles of academic freedom, autonomy, and neutrality seemed simple and adequate to the times. For the small and rather detached universities that predominated in this country up to World War II, these concepts offered a workable rationale to protect faculty members from the meddlings of a distant and conservative world. After the war, however, the role of universities changed radically. The student population grew to more than ten million as half of all high school graduates sought some form of higher education. Vast building programs were undertaken to accommodate these swelling enrollments. Federal budgets for campus-based research also expanded steadily, exceeding $3 billion per year by 1965. As institutions of every kind felt the need for expert knowledge, faculty members became increasingly prominent as advisers to governments, corporations, and great foundations. Whether Republicans or Democrats were in power, professors managed to find their way into Cabinet posts and other important positions. In short, with their huge enrollments, their large faculties and staffs, and their extensive portfolios of corporate stock, universities had become major institutions in America, reflecting the centrality of knowledge and advanced training to the life and progress of a modern industrialized society.

As universities grew in size and influence, their financial needs rose correspondingly, and the search for funds became increasingly vigorous and comprehensive. No longer could educators look only to major industrialists for support. After World War II, even public universities established offices and staffs for the purpose of soliciting foundations, corporations, and the rank and file of their alumni. More important still, public and private institutions alike began to devote more and more time to preparing proposals for grants from the federal government to support research, new facilities, and student aid. In these ways, as society came to rely more and more on universities, universities in turn grew ever more dependent on society for the money required to support their expanding activities.

After World War II, therefore, the image of the ivory tower grew obsolete. Instead, a vast and intricate network of relationships arose linking universities to other major institutions in the society. Under these conditions, the meaning of the traditional academic safeguards began to seem increasingly obscure. In a world transformed by technological innovations, should academic freedom extend to university laboratories that could produce discoveries of awesome power and destructive force? Could universities continue to claim autonomy in setting admissions standards when they controlled access to almost all the major professions in the society? In a country where universities held large accumulations of corporate stock in their portfolios, could they expect to remain "neutral" in disputes over the conduct of American companies?

In the early postwar years of ebullience and growth, these tensions attracted little notice. Academic leaders, faculty members, and public officials were all too preoccupied with the task of developing the nation's research effort and expanding university facilities to absorb a growing tide of prospective students. Commencing in the mid-1960s, however, two movements arose that exposed the latent contradictions with sudden clarity.

The first of these pressures emerged from the federal government's determination to be more aggressive in pursuing a growing list of social goals. In rapid succession, the Congress and the White House took a number of steps to achieve equality among the races, not only by removing overt barriers of discrimination but by encouraging affirmative efforts to improve the educational and employment opportunities of blacks, Hispanics, and other disadvantaged minority groups. These efforts were followed by measures to overcome discrimination against women, to protect the environment, to extend health-care services to the aged and indigent, to improve safety in the workplace, and to alleviate poverty. This ambitious program of reform produced an avalanche of new laws and regulations extending to all major segments and institutions in the society.

In earlier generations, universities and other nonprofit organizations were left largely exempt from social legislation, even from such basic measures as minimum-wage laws, unemployment insurance, and workmen's compensation. Such exemptions seemed tolerable, though somewhat difficult to justify, as long as these institutions were small and self-sufficient. But continued exemption grew less and less tenable after universities began to employ millions of people and to receive huge grants from the government. Once these changes became apparent, Congress soon applied its protective laws and regulations not only to companies but to institutions of higher learning as well.

To the extent that these laws merely involved basic provisions of employment security, such as old-age pensions and workmen's compensation, they were financially burdensome but did not limit the autonomy of the university over basic matters of educational policy. But many of the newer regulations struck much closer to the core of the academic process. Affirmative-action programs affected the procedures and even threatened the criteria employed in selecting faculty. Laws outlawing racial discrimination soon governed the admissions standards used by colleges and professional schools. Regulations to protect human safety began to impinge on various methods of research employed in biological and medical laboratories. Efforts to extend access to health care caused the government to press medical schools to alter their curriculum and training programs in order to prepare larger numbers of primary-care physicians. In short, by 1975, the federal government was beginning to move on many fronts to regulate academic policies in ways that would bring them into closer conformity with national needs.

During the same period, a second form of pressure emerged from an entirely different quarter. As the struggle for civil rights gathered strength in the South, students began to express more concern for social injustice and to work much harder for social reform. In summers, on weekends, during vacations, they moved into cities and traveled to the South, picketing segregated lunchrooms, organizing boycotts against discriminatory employers, helping blacks register to vote and enroll in white suburban schools. As time went on, the civil rights struggle encouraged other neglected groups to express demands of their own—and once again, college students were heavily involved. Consumer problems, environmental concerns, the rights of women and homosexuals—all these and many more became prominent social issues carrying with them their own complement of demonstrations, rallies, encounter groups, publicity, and active political organizations. Overshadowing these many efforts was the massive protest against the Vietnam War. This bitter campaign served as nothing else to mold and clarify the central elements of the new student consciousness—a heightened sensitivity to injustice and human suffering, a distrust of government, and a growing tendency to supplement the political process by grass-roots organizing and ad hoc methods for changing public opinion and mobilizing pressure for change.

In this era of protest, the traditional neutrality of universities was bound to be called into question. Few social problems existed in the society that did not have some link to the faculties, the employment practices, the portfolios, or the admissions policies of the huge, sprawling multiversities. To students, eager to do their part to reform society, what was more natural than to seek out such connections and use them to harness the power and prestige of these great institutions of learning in the struggle against injustice?

As student concerns began to multiply, the number of demands on universities grew. In 1969, Harvard was asked to issue statements condemning the war in Vietnam; to abolish the Reserve Officers Training Corps (ROTC); to stop displacing tenants to make room for institutional expansion; to bar campus visits by military recruiters. Ten years later, the violence had diminished but the social concerns still persisted. One group of students was demanding that the administration cancel a contract with the government of Iran to plan a new institute of science; a second had called for boycotts against companies trading in nonunion lettuce or distributing unsafe products to the Third World; still other organizations urged the divestiture of all stocks in American corporations doing business in South Africa, while several groups demanded that the university cancel an agreement to name a library after a deceased businessman who had made much of his fortune in South African mining operations.

As these issues erupted on campuses across the nation, university leaders had to react in an atmosphere of turbulence and crisis. The results were predictably uneven. In response to the urban strife of the late 1960s, campus administrators produced, almost overnight, a wide variety of research institutes, employee-training programs, consulting activities, and student-service efforts. Conceived in haste, many of these ventures failed to survive and only a few fully achieved their intended purpose. Similarly, faced with student demands to sell their South African holdings, some universities agreed completely, others arrived at complex plans for partial divestiture, most concluded that divestiture should be only a last resort, and a handful refused even to consider the matter. Since few institutions had reviewed such issues with care before events forced them to reach a decision, their answers were seldom well considered. As a result, critics understandably questioned the depth of their concern for the underlying problems. To many onlookers, the positions universities took seemed to depend less on reasoned principle than on the tenacity with which the institution defended its interests or the skill which government bureaucrats and campus activists displayed in exerting pressure on harried presidents and trustees.

In recent years, educators have devoted more care to these issues, and wisely so. For their own self-interest, they need to prepare principled replies to the demands made upon them lest they be hurried into expedient positions or overwhelmed by pressures they do not adequately comprehend. Moreover, academic institutions have special reasons for thinking about their social obligations that go beyond those of other organizations. Universities are concerned with education, and their response to social issues will affect the education of their students just as surely as the lectures and the readings that go on in their libraries and classrooms. If we would teach our students to care about important social problems and think about them rigorously, then clearly our institutions of learning must set a high example in the conduct of their own affairs. In addition to responding to its students, a university must examine its social responsibilities if it wishes to acquire an adequate understanding of its proper role and purpose in present-day society. Like churches, universities experience the constant tensions that result from embracing transcendent goals and ideals while having to exist and be of service in a practical, imperfect world. It is simple enough to reconcile these tensions in an organization that remains in relative isolation from society. But the task grows infinitely harder when the university becomes deeply enmeshed in the affairs of the outside world. Such involvements lead to serious conflicts over the proper policies to pursue. In part, these differences result from the problems that are bound to arise in trying to reconcile the public's urgent, practical demands with the long-term interests of an academic institution. In part, disagreements occur because of differing visions of the good society to which we would like our universities to contribute. Whatever the cause, the issues go to the core of our hopes and aspirations for our universities and help us all to understand what we would like them to be and to achieve.

These concerns are largely responsible for my decision to write this book. I have divided the discussion into three sections. In Part I, I discuss the three basic academic principles that set limits on how far universities can go in responding collectively to society's needs. The first principle involves the concept of academic freedom and the limits it places on the power of universities to interfere with the freedom of scholars to think and write as they choose. The second concerns the university's autonomy over academic affairs and the restrictions on its own independence that result from the growing demands of the state. The third has to do with institutional neutrality and the need to find some form of social responsibility that will avoid unwise political adventures as well as excessive obligations and distractions that could imperil the quality of teaching and research.

In Part II, I look in greater detail at the concepts of academic freedom, autonomy, and neutrality by considering how they affect the university's efforts to use its intellectual resources to address certain problems in the outside world. The problems I have chosen include racial inequality, the risks of scientific research, the need for technological innovation, the decline of ethical standards, and the desire for economic development in the Third World. Of course, the university is concerned with many other important issues, such as war and peace, the preservation of the environment, the delivery of health care, and the status of women. But the problems I have discussed are representative and capture the university in all its important academic roles—selecting students, hiring faculty, shaping the curriculum, performing research, and supplying technical advice.

To conclude the study, I examine proposals in Part III that would have the university attack various social injustices through channels other than its academic programs, such as voting on stockholder resolutions, boycotting suppliers, and taking formal institutional stands on controversial public issues. The review of these methods will complete a rather extensive inventory of the ways by which the modern university can respond to society's needs. Along the way, I hope not only to explore a number of difficult moral issues but also to convey some sense of how a modern university works and what its strengths and limitations are in carrying out its various functions in a difficult and demanding environment. Much of what I write has application to all institutions of higher learning. But I should make clear at the outset that my chief concern is with the major research university rather than the denominational, community, or small liberal arts college. In choosing this emphasis, I do not mean to suggest that research universities are more important than other types of educational institutions. They are simply the institutions I happen to know best.

My subject is a prickly one, embracing topics that have produced much conflict and bitterness over the years. Different groups on the campus have played a prominent part in these debates and have consistently expressed sharply divergent views. Without understanding something of these factions—their perspectives, their various roles within the university, their peculiar biases—one cannot fully comprehend the nature of the discussion or evaluate the positions taken on different sides.

The first of those groups is composed of students and professors who are particularly sensitive to social issues and care deeply about injustices in the world. These "activists" have played a critical role in calling attention to ethical questions affecting the university and insisting that the issues be carefully considered. Without their efforts, important moral problems would have been conveniently overlooked on many campuses. At the same time, activists usually have no responsibility for administering the university and will rarely suffer the consequences of the decisions they recommend. As a result, they have little reason to take account of the financial problems and administrative burdens their proposals might produce. Nor need they worry much about the difficulties of trying to translate their wishes into workable rules that can be applied consistently and explained to others concerned with the institution. For these reasons, those who raise issues of social responsibility are not much given to compromise nor are they particularly sensitive to the practical problems that often arise from their demands.

Although many members of the university pay little attention to such campus controversies, some of the more conservative faculty periodically become involved. When they do, they tend to express a rather traditional point of view. They are frequently irritated by their activist colleagues and grumble that arguments over the Vietnam War or South African investments are peripheral matters that should not be allowed to occupy the time of professors and administrators. At times, they appear to show scant regard for the sufferings and injustices of the outside world. One may even suspect them of harboring an excessive preoccupation with their private scholarly pursuits and a nostalgic concern for preserving a way of life to which they have grown attached. Still, it is often the traditionalists who stand up most strongly for academic freedom and for the essential intellectual standards of the institution. If the activists are the social critics of the university, the traditionalists are its academic conscience, always ready to dissent and to embarrass the administration whenever it seeks to compromise important academic principles in order to pacify students and settle an unpleasant dispute.

Administrators, be they presidents or deans, have duties and concerns that also affect their attitudes toward controversial issues. The nature of their responsibilities forces them to mediate among opposing points of view and to search for policies that they can justify in public and apply to future cases without intolerable difficulty. These pressures often lead them to conclusions that offend individuals who take strong positions on either side of the controversy involved. Administrators are likewise keenly influenced by the constant problem of trying to maintain their institutions in a time of severe financial pressure. Students may overlook the subsidies needed to support their scholarships, their libraries, and their gymnasia. Even faculty members sometimes forget all that is required to provide their salaries, their laboratories, their books and periodicals. But presidents and deans are constantly reminded that the real income of professors declined by more than 15 percent in the 1970s, that parents are troubled by rapidly rising tuitions, and that talented people in the university are continually being denied opportunities to do creative work because of lack of funds. These daily realities cause administrators acute concern for the future of their institutions and for the welfare of their students and faculty. But we should also remember that those same anxieties may make them less sensitive than they should be to ethical considerations that might require them to reject a large gift, or offend a powerful alumnus, or take a position that could attract unfavorable publicity.

Despite their differences, each of the groups contributes in important ways to the debate over the social responsibilities of the university. If any of the three were missing from the drama, something essential would be lost. Yet each carries its own peculiar biases, which obstruct clear vision and make it difficult to reach solutions that are satisfying to all. Having served for several years as a dean and for more than a decade as a university president, I cannot pretend to have escaped this fate. But no one in the university would be likely to take the trouble to write about these issues unless he were identified in some fashion with one of the competing points of view. Thus I can only do my best to guard against the biases of my position and make certain that my readers are all properly forewarned.

Part I

Basic Academic Values

1

Academic Freedom

IN THE SPRING OF 1977, Columbia University announced that it would offer Henry Kissinger a special chair in international relations amply endowed with funds for staff support and research. In the weeks that followed, many students and professors vigorously protested the appointment, citing Dr. Kissinger's involvement in the bombing of Hanoi, the invasion of Cambodia, and the prolongation of the Vietnam War. Eventually, the controversy died when Kissinger declared that he was not prepared to accept Columbia's offer. But the episode left a number of issues unresolved. Dr. Kissinger's attackers insisted that they were not violating his academic freedom by objecting to actions that he took as Secretary of State. And yet, was Columbia at liberty to reject Dr. Kissinger's appointment on the basis of policies he had earlier espoused, simply because he advocated them not as a scholar, but as a public servant? Should the administration have agreed to pass a moral judgment on those policies on the ground that they were no mere opinions but views translated into decisions causing death and destruction to thousands of people? In considering a faculty appointment, should the university evaluate a candidate's behavior in public office if the actions involved matters, such as the bombing of Hanoi, that bore no clear relation to his field of scholarly competence?

These questions remind us that disputes over academic freedom have not disappeared. In fact, they have grown more complicated in an age when faculty members have become involved with important controversies in the "real world." Such problems deserve thoughtful consideration, since they bear directly on the way a university functions and the values that underlie its intellectual activities.

The Case for Academic Freedom

Freedom of expression, in all its forms, can be justified on two fundamental grounds. For the individual, the right to speak and write as one chooses is a form of liberty that contributes in important ways to a rich and stimulating life. To be deprived of such liberty is to lose the chance to participate fully in an intellectual exchange that helps to develop one's values, to make one's meaning of the world, to exercise those qualities of mind and imagination that are most distinctively human. Beyond its significance to the individual, freedom of speech has traditionally been regarded in this country as important to the welfare of society. Throughout history, much progress has occurred through growth in our understanding of ourselves, our institutions, and the environment in which we live. But experience teaches us that major discoveries and advances in knowledge are often highly unsettling and distasteful to the existing order. Only rarely do individuals have the intelligence and imagination to conceive such ideas and the courage to express them openly. If we wish to stimulate progress, we cannot afford to inhibit such persons by imposing orthodoxies, censorship, and other artificial barriers to creative thought.

These reasons provide the intellectual foundation for the guarantees set forth in the First Amendment of our Constitution. Even so, we must acknowledge that our commitment to free speech is more a matter of faith than a product of logic or empirical demonstration. It is always possible that the exercise of this liberty will produce mistakes and misperceptions that will mislead the public and actually result in harmful policies. In contrast to many other countries, however, ours has elected to guard against these dangers not by censorship, but by encouraging open discussion in which ideas can be subjected to criticism and errors can be corrected through continuing argument and debate.

Universities should be unreserved in supporting these principles, since freedom of expression is critical to their central mission. This point deserves a word of elaboration, for now that universities have become more involved in the society and more important to its development, they have acquired different constituencies that view their purpose in somewhat different ways. To parents and students, universities are chiefly places where young people can obtain an education and spend several pleasant, intellectually stimulating years. To the learned callings, universities are the locus of leading professional schools that select able students and train them to serve as competent practitioners. To the government, universities are vehicles to help achieve social goals, such as equal opportunity for minorities, as well as important sources of sophisticated knowledge needed for defense, foreign policy, medicine, and technological development. To corporate and foundation executives, along with public officials, universities are also valuable repositories of expertise from which to gain advice in addressing complicated questions.

Though all of these perceptions are accurate, we could probably obtain most of the services mentioned without having to create a university. For example, independent colleges could provide an excellent undergraduate education, as many of them do already. Separate institutions could be formed to offer professional training adequate to meet our practical needs. And consulting organizations could supply the specialized advice and analysis that public agencies and other institutions so often seek.

While the various functions of the university could be reorganized and redistributed in this fashion, something important would be lost. Neither colleges, nor consulting organizations, nor professional training schools can satisfy society's need for new knowledge and discovery. True, one could look to some sort of research institute to perform this function. But even this alternative would not wholly replace what universities can supply. It is the special function of the university to combine education with research, and knowledgeable observers believe that this combination has distinct advantages both for teaching and for science and scholarship. Experience suggests that graduate students learn best from working directly with able and established professors actively engaged in their own research, while the latter benefit in turn from the stimulation they derive from inquiring young associates. Without the marriage of teaching and research that universities uniquely provide, the conduct of scholarly inquiry and scientific investigation, as well as the progress of graduate training, would be unlikely to continue at the level of quality achieved over the past two generations. In a society heavily dependent on advanced education and highly specialized knowledge, such a decline could be seriously detrimental to the public welfare.

If this unique combination of education and discovery is the chief contribution of the university, how can its progress be secured? Apart from the libraries, laboratories, and other facilities important to research, two ingredients are especially important. The first of these is the ability to recruit the ablest and most creative people that can be attracted into academic life. The second critical element is an environment of freedom in which professors can do their work without constraints or external direction. Highly intelligent, imaginative people tend to resist orders from above and do not do their best work under such conditions. Even less desirable than centralized direction is the imposition of restraints on the kinds of ideas and hypotheses that scholars can publicly entertain, for such restrictions stifle the spirit of venturesome inquiry while blocking off entire fields of investigation that seem threatening to those who have strong interests in maintaining the status quo.

For these reasons, academic freedom is not merely a reflection of society's commitment to free speech; it is a safeguard essential to the aims of the university and to the welfare of those who work within it. Teachers and scholars have a vital stake in continuing to enjoy the liberty to speak and write as they choose, because their lives are entirely devoted to developing and expounding ideas. Universities in turn have a critical interest in preserving free expression, for without that freedom they will be hampered in appointing the most creative scientists and scholars and will suffer from forms of censorship that will jeopardize the search for knowledge and new discovery that represents their most distinctive contribution.

Opposition to Academic Freedom

Despite the force of these arguments, attacks upon academic freedom have continued over the years since the doctrine was proclaimed in 1915. For several decades, the assaults came chiefly from conservative groups disturbed by theories and ideas that seemed to undermine prevailing orthodoxies. More recently, however, the greatest challenges to free expression on the campus have come from students and faculty on the Left who have launched vigorous attacks on professors involved in the Vietnam War or in disputes over matters affecting race. For example, at least one academic association has condemned scholars for conducting research of a "racist" nature.[1] Moreover, in a survey published in 1976, 11 percent of the professors who responded agreed that "academic research on the genetic bases of differences in intelligence should not be permitted, because it serves to sustain a fundamentally racist perspective," and 18 percent supported the proposition that such research "should be discouraged because it can easily serve to reinforce racial prejudices."[2]

Regardless of their political coloration, all attacks on academic freedom rest upon a single rationale. To opponents of free expression, ideas are powerful; they frequently affect public policy and are used to justify important decisions. As a result, misguided theories and specious arguments can cause considerable harm. Granted, one can always try to counter such views with opposing arguments. Yet only in science can errors be disproved decisively, and even there fallacious theories may linger for decades before they are finally put to rest. In matters of social policy, shoddy ideas and dubious theories can persist indefinitely and be exploited by powerful people to justify inhumane and exploitative policies. Hence, those who advocate censorship will acknowledge the value of free speech but argue that there are times when particular theories and opinions threaten to produce such grievous harm that they must be suppressed.

In presenting this view, opponents of academic freedom overlook two glaring weaknesses in their position. In the first place, history reveals that those who try to stamp out heresy often make egregious mistakes. Since the time of Socrates, intellectuals have been penalized under circumstances that seem embarrassing in retrospect. Professors have been dismissed or denied appoint-

---

1. American Anthropological Association, Annual Report, 1972, p. 59.
2. Everett Carl Ladd, Jr., and Seymour Martin Lipset, "Should Any Research Topics Be Off-Limits?" *Chronicle of Higher Education*, 22 (March 15, 1976), 11.

ments for upholding the right to strike, for advocating racial integration, for refusing to testify before the House Un-American Activities Committee, for supporting the recognition of Communist China. As noted a figure as Bertrand Russell was barred from teaching at the City College of New York for propounding "immoral and salacious doctrines" that seemed to condone extramarital sex. Groups that seek to impose their orthodoxies today will presumably concede these errors, but will insist that their own opinions rest on firmer ground. Yet those who attacked professors in the past must also have believed in the rightness of their cause. Insofar as we can tell, their actions stemmed from a sincere belief that it would be harmful to students and to the public at large to employ teachers who expressed ideas and supported policies that seemed at the time to be dangerously misguided. Despite these good intentions, the results were often sadly mistaken, and we should be honest enough to acknowledge that similar errors will occur if we begin to penalize professors for their moral, political, or economic beliefs.

The second fallacy in all attempts at censorship is the implicit assumption that only like-minded people will be able to decide which orthodoxies to impose. Bankers and industrialists proceeded on this premise at the turn of the century when business values predominated in the society. Radicals seem to have acted on the same assumption during the brief period in the late 1960s when their militant tactics threatened to push all opposition aside on campuses across the country. But history suggests that no faction can wield decisive influence indefinitely and that groups with differing views will be ready to wage war against unpopular opinions whenever the opportunity arises. It required no more than a decade to discover how grossly the radicals overestimated their power and how quickly they were followed by fundamentalist groups and conservative forces intent on pressing their own values on television programming, school textbooks, and other means of communication. Ironically, the very professors who disdained academic freedom only ten years ago could soon find themselves clinging to the doctrine to protect themselves against the tide of conservative ideologies.

We need little imagination to perceive how efforts to impose political, economic, or moral judgments on faculty appointments might weaken the university. Any faction with strong ideological views could mobilize pressure to block unwelcome appointments and discourage controversial candidates from accepting offers. Radical activists would protest the presence of faculty members with "racist" or "fascist" opinions. Arch-conservatives would oppose the appointment of Marxists, as they have tried to do in recent years by introducing shareholder resolutions to bar corporate contributions to universities employing Communists on their faculties. Other groups could mount attacks of their own to block the appointment of professors who favor abortion, or believe in the heritability of intelligence, or advocate some other controversial position.

In the struggle between contending groups, it is doubtful whether any faction would emerge fully satisfied with the results. What *is* clear is that the university and its faculty would be badly damaged in the process. Professors would be inhibited from expressing their opinions or even doing research on controversial subjects for fear of being penalized and harassed.[3] Potential appointments would be quietly shelved to avoid provoking acrimonious disputes. In these ways faculty members would be restrained in the exercise of a freedom that is central to their calling. The university would be unable to secure the services of professors who could contribute substantially to the institution. And society would suffer the loss of new ideas and discoveries in fields that proved too controversial to attract able scholars.

Because of these dangers, universities generally agree that they should not penalize a professor or block his promotion or appointment because they disapprove of his political, economic, or moral views. This precept is not always easy to follow, especially when the candidate's field of study falls within the social sciences. In practice, it is all too easy to mask a distaste for a person's ideological beliefs by arguing that his writings are poorly reasoned or superficial. With sufficient effort, however, it is usually possible to

3. One careful study has surveyed the effects on professors of the attacks on Communists and subversives during the McCarthy period. According to this study, almost 20 percent of the faculty respondents reported that they had become less willing to express unpopular views in class and more inclined to avoid controversial subjects in their speeches and writings. Paul F. Lazarsfeld and Wagner Theilens, Jr., *The Academic Mind: Social Scientists in a Time of Crisis* (Glencoe, Ill.: Free Press, 1958), p. 194.

separate ideological judgments from assessments of a scholar's intellectual capacity, and most universities will take the greatest pains to do so.

Although the principles of academic freedom are now widely accepted, the changing fortunes of the modern university have brought new dangers of a subtler kind. These risks are a direct result of the closer contacts that have developed between university faculties and the outside world. Fifty years ago, scholars rarely received federal research grants, spent little time consulting in corporate offices or government agencies, and prepared no proposals for philanthropic foundations. Though their incomes were modest and their research projects limited in scope, professors were largely independent of the outside world. Today, of course, all that has changed. Most faculty members in the sciences and social sciences cannot carry on their research without outside funding. Their personal welfare has often come to depend on fees from corporate consulting and summer stipends from government or foundation grants. Many travel regularly to Washington or to major institutions to share their expertise and make recommendations on significant policy matters. More than a few harbor ambitions of leaving the university periodically to serve in important public posts.

Through these extensive contacts with the outside world, professors have increased their incomes, enlarged their research, and added excitement and variety to their lives. But these advantages have not come without a price. If faculty members depend on outside funds to carry out their research, the subjects they choose to investigate will be influenced by the opportunities available to obtain the necessary resources. When Congress appropriates larger sums for cancer research, hundreds of investigators will shift the focus of their work to the cancer field. When the government loses interest in supporting research on economic development abroad, as it did after the mid-1960s, academic interest in the subject will also diminish. Professors of economics and their graduate students will begin to specialize in other areas even though the problems of underdeveloped countries remain just as urgent as before.

Scholars who consult extensively in Washington will also develop subtle dependencies on their government patrons. Like most human beings, faculty members enjoy the excitement, the prestige, the variety that come with opportunities to participate in shaping the nation's policies. As they grow accustomed to this way of life, they may grow less inclined to dissent from official policies or to advocate positions that might jeopardize their influence or offend their patrons. Slowly, imperceptibly, without even noting the changes taking place, they may become more "pragmatic," "realistic," and "sound" in their judgments of human affairs. Unfortunately, they may also grow cautious, conventional, and less able to take a detached and critical view of the events and policies in which they have become enmeshed.

Fortunately, the effects of money and worldly influence do not extend to all parts of the university. Professors in most disciplines do not participate heavily in consulting or aspire to take a government post. Faculty members in the humanities, law, divinity, and even business administration seldom require much outside funding. Social scientists usually require modest grants for their work, but they can often find several different sources to which they can apply for support. Even in the natural sciences, where large-scale funding is often necessary for research, government grants are available for many types of inquiry, and able investigators can usually find the support they need without undue difficulty.

Despite these qualifications, it would be fatuous to ignore the effect of money and worldly ambition on scholarly writing and research. Many professors are subject to these pressures, and it is quite possible that the resulting dangers pose a greater risk to scholarship than any threats arising from conventional attacks on academic freedom. Yet little can be done to minimize these hazards. One can hardly expect foundations or public agencies to refrain from making judgments about the use of the funds under their control; their resources are limited and they must obviously make choices in deciding how to distribute their money. University presidents can try to build research endowments to support able professors whose ideas do not find favor in the usual granting agencies. But funds of this kind are hard to raise and will never suffice to cover the costs involved in fields where research is expensive. Even less can be done to counteract the human frailties and ambitions that lead scholars unconsciously to lose their detachment and alter their views to avoid offending powerful patrons. In short, we must reluctantly accept the fact that as the research university has grown in influence, a measure of scholarly independence has been lost.

Having recognized these problems, some critics suggest that academic freedom has become an illusion and no longer deserves to be taken seriously. But this is surely an extreme reaction. No one has ever pretended that professors could be totally free in pursuing their scholarly endeavors. On the contrary, the process of intellectual inquiry has always been subject to many influences quite beyond the investigator's control—the limitations of time and experience, the unconscious desire for peer approval, the subtle burdens of conventional paradigms and modes of thought. The conditions of modern life have placed new pressures and inhibitions on intellectual inquiry, but they have also overcome earlier limitations by expanding opportunities for scholars to travel and to acquire more information and experience. In these circumstances, the most that a university can do is to try to free the scholar from artificial constraints that are subject to its control. It can do its best not to penalize a professor for his opinions and to defend his right to express his views from hostile pressures outside the institution. If these efforts cannot produce complete intellectual freedom, they remain no less beneficial. Anyone who seriously doubts this conclusion has only to look at the conditions that prevail in authoritarian countries and ask whether he would be equally content to be a scholar under those repressive conditions.

Practical Problems

Even people who accept the preceding arguments will often disagree about the scope of academic freedom and dispute its application in concrete cases. Over the years, however, a number of points have been clarified. It is generally recognized that academic freedom does not convey a right to teach any subject one wants, or to indoctrinate one's students, or to encourage others to violate the rules of the institution. Moreover, some objections to academic freedom have come to be widely perceived as trivial. For example, concerned alumni sometimes worry that the employment of a particularly controversial professor will damage a university's reputation because the public will assume that the institution accepts, or at least does not oppose, the opinions expressed by members of its faculty. Fortunately, most thinking people now understand that a university does not necessarily endorse the views or behavior of its professors and that any academic institution dedicated to free expression will include individuals on its faculty whose opinions seem unwise or irresponsible even to its own administration and trustees. There will always be those who do not understand this point, and their reactions may even cost the university some significant donations. But this is a price that the institution should gladly pay for the sake of free expression and the right to appoint professors strictly on the basis of their ability as teachers and scholars. Indeed, now that academic freedom is firmly entrenched, any university that deliberately violated the doctrine would do much greater damage to its reputation than any harm it might suffer from appointing a professor with provocative views.

More troublesome is the argument that universities must occasionally consider the political and economic ideologies of candidates in order to achieve a faculty of suitably diverse beliefs and values. This point has been pressed by representatives of both ends of the political spectrum. Some have urged the appointment of more radicals in the social sciences, while others have claimed with equal conviction that university faculties are already left of center and that more conservatives should be selected.

Such arguments have a plausible ring because they seem to be neutrally phrased in terms of balance instead of favoring any particular ideology or view. Nevertheless, they can quickly lead to severe difficulties. If a university does its best to choose the ablest teachers and scholars, it is likely to assemble a faculty with a considerable diversity of opinion. On rare occasions, when two candidates seem to have equal scholarly promise, the final selection may properly turn on a desire to bring a different perspective to the faculty. But it would be a mistake to go beyond these unusual cases by making deliberate efforts to achieve greater ideological "balance." Endless, inconclusive arguments would ensue over what the proper balance ought to be. And even if everyone could agree on the appropriate mix, efforts to achieve this goal would eventually weaken the intellectual quality of the faculty by forcing the university to pass over abler candidates in order to hire representatives of this or that political point of view.

To be sure, an institution may wish to provide opportunities to study a variety of major fields of thought and experience, and this effort may indirectly affect the ideologies represented within its faculty. For example, a decision to offer instruction in socialist economics will increase the chances of appointing a socialist to the extent that socialists are more likely to specialize in this subject. Even so, the underlying decision by the university involves a choice of field and not a determination to appoint a professor of any particular ideological persuasion. Moreover, experience does not show that socialists are always the most competent experts on socialist economies any more than women are necessarily the ablest candidates for a post in women's studies or blacks the best possible choices for appointments in Afro-American history. The essential point in all these cases is that professors must be appointed on the basis of their intellectual competence in their chosen field and not because of their race, sex, or ideology.

Other problems have arisen in deciding whether academic freedom should protect professors who make controversial statements on issues outside their special field of knowledge. William Shockley, who earned a Nobel Prize for his work on transistors, provoked great bitterness for his assertions that blacks were genetically inferior to whites. The biologist George Wald, another Nobel laureate, aroused antagonism for his sweeping criticisms of government policies at home and abroad. Angry people sometimes argue that universities should discourage such pronouncements and that academic freedom has no relevance to those who venture beyond their area of special expertise.

It is not clear what steps critics expect the university to take in order to prevent such statements. Clearly, the institution would lose the services of valuable teachers and scholars if controversial professors were fired or excluded for speaking outside their field of competence. Moreover, few thoughtful people would support an attempt to discourage such pronouncements. Throughout history, great intellectuals—Leibniz, Cournot, Jevons, Whitehead, and many others—have made important contributions to knowledge beyond their original fields of work. At a time so marked by narrow specialization, professors should be encouraged rather than inhibited when they seek to broaden their scope and apply their knowledge to new and unconventional problems.

Efforts to restrict academic freedom in such cases would also encounter severe practical difficulties. Who is to say whether Bernard Shaw was merely a playwright and Bertrand Russell only a logician—and hence incompetent to speak on the great social and political questions of their time? And what is a university to do if it censors a professor who makes controversial statements outside his field only to be confronted by similar assertions from another faculty member speaking within his area of disciplinary competence? Is Shockley to be penalized as a scientist for his views on race and IQ, while Arthur Jensen, a psychologist, enjoys the freedom to publish bitterly disputed conclusions about racial differences in scores on intelligence tests? Even greater complications could arise from the fact that controversial statements—whether or not they fall within the speaker's special field—are all protected by the First Amendment. Although private universities are probably not subject to the Bill of Rights, no one could defend having one set of rules for faculty members in state universities and another and more limited set for scholars employed by private institutions. Indeed, it is hard to comprehend why an institution supposedly dedicated to a free and open search for knowledge should ever impose restrictions on speech more stringent than those allowed the general public under the First Amendment. For all these reasons, it would be absurd for any university to restrict academic freedom to expressions of opinion within a scholar's field of expertise.

More troublesome cases can arise when professors are criticized not for their teaching and research, but for specific actions they have taken. On occasion, commentators have sought to draw a clear distinction between speech and action, suggesting that individuals are protected in arguing for revolution but not in taking specific steps to put their ideas into effect. While this distinction is valid up to a point, it cannot be taken too literally. Speech and thought have little value unless they are communicated, and much communication requires action. Even acts unaccompanied by speech may be a form of expressing opinions. Citizens participate in a silent peace march to convey opposition to a war. Scientists refuse to attend a conference in a foreign land to protest the imprisonment of political dissidents. Such behavior deserves the protection commonly accorded to speech provided it does not interfere unjustifiably with the legitimate interests of others.

Occasionally, acts of protest and conviction will violate the law. In the course of a recent suit alleging sex discrimination, a professor in Georgia went to prison as a matter of principle rather than reveal to the judge how he had voted on the faculty appointment in question. Other professors have been convicted from time to time for practicing civil disobedience to protest the practice of racial segregation or the prosecution of wars they considered unjust. A university may not have to pay such persons if they are sent to jail and even may be justified in replacing a professor who is incarcerated long enough to disrupt academic programs seriously. Similarly, a dean may legitimately require a professor to make documents available or to cooperate in other ways with internal university proceedings even if the faculty member resists on principle. In taking such steps, however, the prudent university will act solely to protect its normal academic interests and not to pass judgment on the opinions or the behavior of the faculty members involved. Upholding social values and interests external to the university is a task that should be left to the civil authorities. Any other course will lead a university into making judgments about the political convictions of professors and will expose the institution to the very risks and pitfalls that originally gave rise to the doctrine of academic freedom.

Much behavior, however, is in no real sense an expression of personal belief. Most persons who steal or defraud are not acting from conviction but simply attempting to promote their own interests. In such cases, surely, a university will not violate academic freedom if it dismisses a professor or refuses to offer an appointment. And yet, although such penalties do not interfere directly with the search for knowledge, they may still expose the university to risks it will not care to run. For example, unless the conduct of a professor has already been reviewed by an appropriate public tribunal, the administration may reach a mistaken conclusion and thus do an injustice to the individual involved. Even if the university acts only when a professor has plainly violated the law, a decision to exclude such a person may harm the institution by depriving it of the best available scholar to teach and write in a given field.

In view of these problems, is there any compelling reason for the university to intervene in such cases instead of leaving this duty to the civil authorities whom society has entrusted with the task of enforcing the law? In certain instances, academic institutions may be compelled to act in order to protect their members from dangers to personal safety or property. An administration may decide that it cannot run the risks involved in hiring a professor who has repeatedly engaged in petty theft or exhibited dangerous psychopathic tendencies. No reasonable person could object if a university denied an appointment on these grounds. One can also imagine a law school hesitating to hire a professor who has been disbarred for defrauding his client, or a medical school wrestling with the problem of appointing an instructor who has cheated the government in claiming Medicare reimbursement. In such cases, the faculty may well be troubled by the prospect of hiring a professor who might provide a poor example to students in need of acquiring high professional standards. In neither instance will the university run any risk of infringing a professor's freedom to express his beliefs. As a result, the institution is entitled to consider whether the adverse effects of hiring such professors will outweigh the contributions they make by exploring and expounding their chosen field of knowledge. Reasonable people will differ in resolving these questions, and the final decision may require the most delicate assessment of the circumstances in each case. But the underlying principle seems clear and should closely parallel the standard applicable to genuine cases of academic freedom. The proper function of a university is to choose for its faculty those persons who are best qualified to perform the educational and scholarly tasks for which they are hired, provided they are capable of observing the elementary standards of conduct essential to the welfare and safety of an academic community. The task of judging those who have transgressed against society is a separate responsibility that should be left to the public authorities, who are better equipped to discharge this function properly.

The ideas advanced in this chapter may seem plausible in theory, but they often prove unpopular when a particularly heated controversy arises. In trying to explain these principles to a hostile audience, one frequently encounters some extreme hypothetical case put forth to test the strength of one's convictions. What if a ruthless deposed tyrant happened to be an outstanding theoretical physicist? What if a profoundly insightful philosopher was known to have presided over a Nazi concentration camp? Each of these individuals may be brilliant. And whereas each has behaved in a grossly inhumane fashion, both may have acted on the basis of sincere personal beliefs. But would a university agree to hire either one for its faculty?

We can readily appreciate the arguments for refusing to make such appointments. In these cases, we are not dealing with a Socrates. By barring known tyrants and acknowledged Nazis, an appointments committee will run no risk of making a mistake in judging their behavior or their opinions. Moreover, although the consequences of hiring such persons may not be fatal, they will surely be unfortunate, since many students are likely to shun their courses and few professors will extend them the minimum courtesy required to allow them to work productively in a collegial atmosphere. In these circumstances, one can argue that the university will accomplish less for teaching and research by making the appointment than it will by turning to another candidate.

Despite the force of these arguments, many thoughtful people may come to a different conclusion. They will acknowledge that there is no real chance that Nazis and tyrants will be proven right in their convictions. But they will be troubled at the thought of excluding able teachers and scholars from the university for reasons that are the proper concern of the civil authorities. And they will also fear that any exception to the normal principles of academic freedom will create too grave a risk that the principles themselves will gradually be weakened by misguided people carried away by temporary passions and prejudices. To these critics, it is only a short step from the Nazi *gauleiter* to Martin Heidegger, who joined the Nazi party for a time but was also a brilliant philosopher who contributed much through his teaching and scholarship.

Although these arguments are hard to resolve, it hardly seems necessary to settle the matter, since in real life such situations are

almost certain never to occur. Tyrants and criminals are not likely
to double as brilliant teachers and scholars, nor will they often be
at liberty to accept a professorship if they have flagrantly violated
widely accepted norms of behavior. Yet some critics will see
parallels in cases that do occasionally arise. Thus those who opposed the appointment of Henry Kissinger may have felt that his
situation was not much different from the extreme examples just
described. What, then, can we make of this bitter controversy?

Clearly, there were legitimate issues that a university could
consider in deciding whether to make such an appointment. One
would obviously have to inquire whether Dr. Kissinger was the
ablest available teacher and scholar to occupy a chair in international relations. Granted his unique experience in the field, some
critics might ask whether his close personal involvement with so
many controversial issues and events in foreign affairs would affect his ability to explore these matters with sufficient accuracy
and scholarly detachment. Others might wish to consider whether
a candidate who had lived eight years in such a prominent post
could devote himself wholeheartedly to the quieter tasks of teaching and research, without spending too much of his time on outside activities of little benefit to the institution and its students.

An appointments committee could also legitimately consider
the nature of the position being offered. Was it a regular professorship or a special chair connoting unusual honor and distinction? If special honors were being bestowed, were they offered because of Dr. Kissinger's accomplishments as a scholar or because
of his fame as a public servant? The latter course would be hard
to defend in an academic institution, since such rewards should
normally be reserved for intellectual achievements. But honors of
this kind would be particularly awkward in the case of Henry
Kissinger. How could a university refuse to judge his public
record on grounds of academic freedom if it simultaneously offered him a special appointment in recognition of his government
service?

However one might resolve such questions, they were all appropriate matters for an institution to consider. But it would have
been clearly improper to deny an appointment to Dr. Kissinger
on the basis of his decisions concerning Vietnam. A university
would not condone Kissinger's policies by offering him a position

any more than it affirms the views of any of the professors on its faculty. If he was truly the best available scholar for a chair in international relations, excluding him on political grounds would deny the university the chance to make its greatest contribution in the field. More broadly, such a decision could have introduced political considerations into the appointments process and inhibited other scholars from volunteering their advice to the government on highly controversial issues of public policy.

Opponents of Dr. Kissinger will doubtless reply that this was a special case because his decisions in public office amounted to complicity in mass murder. But that is a conclusion which could only be reached on the basis of opinions about the conduct of the war and assumptions of fact concerning the nature of the government's dealings with Hanoi. Although Dr. Kissinger's critics may believe that these issues are easy to resolve, many reasonable people obviously disagree. The doctrine of academic freedom is founded on a conviction that it is extremely hazardous for a university to render moral and political judgments of this kind. The dangers involved seem especially severe when the issues at stake have to do with the decisions of a government official during the prosecution of a war. Should Robert Oppenheimer have been excluded from the Institute for Advanced Study because of his part in the development and use of the atomic bomb? Should James Bryant Conant have been prevented from continuing as president of Harvard for recommending the attack on Hiroshima? Should appointment committees have attempted to judge the conduct of professors who helped to plan the saturation bombing during World War II or to engineer the fire raids on Tokyo and Dresden? Universities lack the acumen and the experience to make wise decisions in matters of this sort. Their deliberations are not subject to the procedural safeguards or the judicial supervision normally thought to be important in reaching public judgments that condemn the behavior of others and penalize them in their careers. Indeed, academic institutions do not even have the means to obtain all the facts required to arrive at fair and reasoned conclusions on the merits of our military policies.

Critics may reply that governments cannot really judge the acts of their own officials in prosecuting a war. Even so, universities are hardly equipped to fill the gap. Barring Dr. Kissinger might have appealed to faculty members and students who were not only aggrieved by the war but eager to take some tangible step to make their dissatisfactions felt. Be that as it may, excluding Dr. Kissinger would scarcely have served to rectify the government's mistakes in Vietnam or to prevent similar occurrences in the future, for universities have no way of imposing their standards of behavior on the nation. Thus one is at a loss to discover a compelling social purpose that would justify an administration in disregarding the normal principles of academic freedom and excluding a scholar whom it considered to be the ablest candidate for a position on the faculty.

In the last analysis, the function of the university is not to define and enforce proper moral and political standards for the society. It has not been asked to assume this role nor does it have the power to carry it out effectively. The function of the university is to engage in teaching and research of the highest attainable quality. When it strays from this task and tries to take the place of public officials by rendering its own judgments on political questions, it runs intolerable risks of making unwise decisions, diminishing the quality of its faculty, and exposing itself to continuous pressures from all of the groups and factions that may wish to impose their own political convictions on the university's work.

As this discussion makes clear, academic freedom remains a primary value in carrying out the university's commitment to the development of knowledge. Because this commitment is basic to the purpose of the institution, freedom of inquiry and expression cannot be compromised to preserve the good will of prospective donors or to avoid the anger of opposing factions intent on punishing those with whom they passionately disagree. Instead, it is the special task of educational leaders to explain the importance of academic freedom and to defend it stoutly against opponents who fear the impact of new ideas and exaggerate the dangers of corrupting the young.

We should also recognize that academic freedom has important consequences, not only for the process of intellectual inquiry but also for the governance of the university. Faculty members now enjoy great authority in deciding how to teach and what to investigate, an authority further protected by the guarantee of tenure.

These safeguards provide the legal framework that defines the university as a community of scholars rather than a hierarchical entity such as a corporation or government agency. The practical effect, however, has been to weaken the collective powers of the institution by barring recourse to methods available in other organizations to develop loyalty, cohesion, and unity of action.

No sensible administration would wish to organize the university in any other manner, since the kind of unity achieved by centralized direction could only be purchased at a heavy cost to the process of continuous debate and creative inquiry so important to intellectual progress. Even so, the genial anarchy permitted by the guarantees of tenure and academic freedom represents a major influence on the behavior of the scholarly community. Without understanding this environment, one will not fully comprehend how far a university can go either in seeking to respect the interests of others or in responding constructively to the problems of the outside world.

2

Institutional Autonomy and the
Demands of the State

WHILE ACADEMIC FREEDOM has caused power and influence to migrate from the central administration to the faculty, professors and administrators have both been losing some of their independence to the mounting requirements of the state. This turn of events was foreseen more than two decades ago by Dwight D. Eisenhower. In his last major speech before leaving office, President Eisenhower uttered his famous warning against the dangers arising from a mushrooming government bureaucracy. His graphic description of a vast "military-industrial complex" won a permanent place among the catchwords that characterize our society. But who among us still recalls the concern he voiced over the threat of big government to higher education? Those words struck no spark in an era when universities could enjoy the fruits of Washington's largesse with few restrictions or controls. Today, the President's warnings seem prophetic. After generations of almost complete immunity from regulation—free even of such basic measures as workmen's compensation and unemployment insurance—universities find themselves subjected to a host of rules covering a long and growing list of campus activities.

This transformation produced all of the familiar confusions, inconsistencies, and red tape that often accompany federal regulation. In the 1970s speeches by university presidents began to be laced with disapproving references to the "myriad pedantic and sometimes contradictory requirements imposed by government regulation"; the "continuing swirl of adversary conflict"; and the "formidable bureaucracy" that "must be served with a constant diet of reports and data."[1] Beyond these irritations, however, a much more basic issue has emerged. If Washington means to assert its authority over higher education, how can we best reconcile the legitimate concerns of government with what were once described by Justice Felix Frankfurter as "the 'four essential freedoms' of a university—to determine for itself on academic grounds who may teach, what may be taught, how it should be taught, and who may be admitted to study"?[2]

Universities have worked for generations to establish their autonomy over academic affairs, and Frankfurter plainly spoke for all of higher education when he declared: "For society's good, political power must abstain from intrusion into this activity of freedom, except for reasons that are exigent and obviously compelling."[3] Despite these words, each of the university's "four essential freedoms" has become the subject of considerable federal scrutiny and regulation. In the selection of students, the government has outlawed discrimination based on race, color, sex, or national origin; Congress has imposed quotas on medical schools to secure the entry of Americans studying abroad; and the Supreme Court has trimmed the power of admissions officers to prefer minorities in choosing their students. In hiring faculty, universities must comply with affirmative-action requirements as well as rules forbidding discrimination based on race, sex, national origin, religion, or age. Congress has moved to influence the curriculum by using the power of the purse to encourage dental schools to require their students to train for six weeks in an underserved area, and the Veterans Administration has demanded that colleges meet minimum standards if students are to receive educational benefits. In the laboratory, federal law prohibits certain types of fetal experiments; the Department of Health and Human Services has imposed detailed procedural safeguards for all investigations involving human subjects; and the National Institutes of Health have promulgated comprehensive guidelines to regulate recombinant DNA research.

Much of this new regulation does not take the form of conven-

1. William McGill, address at the University Club, New York, February 8, 1975, mimeographed, pp. 14, 18–19.
2. Sweezy v. New Hampshire, 354 U.S. 234, 263 (1957).
3. Ibid.

tional lawmaking. Instead, Washington typically intervenes by creating rules and attaching them as conditions to the receipt of federal funds. The influence exerted by such rules is limited when public officials merely offer to pay the costs of a new activity and stipulate the terms by which it shall be carried out. In these cases, universities are free to decide whether or not to seek the funds to establish the program. But the government exerts a leverage akin to the force of law when it attaches conditions *retroactively* to the continued receipt of federal money—for example, when it decrees that it will no longer provide student aid to institutions that fail to provide adequate facilities for the handicapped. The more the university depends on the funds involved, the greater the compulsion to adhere to the government's requirements. When Congress threatens to remove *all* federal grants from institutions refusing to comply with its conditions, no major university can withstand the pressure, because it is impossible for medical schools to operate or major research programs to continue without substantial government support.

In pondering these intrusions, many educators insist that the government has already gone too far and that further interference will almost certainly be unwarranted. Yet even a die-hard opponent of federal regulation will concede that the courts should prevent universities from discriminating against professors because they are black and that the National Science Foundation has the right to determine how to allocate government funds between basic and applied research. The problem lies in deciding where to draw the line. How much autonomy should universities have in carrying out their academic functions? Under what circumstances should the government intervene? And when the government acts, what methods of regulation should it employ to achieve its ends with minimum damage to the academic enterprise?

These issues are not simply matters of private concern to colleges and universities. They are important to the nation as well, for colleges and universities are society's principal source of the new knowledge and advanced education that have come to be essential to a modern society. Thus the critical task is not merely to find an adequate compromise between public needs and the private interests of the academy, but to decide how government and universities can work in harmony so that higher education will be able to make its greatest social contribution. And therein lies the problem. Now that higher education plays such an important role, government is more and more inclined to intervene to make certain that colleges and universities serve the public well. Yet we know that government can easily clasp education in a deadly embrace that stifles its creativity and vigor; this much is painfully evident from the experience of universities in other societies. In order to avoid such dangers, public officials need to consider the role of state and university in a larger perspective instead of continuing to act in a piecemeal fashion, intervening here and withdrawing there in reaction to a disconnected series of specific problems and special concerns.

The Justifications and Costs of Federal Regulation

Despite Justice Frankfurter's plea for academic autonomy, one can scarcely deny the need for at least some government regulation. When academic programs clash with other values, educators are not necessarily the best arbiters to resolve the conflict. Scientists may need freedom to do their best work, but this scarcely means that they should have the right to decide how much of the taxpayers' money should be spent on research. Nor would Congress be well advised to do away with unemployment-compensation laws in universities in the hope that academic administrators will always take enough money from faculty salaries and scholarships to make adequate provision for employees who happen to lose their jobs.

We should also not suppose that the aggregate efforts of many hundreds of institutions and many thousands of professors will automatically distribute themselves in a pattern that matches the country's needs. For example, we cannot assume that social scientists will divide their efforts appropriately between different fields of research or that market forces will automatically lead colleges and universities to train physicians or doctoral students in numbers corresponding to society's needs. If the government is subsidizing university programs or if these programs are important enough to the public, officials will naturally wish to intervene whenever the results stray too far from the nation's interests.

Finally, although educators have special competence to resolve many kinds of academic issues, they can make egregious errors in particular cases. Institutions may offer worthless instruction because of incompetence or financial pressure. Professors or administrators may act unfairly through inadvertence, bad judgment, or outright prejudice. Such actions often do harm to individuals, especially today when receiving tenure, gaining admission to professional schools, and acquiring degrees of every kind are important to many careers. One may therefore concede universities a broad discretion in academic matters yet still argue for the government's right to protect the occasional victim who suffers from a practice or decision that is demonstrably wrong.

These arguments lend support to many kinds of government intervention. At the same time, just as educators may have inflated notions about the proper scope of institutional autonomy, so may public servants exaggerate their ability to benefit the public by enacting rules and restrictions. Experience teaches us that government intrusion has serious limitations and costs that are inherent in the very process of public regulation.

To begin with, the officials who enact and interpret our laws often make mistakes. They may err because they do not adequately understand the institutions they seek to regulate. They may burden universities with inappropriate regulations designed for the different circumstances of industrial firms. They may also feel driven by constituency pressures to act even if they do not know enough to devise a sound solution for the problem at hand. At times, they may make questionable decisions in the face of political pressure or accept doubtful compromises to achieve the consensus needed to enact legislation.

Such errors can be particularly costly when they are made by Congress or a federal agency. Since universities work in the realm of ideas, it is especially important to preserve their freedom against unwise and unjustified political intervention. The costs of making a mistake are also magnified by the long reach of government authority. If a single university stumbles, the consequences are limited in scope. When federal officials err, the harm is infinitely greater because the government normally acts through policies and rules that extend to many, if not all, academic institutions. The resulting burdens not only will be widespread but may be long-lasting as well, since vested interests and inertia often combine to delay the repeal of dubious legislation or even to postpone reform indefinitely.

Regulation can also harm the educational process by imposing uniform rules that chip away at the diversity so important to our system of higher learning. Progress in education depends on constant experimentation carried on through the innumerable trials and errors of many separate colleges and universities. These institutions need freedom to innovate. They also require enough independence to produce the variety needed to serve a vast student population of widely differing abilities, aspirations, and tastes. When the government intervenes by fixing uniform rules, it works against these values. No one can count the resulting costs with precision. But observers who have studied the achievements of our leading private institutions ascribe their success primarily to their relative freedom from governmental supervision.[4] Conversely, authorities in Europe have begun to recognize the dangers of highly centralized systems of higher education and are seeking to introduce greater diversity by giving more autonomy to individual universities.[5]

Government intervention may not only undermine diversity, inhibit innovation, and result in costly errors; it may also force universities to spend large sums in complying with federal regulations. At times, these expenditures result from building alterations to equalize athletic opportunities for men and women or renovations to make laboratories conform to changing safety requirements. More often, the burdens take the form of added staff and effort to fill out forms, compile data, cope with on-site investigations, and meet the many procedural requirements that follow in the wake of federal laws and regulations.

The cumulative costs of compliance are already running into millions of dollars each year for large universities, and the relative burdens are undoubtedly greater for smaller institutions. In contrast to corporations, universities cannot readily pass along these expenses by raising prices to consumers. State institutions may not receive authorization for higher tuitions, and private colleges

4. Edward Shils, "The American Private University," *Minerva*, 11 (January 1973), 6.

5. Burton Clark, "The Insulated Americans: Five Lessons from Abroad," *Change*, 10 (November 1978), 24.

are often unable to raise charges any further and still compete with their heavily subsidized public counterparts. As a result, many academic institutions have undoubtedly had to defray the cost of complying with federal regulations by reducing their budgets for teaching and research. In today's fiscal climate, this state of affairs seems destined to continue for the foreseeable future.

If regulations cost money, administrators can try to find the necessary funds by cutting back their least valuable programs. But regulations often impose burdens that cannot be overcome in this fashion. For example, the recurring threat of new interventions and new controversies demands the personal attention of top university officials and distracts them from their academic duties. In the 1970s, this process reached such a point that regular meetings of university presidents were devoted almost entirely to issues of government relations rather than questions of education and research. Similar burdens weigh upon professors as well. In most major universities, government forms and reports consume thousands of faculty hours each year, hours that are taken in large part from research, class preparation, and counseling with students. Obviously, the time presidents spend on federal relations cannot be made up by hiring added staff nor can the effort expended by an outstanding scientist be replaced by simply hiring another faculty member.

It is easy to dismiss these problems as "errors" attributable to faulty coordination, poor organization, or inept bureaucrats hired by the previous administration. And it is doubtless true that many of these difficulties can be reduced by working harder to devise better regulatory strategies, to draft clearer regulations, and to attract abler public servants. Nevertheless, we should realize by now that these problems are not simply "errors" that can be overcome by conscientious effort. They are an intrinsic part of the regulatory process, and we should account for them as systematically as we can in considering the appropriate limits to federal intervention.

At present, government officials spend far less time assessing the costs of administering new regulatory measures than they spend examining the underlying problems that have produced the demand for intervention. University representatives can argue against proposed legislation by calling attention to problems of implementation. But neither they nor the Congress can weigh these burdens in detail, since no one will yet have drafted the regulations needed to carry out the legislative intent. For example, who could have anticipated the 10,000 words of regulatory prose that emerged from just 45 words of legislation requiring adequate opportunities for the handicapped? Even after new laws have been enacted, public officials rarely do all they can to minimize the resulting burdens. In particular, few agencies work closely enough with affected groups to take full advantage of their ability to help anticipate problems and negotiate satisfactory compromises. True, new executive orders have been issued commanding federal agencies to prepare "impact statements" before issuing regulations. Even so, since no one knows enough to devise reliable estimates of future regulatory costs, it is quite unclear that the new requirements will have much beneficial effect.

To counter these deficiencies, Congress could make wider use of its power to review draft regulations before finally approving regulatory legislation. In addition, government agencies might make a practice of appointing advisory committees composed of representatives from universities and other interested groups and then work closely with these committees from the very outset of the drafting process—or even before suggesting new legislation. Such procedures would doubtless lengthen the time required to enact and implement new laws. But there is simply no way to decide whether new rules are really desirable without considering all the costs that further intervention will entail. Nor is it likely that the affected parties will gain much confidence in the regulations or have a stake in making them succeed unless the various groups with their conflicting interests come together in advance and try to reconcile their differences through patient, informed discussion. After all the difficulties encountered under recent regulatory legislation, the government might save time in the long run, as well as do more to promote the public interest, if it undertook such consultation before embarking on ambitious new programs.

Strategies of Regulation

When public officials review new proposals to regulate higher education, they must do more than ask what they hope to gain by intervening and what the accompanying costs might be. They should also consider what strategies will achieve their goals with the least possible harm to the academic enterprise. In reviewing this question, the government can choose among at least four alternatives. It may issue *commands* to force universities to stop doing something, or to take some affirmative step, or to conform to a series of substantive rules or standards. Officials can also impose *procedures* that require universities to review certain decisions or study particular problems with special care. A third method available to the government is to offer *subsidies* to elicit some hoped-for action from universities, such as building new facilities or performing particular types of research. Finally, public officials can try to strengthen *market forces* and thus rely on greater competition to achieve the desired ends.

Although each of these alternatives presents special advantages and risks, officials do not always take sufficient time and care to select the most appropriate method. As a result, poor choices of strategy are a major cause of unwise interventions and unnecessary administrative burdens. To put the matter more positively, the government has an opportunity to do a much better job of reconciling the interests of higher education with other public concerns by making sounder choices of regulatory technique.

STRENGTHENING MARKET FORCES   Officials may be able to avoid making difficult and unpopular decisions by strengthening market forces and relying on individual choices within a competitive system. Thus, if Congress wished to improve graduate education, it might do better to give generous stipends to able students—and allow them to choose their own graduate programs—rather than attempt the prickly task of designating "outstanding" institutions to qualify for direct federal support. Similarly, an agency intent on protecting students from substandard educational programs might wisely prefer to order universities to make more information available to applicants instead of embarking on the treacherous course of establishing minimum standards of educational quality.

Although market strategies have their virtues, they also have severe limitations. Many social ends cannot be achieved through the operation of market forces. Better information about job opportunities may help women and minorities to locate academic posts, but it will hardly do away with the need for rules outlawing discrimination. Nor will market forces ensure that handicapped students achieve full access to higher education or that laboratories observe a due regard for public safety. Furthermore, because universities do not constitute a free market in the ordinary commercial sense, efforts to rely on market forces will often prove impossible or prohibitively expensive. For example, independent colleges cannot charge tuitions that are competitive with those of the heavily subsidized public institutions. Although the government could strengthen worthy private colleges to some extent by giving more federal aid to students, Congress would find it expensive and politically unattractive to devise an aid policy that would actually offset the higher tuitions of private colleges and allow them to vie equally for students on the basis of academic quality. For all these reasons, though efforts to strengthen market forces may have a limited, supplementary role in helping to achieve public ends, they will rarely succeed in removing the need for more direct forms of government intervention.

SUBSIDIES   Subsidies offer a remarkably versatile means of bringing about constructive change. They can be used to increase the supply of minority faculty, to develop new training programs, to encourage particular forms of research—indeed, to strengthen almost any form of worthy endeavor and call forth almost any effort to further the public interest. Their special virtue lies in their capacity to elicit behavior from universities in a way that minimizes compulsion and preserves diversity by allowing each institution to refrain from participating if it finds the proposed activity unsuited to its needs and objectives. Subsidies do cost money. But the expense is usually justified because the government will be seeking to use universities to accomplish ends that benefit the public.

Notwithstanding these advantages, offering subsidies can lead to several problems. Public officials may impose such meticulous accounting requirements that faculty members will have to spend many hours filling out forms instead of doing their regular academic work. Government funds may distort the priorities of a university, or create gross differences in salaries and perquisites within the institution, or divert faculty energies excessively from teaching to research. Subsidies can also create dependencies and vested interests that make it hard to withdraw the funds when the need has passed. Above all, government officials may overreach themselves by setting detailed criteria to govern the use of public funds. Such criteria will not have the force of law, since universities need not apply for the money. But the quality of work will suffer nonetheless if officials with limited experience try to impose their own judgment on academic matters by prescribing in detail how research should be carried out or how a training program should be organized.

Even if government funds are administered with sensitivity and good judgment, offering money to universities is not an appropriate way of achieving all legitimate objectives. Subsidies work best when the government's aim is to persuade institutions to undertake new activities; they are not a good device for stopping universities from engaging in some form of undesirable behavior. It is distasteful to pay institutions for refraining from unjustifiable acts and prohibitively expensive to reward them for satisfying some minimum standard that almost all would routinely achieve in any event. In these situations, the government can normally achieve its ends only by resorting to more intrusive forms of regulation.

PROCEDURAL REQUIREMENTS The government often insists that educational institutions undertake some sort of review to ensure careful consideration of particular programs or decisions. Thus courts have required universities to offer a fair hearing to professors before discharging them for misconduct, and the Labor Department has insisted on reasonable grievance procedures for women and minorities who allege that they have suffered from discrimination. By requiring such review, officials can see to it that disputes are settled inexpensively and can encourage universities to act with care and deliberation while still allowing academic officers to make the actual decisions involved. In this fashion, the government induces universities to act according to the public interest without running the risk that inexperienced public officials will render academic judgments they are ill-equipped to make.

Procedural requirements work best in situations where certain characteristics exist. The elements of a fair procedure must be accepted and widely understood so that the government is largely confirming established practice rather than imposing detailed procedures that may be unsuited to academic institutions. In addition, the expense involved must not be out of proportion to the importance of the underlying problem. For example, it would clearly be burdensome and unwise to require universities to review every dispute over an examination grade or every protested decision from the admissions office. Finally, the values at stake must be shared sufficiently widely that universities will normally reach decisions that conform to the public interest if they are simply made to take the time to study the issue with care. Thus in matters of personnel, compulsory grievance and hearing procedures have been effective precisely because few universities will support a department chairman or an administrator who is shown to have discriminated against women and minorities or to have fired a member of the staff for insubstantial reasons.

If the foregoing elements are not present, procedural requirements are likely either to do little good or to create burdens and costs that exceed any benefits achieved. Moreover, procedural requirements tend to be rigidly applied in ways that add to their cost. Although legally mandated procedures may be inappropriate or unnecessary for many institutions, the government will rarely agree to make exceptions unless there are clear-cut reasons for doing so—reasons that do not force officials to make subjective, controversial judgments. For example, the Department of Education insists that every institution desiring federal aid must be accredited and that every accreditation must include an elaborate self-study in which the institution defines its goals and assesses its ability to meet them. At first glance, this requirement seems innocuous enough. But most institutions clearly deserve accreditation, and many of them will not need to undergo a costly self-examination, because their programs are plainly in good health, or because the time is not ripe for such a review, or because a more limited, focused assessment would be more appropriate. Even so, they must comply and thereby incur needless costs and distractions.

The burdens imposed by any one set of procedural rules may be assumed without great difficulty. But the costs of compliance quickly mount as requirements multiply and institutions have to submit increasingly elaborate plans for affirmative action, facilities to assist the handicapped, and other federal purposes. Applicable rules and guidelines grow steadily more complex as ambiguities and unanticipated questions accumulate. Confusion increases as procedures are administered and interpreted by inexperienced public officials. Frequent changes occur as new administrations arrive with ideas of their own on how to administer the rules. In the end, the cumulative burdens of complying with the mandated procedures can easily run to millions of dollars in a large research university. For all these reasons, procedural strategies can be a useful tool only if they are used sparingly and limited to the kinds of problems that lend themselves to this type of intervention.

SUBSTANTIVE RULES   The most intrusive form of regulation is to issue an order, either by legal command or by attaching retroactive conditions to the continued use of federal funds. In framing orders, the government is generally on safest ground when it simply prohibits a specific act that offends some compelling public interest, such as the interest in avoiding racial discrimination. Even in these seemingly clear cases, rules can create problems, either because officials occasionally err in deciding whether discrimination has occurred or because of the costs and delays incurred in defending ill-founded law suits. But almost everyone would agree that these burdens are worth imposing in order to minimize a particularly repellent form of injustice.

When the government issues rules that reach beyond the classic forms of discrimination and abuse, it may not only increase litigation—with all the attendant vagaries, uncertainties, and costs—it may also make mistakes that impose much heavier burdens on large numbers of institutions. In 1974, for example, Congress enacted the so-called Buckley amendment, which sought, among other things, to protect students from unfair or malicious letters of recommendation by giving them access to their admissions files and other records. Although this legislation may occasionally have helped to avoid an injustice, most experienced observers believe that these gains have been far outweighed by the tendency of the amendment to discourage candor on the part of those who write letters of recommendation. Much more serious consequences are likely to result from the recent federal rule forbidding mandatory retirement before age seventy. Although this requirement may work well enough in industry, it will affect university faculties adversely by further reducing academic job opportunities already depleted by the decline in student population that will continue over the next generation. In these circumstances, the retirement law seems destined to allow existing faculty a few extra years of service at the cost of retarding affirmative action, frustrating the careers of many able young teachers, and keeping universities from renewing themselves by bringing new blood to their faculties.

Even plausible rules can interfere in questionable ways with particular universities. Regulations that work reasonably well in most instances may unexpectedly prove to make little sense when applied to institutions with special circumstances or unusual programs. For example, it was trivial and silly for Washington officials to take action to prevent colleges in certain midwestern states from having six players on their women's basketball teams instead of the five traditionally found on men's teams. Similarly, rules that seem sensible to most people may conflict with values and practices that matter greatly to particular groups of institutions. Thus restrictions against age discrimination may interfere with the practices of medical schools that favor younger applicants because they will have longer periods of service in their profession. Prohibitions against all discrimination based on sex may hamper women's colleges that prefer to appoint women faculty in a sincere belief that role models are important to their educational mission. Rules condemning the dismissal of unmarried pregnant women may frustrate the efforts of conservative colleges to impose strict standards of behavior on their faculty. One may agree or disagree with these academic policies. But the very essence of diversity is the freedom to experiment, to make mistakes, to cling to values not commonly shared within the society. Such freedoms have their place, especially in a society that respects the virtues of pluralism. Yet diversity is inevitably diminished by an accumulation of rules that translate majority preferences into federal commands.

Still further complications arise when the government does not merely condemn particular practices but tries to compel faculty members to perform their academic work in specified ways. Public officials can order that a particular course be given, but they cannot make sure that the classes will be adequately taught. A court can force a university to grant tenure to an aggrieved faculty member, but a judge has no power to require colleagues to offer the cooperation and respect that are necessary to enable most professors to be effective and satisfied in their work. In short, no official can order professors to act with enthusiasm or conviction. And this is a serious defect, for few academic pursuits are worth much if they are carried on in any other way. As a result, requirements tend to be less effective than subsidies as a means of persuading universities to respond in some affirmative fashion.

The problems just described are greatly compounded when the government moves beyond particular rules and imposes a series of substantive standards to regulate complex matters—such as the admission of students or the selection of faculty. Since such standards embody a multitude of rules, they carry the gravest risk of perpetrating errors, narrowing diversity, and stifling innovation. Congress can try to relieve these problems by framing broader standards and then giving discretion to agencies in the executive branch to apply these measures flexibly in specific cases. But this strategy merely introduces a new set of dangers. Mistakes will occur because government personnel often lack the training and experience to use their discretion wisely in making decisions affecting education and research. Regional offices in a single agency will arrive at conflicting policies, causing uncertainty and confusion. Understaffed and overburdened by the task of applying general rules to complex institutions, public officials are likely to subject universities to frustrating delays and recurrent demands for new data, new forms, and new explanations. Since all these defects are inimical to the educational process, standards represent a last resort, to be imposed only when the need for intervention is compelling and no other regulatory device exists that is adequate to solve the problem.

Some Modest Proposals

With this review of the most important regulatory strategies, what guidelines can be used in seeking to reconcile the university's need for institutional autonomy in educational matters with the government's duty to protect the public interest? The task is assuredly not an easy one, for each regulatory proposal tends to stand or fall on its own peculiar facts. Nevertheless, a few tentative suggestions can be made, if only to provoke discussion.

AVOIDING INAPPROPRIATE INTERVENTION   Two kinds of federal rules threaten the academic process in such fundamental ways that we can safely regard them as inherently wrong. The first category includes attempts by the government to regulate the content of ideas and knowledge that members of the university community seek to discover, disseminate, or learn. Thus officials of the Department of Health, Education, and Welfare erred in 1974 by proposing regulations that required universities to review course materials "to ensure that they do not reflect discrimination on the basis of sex." Clearly, such requirements would have forced academic administrators to censor the teaching of their professors in disregard of accepted principles of academic freedom and the First Amendment.[6]

The government should likewise refrain from discouraging research that might result in the discovery of some unsettling piece of knowledge, or from putting pressure on the university to hire or fire professors because of their opinions, or from prohibiting certain types of people from studying in an academic institution through concern for what they might learn or say. These limits on government power are much in keeping with the First Amendment aims of maintaining freedom of speech and an open mar-

6. The HEW initiative and subsequent decision to withdraw the controversial provision are described by Richard W. Lyman in "Federal Regulation and Institutional Autonomy: A University President's View," in Paul Seabury, ed., *Bureaucrats and Brainpower: Government Regulation of Universities* (San Francisco: Institute for Contemporary Studies, 1979), pp. 35–37.

ketplace of ideas. They seem especially important to academic institutions, because attempts to impose an orthodoxy on higher education strike directly at the process of discovery and social commentary that is essential to progress in a free society.

The second suspect category includes cases in which the federal government tries to overrule university decisions about academic matters not to promote some separate interest of legitimate public concern, but simply because public officials believe that they can do a better job of deciding what is needed to accomplish academic ends. For example, it would be inappropriate for Congress to insist that lawyers should be taught by one pedagogic method rather than another, or that particular courses should be put in the curriculum to improve the quality of undergraduate education, or that certain criteria should be followed in order to make better faculty appointments.

In listing these cases, I do not mean to suggest that public officials can never decide academic issues more wisely than universities—any more than the Supreme Court would insist that government censors could never succeed in finding a book or idea that actually deserved to be suppressed. My conclusion simply rests on a conviction that if the government freely substitutes its judgment and overrules universities on academic issues, the results, on the whole, will be damaging to the quality of higher education. The results will be harmful for a multitude of reasons: because government officials will not know as much about academic issues as educators and faculty members; because government rules are likely to impress uniformity and rigidity on a field of activity that needs diversity, experimentation, and change; because teaching and research do better under conditions of freedom rather than external direction; and because efforts to determine the academic policies of three thousand separate institutions are likely to be expensive and difficult to enforce. Universities will doubtless make mistakes if they are left to their own devices. But our decentralized system limits the impact of these errors by making it possible for aggrieved professors and students to move to other colleges and universities if they are deprived of the appointment, the opportunity for admission, or the course of study that they feel they deserve.

Beyond these questionable categories lies a wide variety of cases where Washington acts not to censor ideas nor yet to impose its own academic judgments, but to promote some other public aim that is somehow affected by university policies and practices. In situations of this kind, educators often lack the objectivity and experience to balance their academic concerns against the separate interests that affect other groups in the society. Hence, public officials can properly consider whether or not to intervene, and although we may sometimes attack their decisions as unwise, we cannot regard their actions as inherently wrong or illegitimate.

PROMOTING NEW SERVICES   On many occasions, the government will seek to further some separate public purpose by inducing universities to provide a new or expanded service. For example, Congress may decide that society needs more doctors, more classrooms, or more research on energy. In these cases, the government should normally elicit the desired service by offering a subsidy, taking care to avoid excessively detailed requirements governing the methods used to provide the service, and relying on university consultants wherever possible to help make any academic judgments involved in awarding public funds.

By and large, the government has followed these guidelines reasonably well. But federal officials have sometimes chosen to elicit new services not by offering a subsidy, but by using compulsion to force universities to perform. Thus Congress has threatened not to renew capitation funds for any medical school that would not agree to increase its class size or accept a quota of American students who had begun their studies abroad. Such tactics interfere needlessly with institutional freedom, for Congress could have achieved its purpose by simply offering to cover the cost to any schools that agreed to expand their classes or accept American students studying in other countries.

Requirements should be preferred to subsidies only when there are strong reasons for insisting that all institutions in a given group join in providing the desired service. Affirmative-action efforts and renovations for the handicapped offer apt examples. Even so, neither program is designed primarily to ensure fair treatment of the university's own students and staff. Both are animated by the more ambitious aim of expanding opportunities for all women, minority groups, and handicapped persons throughout the nation. Hence, Washington may impose regulations, but it should agree to pay for the costs involved, since both programs make use of universities in order to achieve broader goals of value to the entire society. If it ignores this principle, Congress will not only act unfairly; it will often do more harm than good, since it cannot know what activities universities will have to sacrifice in order to finance the new programs. Thus federal requirements for the handicapped have often caused universities to install costly ramps and elevators that yield benefits so infrequent and speculative as not to compare with those that might have resulted from continuing to use the diverted funds for scholarships or other educational purposes. For these reasons, only in cases such as minimum wages, social security, or workmen's compensation—where Washington is simply setting the minimum terms that universities must observe toward their own students and employees—should academic institutions be required to assume the cost of providing new benefits as a normal operating expense.

PREVENTING ABUSE On many occasions, the government will wish to intervene not to promote a new activity, but to prevent universities from behaving in some undesirable way. For example, Congress may wish to establish safety measures for the disposal of hazardous materials or standards of accountability to avoid the waste of public funds. In such cases, the government can hardly avoid enacting rules; the principal question is how to accomplish the task in a manner that will adequately protect the public without imposing excessive burdens of time and money on universities.

During the 1970s, the pendulum swung too far in the direction of strict accountability. Agency officials came to believe—with good reason—that they had more to fear from a Congressional hearing on wasted research funds than they could gain by protecting able investigators from a stifling burden of accounting forms and time sheets. Yet it is far from clear that the public obtained a good bargain.

For example, many of the current accounting requirements seek to prevent professors from using some of the research funds from one grant to support graduate instruction or research under some other governmentally supported project. Public officials are surely justified in asking investigators to avoid unauthorized shifts of this kind. Yet one wonders how much time and scrutiny should be expended in making sure that these transfers will not be made. Since all of the projects for which the federal funds are being used have been approved by the government, it is not clear how much can be gained by creating more and more minute and costly requirements to ensure that each federal dollar is used only in the precise program for which it was specifically authorized. What *is* clear is that scientists already spend a large and growing fraction of their time preparing more and more detailed research proposals, filling out safety and affirmative-action reports, serving on various oversight and review committees, and attempting to comply with increasingly intricate reporting and accounting requirements. The cost of adding to these burdens cannot be measured in money alone. In any society, the number of creative scientists is extremely small. When we divert too much of their time from research to administration, we lose a precious resource that cannot be replaced by simply hiring more investigators, even if universities could afford to do so.

The government may also consider preventive regulation to discourage shoddy educational practices that could harm unwary students, expose the public to incompetent professionals, or waste federal scholarships on worthless academic programs. But efforts of this kind can cause problems beyond the ordinary costs of administration. The educational process is sufficiently subtle and intangible that it is difficult to measure success or quality by any objective standard, such as minimum class hours, faculty-student ratios, or numbers of books in the library. Attempts to impose such standards also carry a serious risk of imposing rigidity and uniformity where there should be diversity and experimentation, of producing incongruous results for institutions with special missions and needs, and of creating doubt and confusion over what the requirements mean.[7] Moreover, standards of this kind

7. These dangers have been aptly demonstrated on the few occasions when the government has imposed procedural or substantive standards for assessing educational quality. One example is the requirement that every accreditation be accompanied by a self-study on the part of the institution under review. Another is the Veterans Administration rule barring full-time G.I. benefits from any academic program that does not require at least twelve hours of classroom attendance each week. This standard ruled out a Wayne

normally generate all manner of artful stratagems to circumvent the law, and thus provoke the government to assume increasing enforcement costs and to issue detailed educational judgments that are beyond its competence to make.

Because of these problems, the government should seek remedies other than imposing academic standards to guard society from inferior educational programs. Individual students can be protected by requiring each institution to provide more accurate information to the public about its academic programs, and by prohibiting unreasonable refund practices that inhibit students from leaving institutions that do not meet their expectations. Though no conceivable remedy is perfect, officials can do more to shield the public from incompetent practitioners by insisting on adequate testing and licensing requirements for the professions than by imposing minimum standards on universities. The government may seek still further protection to ensure that federal scholarship funds are not diverted to incompetent institutions. But in most cases officials have wisely looked to private accrediting agencies to make the academic judgments required. Of course, errors can also be made by these independent organizations. But private accreditation tends to attract able, experienced faculty members who perform the service as a professional obligation rather than a government job and who are often capable of giving helpful advice even to strong institutions. For these reasons, government officials should continue to look to this source— and rely on simple safeguards regulating procedures and membership to ensure that accrediting bodies are organized and staffed to perform responsibly.

A final reason for preventive regulation is to protect individuals from injustice. In flagrant cases, such measures serve a useful purpose. During the 1970s, however, the government was increasingly asked to impose new measures to guard students and faculty from unfair treatment in admissions, hiring, disciplinary proceedings, and almost every other area of academic life. The opportunities for intervention are virtually limitless. Only a few years ago, a conference committee drawn from both houses of Congress

State University program for intensive weekend study that had previously been approved by private accrediting agencies and cited positively by UNESCO.

agreed to consider a proposal to deny all capitation grants to medical schools that discriminate among applicants on the basis of their views about abortion. We can agree that such opinions should be irrelevant to gaining admission to study medicine. The same could doubtless be said of a student's views on national health insurance, fetal research, recombinant DNA experiments, transcendental meditation, or the future of the Republican party. But is it really wise for the federal government to try to prohibit universities from considering particular items in the endless list of inappropriate criteria for admission? Any effort by Congress to proceed down this path would surely expose higher education to more and more of the dangers earlier described—the vagaries, costs, and uncertainties of litigation, the gradual narrowing of diversity and innovation, and the risk of enacting questionable rules, such as the Buckley amendment, that bring unexpected side effects far worse than the harm they seek to remove.

It is true, of course, that rules to ensure fairness may succeed in preventing a number of unwise and arbitrary acts on the part of universities. But the effects of these missteps are considerably reduced by the opportunities available to students and faculty to seek admission or employment at other institutions. Hence, the government should exercise great caution in enacting rules of this kind. No one would dispute the decision to intervene in cases—such as discrimination against women or blacks—where there is a principle at stake of such compelling importance that even occasional transgressions must be halted. Similarly, judges may wisely insist on protecting existing students and faculty by requiring that they not be dismissed or seriously penalized on grounds for which they had no reasonable notice or without an opportunity for some sort of review by the institution. But Congress should resist the temptation to enact new rules simply to prevent actions on the part of universities that government officials happen to consider unreasonable. The list of such prohibitions would be endless, and the resulting web of rules would almost certainly lead to costs out of all proportion to the actual benefits achieved.

To some readers, these suggestions may seem to leave too little scope for public regulation. For it is always tempting to suppose that present practices could be improved with a bit more control over the freedom of universities to decide who should pass through the gateways to the great professions, or what students should learn in order to prepare themselves for an important occupation, or how best to harness the power of science as a force for good rather than evil. I have tried to mark the pitfalls that beset this course. They are serious and deserve our continuing concern. One has only to look to our public primary and secondary schools to observe the damage that can be done by trying to achieve all manner of public purposes by relying more and more on government rules enforced by the adversary methods and the cumbersome procedures that are characteristic of our legal system.

It would be unfortunate to follow this example in our colleges and universities. As noted earlier, we need a strong system of higher education because of the importance of knowledge and advanced education to almost every significant aspect of modern society. If our colleges and universities were demonstrably mediocre and insensitive to national needs, we might have little to lose and something to gain by attempting more government intervention. With assistance from the federal government, however, we have built a system of higher education universally regarded as the best in the world in terms of the quality of research, the eminence of our leading universities, the access provided to all racial groups and income strata, and the responsiveness of the system to widely varying student needs. This does not mean that our colleges and universities are perfect, or even nearly so, nor does it imply that higher education should be immune from regulation. The point is simply that our colleges and universities have become a highly successful and valuable national asset, and we should therefore take care not to diminish their usefulness by burdening them with more and more restrictions.

Despite the actions I have criticized in this chapter, the government has not done badly up to now in observing a proper restraint toward higher education. Notwithstanding all of the near-escapes from ill-advised regulations, public officials have intervened not wantonly, but almost always to achieve some manifest public benefit or to resolve a problem of obvious public concern. A new administration could doubtless do much useful work to devise less intensive methods to achieve the government's ends and to reduce the administrative burdens that often accompany current regulations. Even so, the proper agenda for the future does not call for the wholesale repeal of existing rules. It does call for an imaginative effort to replace cumbersome regulatory schemes with simpler, more imaginative strategies and for continued vigilance against fresh incursions on the autonomy of universities over basic academic programs.

With the advent of the Reagan administration, the risk of further regulation may seem small. But administrations come and go, while there will always be fresh temptations to intervene, to tinker, to seek better solutions than educators have been able to devise. When such occasions arise, I would argue strongly that society will be served best if the government observes a clear presumption against further regulation. This presumption should by no means be absolute. What it should require is a clear and convincing showing that other interests are compelling enough to justify intervention and that the government has chosen the least intrusive method to achieve its legitimate ends. If federal officials can observe these limits, they will have the authority they require to curb serious abuses and to offer adequate incentives to bring educational resources into line with important public needs. At the same time, each university will retain wide latitude to determine for itself how it can respond most appropriately to the changing needs and opportunities that constantly appear in the outside world.

3

The Purposes of the University and Its Responsibilities to Society

SINCE WORLD WAR II, universities have scarcely lacked for opportunities to serve society. As the possibilities continue to multiply, educators have engaged in spirited debates over the proper course for their institutions to follow. Which functions can be properly discharged by the academy and which should be left for other agencies to perform? How far can universities go in adding useful programs and services without unduly burdening and distracting their faculty and staff? Should they merely respond to the demands placed upon them or should they take more initiative in deciding what society needs and how the university can best use its resources to encourage constructive change?

The Emergence of the Multiversity

Different strands in the history of American higher education point at different answers to these questions. In the nineteenth century, our academic institutions drew much of their inspiration from European models. From Germany came the idea of a university dedicated to research conducted by the specialized professor with the help of student apprentices. From England came a strong emphasis on the teaching of undergraduates and a broad conception of education that embraced the moral and emotional as well as the intellectual development of the student.

Both the English and the German traditions conceived of academic institutions standing somewhat aloof from the public. Both emphasized the value of learning and discovery for their own sake. Universities might influence society profoundly either by making discoveries that others could apply to practical uses or by assembling a young elite and helping them to acquire informed and inquiring minds. In these ways, higher education doubtless "told silently on the mind of the country," in Matthew Arnold's words. But any social changes that ensued were merely the by-products of the university and not its *raison d'être*.

It was precisely on this point that the American experience departed most sharply from its European models. Americans tended to look on higher education as a means for providing the knowledge and the trained manpower that a rapidly developing society required. In 1862, Congress embodied this spirit in the Morrill Act, which offered grants of land to each state for "the endowment, support, and maintenance of at least one college where the leading object shall be ... to teach such branches of learning as are related to agriculture and the mechanical arts, in such manner as the legislatures of the states may respectively prescribe, in order to promote the liberal and practical education of the industrial classes in the several pursuits and professions in life." As time went on, land-grant colleges and universities, especially in the Midwest and Far West, provided services that extended far beyond professional and vocational training. Extension services and field stations supplied farmers with information on the newest agricultural techniques. Law teachers helped to draft new commercial codes, while economists advised state officials on labor and social legislation. Special programs during the evening hours offered instruction to hundreds of thousands of adults, helping them to explore intellectual interests or to prepare themselves for better careers. As one president of a land-grant institution observed during the 1930s: "The state universities hold that there is no intellectual service too undignified for them to perform."[1]

For several decades, private institutions lagged behind the land-grant example. As late as 1940, most of them remained rather detached from society, carrying on their research and educating their students without much traffic with the outside world. During the next five years, however, the demands of a global conflict led all universities to participate in the national war effort.

1. Lotus D. Coffman, *The State University: Its Work and Problems* (Minneapolis: University of Minnesota Press, 1934), p. 205.

Ironically, it was through the development of weapons that academic scientists proved how valuable their talents could be to the modern industrial state. The lesson was not lost on our political leaders.

After 1945 the federal government built on its wartime experience by providing the mechanisms and the money to support a massive program of basic research on the nation's campuses. As time went on, Washington took further initiatives to encourage universities, private as well as public, to meet important national needs. Congress began to make large appropriations of funds for medical research to discover treatments and cures for cancer, stroke, and other major diseases. As America's role in the world increased, additional sums were given to produce specialists on far-off regions of the globe. Medical schools received handsome bonuses in return for expanding their enrollments to enlarge the supply of doctors. Fellowships poured forth to train more Ph.D.'s to teach the swelling ranks of college students, and construction grants were provided to build new dormitories and classrooms.

Foundations also flowered during the postwar period. At first, they frequently offered large grants of unrestricted money to improve the quality of universities. But staff members quickly pressed their boards to abandon this practice in favor of offering funds for specific university projects that addressed important social needs. Like the government, foundations were soon contributing to a wide variety of service programs. With this support, professors were able to teach and offer technical advice in underdeveloped countries; schools of education mounted model curricula for high schools in suburbs and ghettos; law students founded legal offices in poor communities; and research projects multiplied, evaluating old remedies and offering new ones for almost every conceivable social ill.

The broad support for public service ultimately produced that distinctively American creation—the multiversity. By 1962, according to one of its most persuasive advocates, the University of California

> had operating expenses from all sources of nearly half a billion dollars, with almost 100 million for construction; a total employment of over 40,000 people, more than IBM and in a

far greater variety of endeavors; operations in over a hundred locations, counting campuses, experiment stations, agricultural and urban extension centers, and projects abroad involving more than fifty countries; nearly 10,000 courses in its catalogues; some form of contact with nearly every industry, nearly every level of government, nearly every person in its region. Vast amounts of expensive equipment were serviced and maintained. Over 4,000 babies were born in its hospitals. It is the world's largest purveyor of white mice. It will soon have the world's largest primate colony. It will soon also have 100,000 students—30,000 of them at the graduate level; yet much less than one third of its expenditures are directly related to teaching. It already has nearly 200,000 students in extension courses—including one out of every three lawyers and one out of every six doctors in the state.[2]

One can justify this sprawling network of activity and all the services it provides on at least two grounds. In the first place, universities have a near monopoly on certain types of valued resources. They alone can award the degrees that are all but indispensable for a number of desirable careers. In addition, they possess forms of expertise and capacities for research and education that cannot readily be duplicated by other institutions in society. Consequently, one can argue that universities should use their special resources to meet important social needs just as public utilities have a duty to make their services available to all customers who desire them.

In addition, institutions of higher education receive heavy subsidies from the government. State universities obtain the bulk of their operating revenues from public funds supplied by the taxpayers. Private institutions may rely less on direct government support, but even they often obtain from a fifth to two thirds of their income from government grants for student aid and research. In addition, they gain assistance indirectly through relief from taxes, including exemptions from the normal levies on private gifts and bequests. Because of this massive public support, universities have reason to acknowledge a reciprocal duty to make

2. Clark Kerr, *The Uses of the University* (Cambridge, Mass.: Harvard University Press, 1963), pp. 7–8.

their services available to help address important social problems.

In many ways, the modern multiversity has more than made good on these expectations. Indeed, writers have often hailed it as a *tour de force* and a great achievement. According to the distinguished British educator and critic Sir Eric Ashby: "The great American contribution to higher education has been to dismantle the walls around the campus. When President Van Hise of Wisconsin said that the borders of the campus are the boundaries of the state, he was putting into words one of the rare innovations in the evolution of Universities. It is one which has already been vindicated by history. Other nations are now beginning to copy the American example."[3]

Despite this approbation, there has long been opposition on many campuses to the strong service orientation of American universities. These criticisms were muted during the halcyon years when federal funds were plentiful and professors moved boldly from one new venture to the next. By the late 1960s, however, after student protests erupted on the campus and established authority was assailed from every side, opponents began to voice their concerns in no uncertain terms.

Critics of a traditional persuasion expressed their sharpest displeasure over the precipitous growth of the multiversity and its formless pursuit of multiple goals. By constantly adding new services and activities, universities had spawned huge, insensitive bureaucracies. Detractors often accused them of losing their sense of purpose and cohesion in a welter of disparate institutes, centers, and socially relevant projects. Within this maze of activity, crowds of students were said to wander aimlessly, neglected by professors who felt more loyalty to the government agency that funded them than to the university in which they temporarily made their home. In the eyes of the traditionalists, a sharp change of direction was urgently required. Universities must begin to cut back on social problem-solving and devote more time and effort to teaching and scholarship for their own sake. Otherwise, by tak-

3. "The Case for Ivory Towers" (Paper delivered at the International Conference on Higher Education in Tomorrow's World, the University of Michigan, Ann Arbor, April 26–29, 1967), p. 4.

ing on more and more "relevant" tasks that other agencies could just as easily discharge, they would soon be unable to maintain high standards of quality in the vital functions that they alone could perform.

From another quarter came an entirely different attack upon the multiversity. According to social activists, higher education served society only by passively accepting the agenda put before it by government agencies, corporations, and other powerful interests. In pursuing this policy, academic officials reached the height of hypocrisy when they proclaimed the neutrality of their institutions. In fact, the activists said, universities behaved like "hired guns," willing to further the ambitions of any group with enough power and money to have their bidding done. Faculties approved ROTC programs to help the military, organized industry-associates programs to benefit corporations, provided extension services to assist powerful farm groups, and through such "contributions" abandoned their neutrality and offered tacit support to all the vested interests that controlled American society.

By 1970, then, the issues were clearly defined. Should universities turn inward and dedicate themselves to learning and research for their own sake, benefiting society only indirectly through advances in basic knowledge and the education of able students? Should they continue instead to respond energetically to society's requests for new services, new training programs, and new forms of expert advice? Or should they take the initiative and set their own agenda for reform by deciding for themselves which programs to mount and which projects to encourage in order to bring about social change?

One can easily misinterpret this debate and misconstrue the motives of the participants. Everyone involved—traditionalists, multiversity enthusiasts, activist reformers—believed that universities ought to serve society. They differed only in their estimate of the burdens these institutions could carry and the ways in which they could make their most important contributions. It is precisely these differences that lie at the core of any serious discussion of the proper social responsibilities of the university.

The Traditionalist Critique

The traditionalist thesis is blurred by a tendency to blame the multiversity for all the contemporary ills of higher education. In fact, larger social forces continually shape our academic institutions in ways that are often beyond the power of educational leaders to resist. For example, it is difficult to hold public universities responsible for their unwieldy size, for much of their growth has been due not to policies adopted by campus administrators, but to increases in the student population coupled with decisions by most state legislatures to increase enrollments to 25,000 or even 40,000 students. Similarly, much of the outside activity of professors must be attributed to society's demand for expertise, which led to consulting fees and other rewards and inducements that university leaders were powerless to control. It is even unclear how much the multiversity, as such, contributed to the unrest of the late 1960s. Student protest did not occur at several large universities but did arise at many small independent colleges. Hence, the turmoil cannot have resulted primarily from the size and social entanglements of the university, but must be attributed to causes such as the draft and the Vietnam War, which provoked a particularly strong reaction among students of exceptional ability, regardless of the nature of the institution they attended.[4]

Despite these qualifications, imbedded in the writings of traditionalists such as Jacques Barzun, Robert Nisbet, and Sidney Hook are two lines of argument that warrant careful examination. To begin with, traditionalists contend that the wholesale effort to serve society's needs has exposed higher education to pressures and temptations that threaten to corrupt academic values. Eager to address social problems and beguiled by the

4. A leading expert on student unrest observed as early as 1967 that "student protesters do not seem distinctively dissatisfied with their educations" and "probably receive relatively *more* individual attention and a *higher* caliber of instruction than do nonprotesters. Furthermore, protests generally tend to occur at the best, rather than the worst colleges, judged from the point of view of the quality of undergraduate education. Thus, despite the popularity of student slogans dealing with the impersonality and irrelevance of the multiversity, the absolute level of educational opportunities seems, if anything, positively related to the occurrence of protest: the better the institution, the more likely demonstrations are" (Kenneth Keniston, "The Sources of Student Dissent," *The Journal of Social Issues*, July 1967, p. 108).

ready availability of funds, faculty members and administrators have often moved too fast to create urban institutes, criminology centers, environmental programs, and other ventures of doubtful intellectual merit. As a result, campuses have become cluttered with research projects that could be carried out as well by consulting firms, while students have been enrolled in educational programs that do not proceed from any well-developed body of knowledge. Traditionalists also charge that many professors spend too much of their time consulting with corporations or advising government officials on specific policy issues. By doing so, faculty members not only neglect their teaching and research but run the risk of losing their detachment and their objectivity. Tempted by the prospect of influencing events, they can easily become partisans and advocates instead of scholars seeking to understand the underlying social forces at work.

One might overlook such problems if they existed only in minor programs and institutes at the periphery of a community of scholars dedicated to teaching and learning. But socially relevant pursuits quickly spread and can eventually corrupt the entire academic enterprise. With the help of willing donors, professorships in the policy sciences multiply rapidly while departments of philosophy languish; problem-oriented institutes spring up and flourish while classics and medieval studies struggle to maintain a meager existence; established professors find it hard to resist the lure of consulting and topical projects at the expense of more fundamental research. As larger proportions of the faculty become engaged in helping to solve social problems, accepted notions of academic responsibility may decline throughout the university. At first, the deterioration will occur in little ways—seeing students less promptly, avoiding departmental chores—matters that are not covered by any job description but that make a difference to the morale of an institution and to the quality of its educational environment. In later stages, teaching loads diminish and the use of graduate student instructors begins to increase. In the end, traditionalists fear, the excitement and rewards of social involvement will gradually erode the status, the esprit, and eventually the loyalty and dedication of teachers and scholars who still devote themselves to traditional academic pursuits.

Should this deterioration occur, much will be lost to the university. Solving practical problems may have immediate importance, but the search for basic knowledge and understanding serves an even greater purpose. Indeed, this quest may grow more important, and not less so, in periods when the society becomes particularly anxious and preoccupied with the issues of contemporary life. As Saul Bellow remarked on receiving the Nobel Prize in 1976: "When complications increase, the desire for essentials increases too . . . Out of the struggle at the center has come an immense, painful longing for a broader, more flexible, fuller, more coherent, more comprehensive account of what we human beings are, who we are, and what this life is for."[5]

The force of Bellow's words emerges with particular clarity when we look back over our history and reflect on the legacy we have received from earlier times. At any given point, a society will be preoccupied with particular problems of immediate importance. But in the longer run, it is not the battles, the elections, the intrigues of the moment that continue to command our admiration and respect. In numbering Athens and Florence among the great achievements of Western civilization, we are moved not by their material conquests or their diplomatic triumphs, but by their enduring works of intellect and imagination that remain to shape our understanding of ourselves, our values, our potentialities and limitations, our deepest aspirations and dilemmas.

If we allow the pursuit of knowledge and understanding to slacken in our universities, the damage will be irreparable, for such intellectual pursuits cannot be carried on effectively in any other setting. Not that our campuses can claim a monopoly on creative work. Artists, composers, novelists, and poets have seldom found the academic environment congenial to their labors. But in the broad domains of basic scientific inquiry, humanistic scholarship, or the analysis of society and its institutions, universities offer the most fertile ground for contributions of lasting importance. Because these endeavors are so valuable, we should not put them at risk by forcing them to coexist with activities that threaten to compromise their integrity and undermine their standards. And it is precisely such compromises that the traditionalists fear once universities embark on a determined effort to influence society and find solutions for its immediate problems.

5. *New York Times*, December 13, 1976, p. 9.

The second theme in the traditionalist critique is more mundane and administrative in nature, yet it too deserves careful consideration. Because the problems of society are so numerous and the need for knowledge and expertise so pervasive, the service-oriented institution will constantly be pressured to add more and more activities and programs. If the university is tightly organized, the central administration will expand in size to accommodate the lengthening list of endeavors. Layers of authority will be added, and bureaucratic methods will replace informal patterns of support and supervision. As procedures grow more rigid and routinized, more time will be required to make even simple decisions, and the processes of administration will become less capable of responding sensitively to the separate needs and purposes of the varied units within the institution.

Universities can try to combat these problems by a policy of decentralization that permits smaller units to maintain a clear sense of purpose and to respond more quickly and sensitively to the needs of their members. Yet decentralization has its limits and creates certain problems of its own. For one thing, it tends to inhibit cooperation between units and aggravates the sense of fragmentation resulting from proliferating programs and functions. In addition, the diffusion of power leads to the creation of many small bureaucracies so that the total number of administrators may actually increase, and more and more time must be taken for negotiation between different administrative groups.

Even if the institution pursues an aggressive program of decentralization, administrators cannot easily divide functions such as maintenance, construction, and purchasing. As government regulation increases, the list of these functions steadily lengthens, since the central staff must exercise enough control to make certain that every unit observes the legally mandated rules that accompany such activities as affirmative action, fringe-benefit programs, and accounting for federal grants. Similarly, under any form of organization, certain officials, particularly the president, must still retain responsibility for the entire institution. As the number of functions grows, the burden on these key officials is bound to increase. Presidents and deans will find it harder to maintain contact with students and faculty or to devote close attention to every program and institute in their vast domain. Serious problems will go undetected for far too long. More time will be devoted to rescuing floundering projects and less will be given to helping adequate programs become better. Fewer opportunities will arise for serious reflection about the future of the institution, and important long-range questions will be neglected in order to attend to immediate crises. In short, the quality of leadership, as well as the effectiveness of administration, will gradually decline.

The traditionalist critique points to a number of dangers and abuses that undoubtedly exist in contemporary universities. But the proponents devote much more effort to explaining defects than they do to recommending solutions. Pressed to its logical conclusion, their criticism seems to call for a more cloistered institution paying little attention to the immediate problems of society. The specialized training and expert advice that the nation requires would presumably be left to other institutions—vocational schools, consulting firms, institutes of applied research, and think tanks of various kinds.

Such extreme solutions, of course, are hardly practical. The cost of reforming our universities would be far too great at this stage in their development. Legislators and donors would hardly wish to pay the price. And it is even unclear how many professors would freely choose to cast their lot with institutions so detached from the problems of society. Nevertheless, we cannot simply dismiss such a serious argument for pragmatic reasons alone. If the only grounds for disagreement with the traditionalist model were its practical limitations, we might still make different choices about the future development of the university in order to nudge it gradually along quite different lines. As a result, we would do well to consider what might be gained and lost if we were somehow able to replace our multiversities with institutions entirely dedicated to learning for its own sake.

To achieve this goal, universities would probably have to do away with their professional schools, since such schools cannot perform their function without preoccupying themselves with the practical problems of their vocations. After all, what is more practical than a teaching hospital or a law school accounting class? To be sure, professional schools would have to exist in some form because they are indispensable to a modern society. But they could presumably be established as independent institutions entirely separate from the university. The question is: what sort of difference would this separation make?

Most educators are convinced that professional schools can reach a high level of quality only when practical teaching and applied research are combined with basic inquiry and instruction of a kind that can only exist within a university setting. Thus every medical school contains strong programs of basic science as well as clinical research. Every leading business school employs economists, political scientists, and even psychologists and historians. Every outstanding law school seeks to develop in its students an awareness of jurisprudence and legal history as well as a mastery of practical skills. Of course, independent professional schools could seek to employ their own complement of basic and social scientists. And yet, one wonders whether able scholars would be comfortable in a professional school totally removed from their parent disciplines and totally separated from the atmosphere, the traditions, the intellectual values of the university. Would they do their best work in such an environment? Would they even accept an appointment? Our past experience offers little reassurance on this score. Although there are several outstanding institutions of learning that possess no strong complement of professional schools, one can scarcely point to a single distinguished professional school that is not linked to a university with an able faculty of arts and sciences. All in all, therefore, it seems likely that separating such schools from the university would eventually do considerable damage to the quality of professional education.

Traditionalists are even more adamant in condemning most of the research institutes that have sprouted during the past thirty years either to address social problems or to increase our understanding of other areas of the world. Skeptics can easily point to undistinguished ventures of this kind, enterprises with pretentious titles staffed by scholars of very modest talents. Yet much of this criticism should be directed at the haste with which these enterprises were established and not at the concept of the institute itself. In reality, much good work has emerged under the aegis of institutes and other similar organizations. Properly administered, such ventures can relieve professors of many of the petty bureaucratic burdens associated with seeking and administering research grants. Much more important, institutes can serve a valuable purpose in bringing together excellent scholars from different disciplines who might otherwise languish in distressingly specialized departments. Indeed, organizations of this kind are almost the only structures in the contemporary university that help to forge links between the separate fiefdoms of contemporary knowledge and learning. If institutes had to exist outside the university, they could no longer serve this integrative function. Moreover, they would find it even more difficult than the professional schools to attract creative people and provide them with the libraries and graduate students that are needed to sustain distinguished work. In the process, something of value would again be lost.

Institutes aside, what can be said of all the faculty efforts to offer social criticism and expert advice on specific issues of immediate concern? Such tasks could likewise be left to specialized institutes, consulting firms, or even thoughtful journalists and writers. But the remedy would not be without cost. There are important forms of technical advice that can be supplied only by scientists working at the frontier of their field. For example, only a leading biochemist can advise a drug company on the long-term implications of recombinant DNA research. There are other forms of consultation and social criticism that typically call for years of study and reflection of a kind that cannot be readily achieved by those who work outside a university setting. Thus academic scholars are often the persons most qualified to provide the government with competent medium-term analyses of political and economic trends in remote countries of the world. It is for reasons such as these that so many professors are solicited for advice by corporations, foundations, and government agencies, despite the existence of consulting firms and private institutes that offer advisory services of every kind.

In short, the cloistered university could probably exist only at a heavy cost to the quality of professional education, applied research, social criticism, and expert advice—activities that are all important to our society. One may still insist that the price is worth paying to preserve the value of traditional scholarship and learning. After all, these pursuits are also important—probably more so in the long run than the service-oriented activities of the multiversity. Yet this argument too seems less persuasive on careful examination than it appears to be at first glance.

With respect to the quality of teaching, one wonders whether service activities are truly the principal villain. Certainly, if teaching loads have dropped, they have dropped furthest not in the social sciences, where consulting and public service are most pronounced, but in scientific disciplines, such as mathematics and experimental physics, where the interests of undergraduates have steadily given way to the demands of pure research. As for the quality of research, one wonders whether traditionalists are correct in claiming that service-oriented activities inevitably corrupt the pursuit of knowledge for its own sake. In science, for example, with all the time devoted to consulting and administering grants, would anyone assert that the pace of new discovery has slackened during the postwar years?[6] In the humanities, scholarship is often marred by trivial work and even at times by a disturbing loss of purpose and morale. But is it not hazardous to blame the excesses of the multiversity rather than much deeper causes in our culture? Even in the social sciences—where the dangers of excessive relevance are most pronounced, the involvement in practical issues most widespread, the loss of detachment most severe—the effects on scholarship are still uncertain. If professors have lost some of their objectivity by trying to shape the society they purport to describe, they have also gained something in experience and first-hand knowledge.

In the end, therefore, traditionalists seem to have exaggerated the drawbacks of the modern university. Much excellent work has been done in these institutions over the past thirty years, both by scholars who keep their distance from the practical world and by social scientists who manage to combine fundamental research with efforts to address immediate problems. Although some professors have doubtless been diverted from serious writing and others have lost some of their objectivity, the level of scholarship in the best of our universities hardly suffers by comparison with the quality of work in the more traditional universities of Eu-

6. It is instructive to compare the traditionalists' concerns with much earlier laments over the state of American science. In 1906, for example, a statistical study indicated that the United States was producing one seventh to one tenth of the world's scientific research, and observed that American scientists "have not produced one tenth of its recent great discoveries or of its contemporary great men" (J. McKeen Cattell, "A Statistical Study of American Men of Science," *Science*, 24 [December 7, 1906], 742).

rope—or even with that of the rare, privately endowed research institutes that offer generous salaries to able scholars and insulate them almost completely from the normal burdens and distractions of academic life.

On the basis of this record, few sensible observers could be confident that society would be better off in the long run by radically altering the nature of our universities. In reality, the concerns expressed by traditionalists are scarcely new; most of them have been voiced for at least a hundred years by those who have resisted the efforts of practical men seeking to cast the academy in a utilitarian mold.[7] Nevertheless, critics continue to speak as if our campuses had slipped from a state of grace achieved in some unspecified golden age. In making these charges, they ignore a substantial body of evidence suggesting that in terms of the quality of students, the accessibility to applicants from all income groups, the achievements of research, and the level of intellectual challenge demanded in the classroom, our leading institutions are better today than they were in prior generations.

To say that these complaints are not new, however, or even to point out that they are often exaggerated and loosely reasoned, is not to say that they are entirely wrong. Even the most enthusiastic university president would admit that each abuse identified by the traditionalists exists to some degree on every campus. If their complaints seem too shrill and their remedies too sweeping and impractical, one must sympathize strongly with the scholarly ideals they mean to emphasize—the dedication, the objectivity, the uncompromising search for knowledge uncorrupted by consulting fees or publicity-seeking. And so, though drastic solutions seem ill-advised, it is surely important to do everything possible to ensure that efforts to serve society do not extend so far that they result in shoddy programs, cumbersome administration, partisan scholarship, and excessive amounts of consulting and government service.

The last of these problems is probably the hardest to correct. At present, university policies actually encourage outside activities

7. For examples of such complaints in the early years of this century—the rise of the campus bureaucracy, the overemphasis on utility and social service, the gulf between students and faculty—see Lawrence R. Veysey, *The Emergence of the American University* (Chicago: University of Chicago Press, 1965).

by allowing professors to collect their regular salaries and simultaneously receive additional compensation for consulting, serving on boards of directors, or engaging in other pursuits away from the campus. Alas, even President Robert Hutchins could not persuade the University of Chicago faculty to remedy this problem, and fresh efforts would undoubtedly meet such strong resistance that one must probably write them off as impractical. At the very least, however, an administration can work with the faculty to set sensible limits on outside activities. Deans can insist on reasonable instructional loads and avoid the temptation to recruit famous professors by promising relief from teaching. Efforts can also be made to reserve distinguished professorships, exceptional merit increases, and other forms of special recognition for faculty members who make the greatest contributions to teaching and scholarship. The outside world already supplies ample excitement, prestige, and material rewards to professors who seek to influence events and offer their advice to those in power. Within the limited means at their command, presidents and deans should surely do whatever they can to emphasize the fact that a university reserves its highest honor and esteem for those who contribute the most to the central mission of the institution.

A few rough guidelines can also help to prevent an institution from encumbering itself with programs and projects of doubtful merit. To begin with, research universities should avoid undertaking tasks that other organizations can discharge equally well. A serious review will often show that educational and intellectual functions are more appropriately performed by state and community colleges, or by urban universities that have deliberately chosen the mission of providing a wide range of services to their surrounding areas. Still other programs can be carried out by consulting firms, corporations, or government agencies. In view of these alternatives, one must ask in every case whether the service to be rendered actually requires those special qualities that set research universities apart: extensive libraries, well-equipped laboratories, faculties enjoying great independence and diverse intellectual interests—and, above all, the presence of scholars who may have little practical experience but have enjoyed unusual opportunities for sustained reading and reflection about their chosen field of study. A moment's thought should reveal activities on most university campuses that deserve careful scrutiny with these criteria in mind—schools of hotel management; doctoral programs in physical education, radio and television communications, leisure studies, or family ecology; masters programs in textiles and clothing, or in home economics; and other doubtful enterprises too numerous to mention.[8]

A second guideline in considering new ventures is that every additional program should enhance the institution's teaching and research activities. An example that plainly meets this test is the teaching hospital, where the university helps to attract able physicians and provides a staff of interns and residents in return for gaining access to a practical setting indispensable for instruction and clinical research. Another illustration is provided by some, though not all, programs for midcareer instruction. In business schools, for example, executive programs often supply valuable instruction for participants while providing an excellent means of exposing faculty members and their teaching materials to experienced managers who can contribute valuable insights gained from years of practical experience.

A third, and closely related, principle is that new projects should not normally be approved unless they can first be shown to command the enthusiasm and active support of existing members of the faculty. In my experience, many of the greatest programmatic failures in universities have occurred when a dean or president has identified an important opportunity and received substantial funding without first ascertaining whether able professors are actually willing to devote substantial time and effort to the enterprise. Occasionally, the administration may succeed in recruiting new personnel to carry out such projects successfully. More often, however, capable people cannot be found or will not

8. For example, many universities in the 1960s established urban "observatories" and other organizations to provide research and consulting services to city officials. Surveys conducted in 1970 among the chief administrative officers of 859 cities revealed that 72 percent found private consulting firms to be a very helpful source of advice, while only 39 percent felt the same way about universities (International City Management Association, "Science-Technology Advice to Local Governments," *Journal of the ICMA*, November 1970, 33–35). With this record, one wonders whether such university advisory services deserve to be maintained.

be genuinely welcomed by the existing faculty. In either event, the venture is virtually bound to fail.

While each of these guidelines provides a separate justification for a new academic program, they will be closely linked in almost all situations. Despite the talk about a confusion of goals in our universities, teaching and research are still the central concerns of almost all professors. Few programs will evoke a sustained commitment from the faculty unless they are capable of enhancing the teaching or the scholarship of the professors involved. Conversely, most service programs that are closely related to teaching and research will for that very reason have a special quality that cannot be duplicated in other kinds of institutions.

These criteria offer useful guidelines to check the excessive growth of service activities. Yet pressures constantly arise to make exceptions to the rules. In times of financial stringency, for example, a university may be strongly tempted to take on new extension programs in order to utilize its facilities fully, even though the courses involved are peripheral and could be done as well or better by another institution. An academic institution may also feel impelled to mount particular projects to meet community needs, such as programs to advise local officials or to assist in educating the underprivileged, even though such efforts may not fit very well with the professional interests and capabilities of the faculty. If these pressures prove impossible to resist, university officials should at least recognize the dangers of accumulating programs of this kind and try to structure them to minimize their burdens. Better yet, the administration should make every effort to solve its financial or community problems by developing programs of a kind that will allow the institution to make a distinctive contribution while simultaneously benefiting its basic teaching and research.

The Activist View

Within the limits just described, universities have an obligation to use their academic resources to respond to public needs. But who is to define these needs and determine the priorities to assign among them? Universities could avoid these questions out of respect for academic freedom and institutional neutrality. In that event, presidents and deans will serve as little more than brokers, joining the interests of faculty members to those of government funding agencies, foundations, and donors. By responding so readily to the requests of outside groups, however, the university may be attacked for clinging to a specious neutrality that amounts to little more than a tacit endorsement of the status quo and a willingness to support initiatives defined by the wealthy and the powerful.

Many writers have assailed universities on precisely these grounds. In the words of Zella and Salvador Luria: "Passive acceptance of the goals and values of society deprives the university of the claim to intellectual leadership and encourages its involvement in ventures of dubious ethical and intellectual value."[9] Harsher critics would go further and allege that the modern multiversity has become a handmaiden of the establishment, transmitting its values, carrying out its purposes, and helping to perpetuate its least desirable features. The implication of such remarks is that someone—presidents, faculty members, students?—ought to take more initiative to frame a conception of the good society and to pursue this vision aggressively by refusing to support certain programs while striving to develop others.

In keeping with this vision, many activists have urged universities to sever their ties with government agencies and other organizations that allegedly engage in harmful and exploitative activities. In the late 1960s, for example, enormous pressure was exerted in an effort to halt further involvement with ROTC programs, war-related research projects, and campus recruitment by the Pentagon, the Central Intelligence Agency, and leading defense contractors. In seeking to cut these links with the outside world, activist leaders took a course that bore some resemblance to that of the more traditionalist critics. But the motives of the two groups were entirely different. While traditionalists sought to minimize outside involvements in order to maintain the quality of essential academic functions, many activists had little regard for these values and mounted their protests for other reasons. In part, they wished to enhance the moral position of universities by avoiding all complicity with activities and organizations they

9. S. E. Luria and Zella Luria, "The Role of the University: Ivory Tower, Service Station, or Frontier Post?" *Daedalus*, Winter 1970, p. 78.

considered to be destructive and inhumane. But the more radical among them had larger ends in mind. Through their mass rallies and their building take-overs they hoped to raise the consciousness of their audience, build a student proletariat, and ultimately reform the entire political and economic structure. In the words of Immanuel Wallerstein, "The government needs the university, as it needs the church, as it needs the arts, as it needs the major political and economic structures . . . to say over and over again that it is worthy of support. If enough of these institutions, through their leaders, refuse often enough to do so, the government, the regime, will fall."[10]

Other writers of a less militant persuasion have urged the academic community to take a more active part in working for liberal reforms. For example, John Kenneth Galbraith has asserted that educators fail to recognize how much power they possess in a modern, technological society. In his words, higher education has gradually amassed considerable influence "from its rapidly increasing numbers with consequent political implications; from its privileged access to scientific innovations; and from its nearly unique role in social innovation." But educators will need to do more than write articles and deliver speeches if they are to use their power to bring about constructive change. According to Galbraith, "redirection of the weapons competition, social control of environment, a wider range of choice by the individual, emancipation of education—require some form of political action." Although scholars tend to shrink from such a role, "it is possible that the educational and scientific estate requires only a strongly creative political hand to become a decisive instrument of political power."[11]

Professor Galbraith did not specify how this latent political force could actually be organized or who should take the lead in

10. *University in Turmoil: The Politics of Change* (New York: Atheneum, 1969), pp. 32–33. Not all radical thinkers shared these objectives. Although almost all sought to avoid complicity with what they considered to be repressive forces in the society, some openly fought against the effort to use the university as a vehicle for social intervention. In this respect, their views were quite close to the traditionalist position. This point serves to make clear that traditionalists are not necessarily politically conservative, nor are all political radicals necessarily identified with what I describe as the activist position.

11. *The New Industrial State* (Boston: Houghton Mifflin, 1967), pp. 386, 294–295.

carrying out that task. But others have suggested concrete steps to enlist faculties in the service of social reform. According to Jerald Johnson:

> One needs very little imagination to envisage teams of teachers upgrading inner-city schools, physical education and theatre and dance personnel designing programs suited to spaces with little grass, sociologist-psychologist teams creating new, more compassionate ways to enforce laws, biologists inventing easy-to-use methods of doing away with rodents, and home economists creating inexpensive accouterments for home decorating. Why aren't these things being done now? Perhaps because the university places little value on this kind of activity and thus chooses not to reward, much less encourage, this type of effort. But as a collective unit the faculty wields great weight. What would be the result if the faculty chose to reward public service in the same manner that . . . it now rewards research and publication?[12]

Even today, of course, professors are free to use a portion of their time advising urban agencies and assisting community groups. Some faculties actually combine professional education with public service; medical schools often help to staff ambulatory clinics and emergency rooms, while law schools establish legal offices where students represent indigent clients under faculty supervision. In Professor Johnson's view, however, these efforts are insufficient to meet the need, and further inducements are required. Presumably, universities should provide these incentives by recognizing social service in reviewing faculty members for promotion and by allowing professors to work on useful community projects as a regular part of their academic duties.

Such encouragement might succeed in shifting substantial amounts of faculty time away from traditional forms of teaching and research toward practical, community-oriented tasks. But would this displacement of effort be wise? If we are to believe the frequent complaints that professors already neglect their students and spend too little time in the more traditional forms of research, it will only make matters worse to give explicit rewards for service activities in the community.

12. "The University as Problem Solver: Creativity and the Ghetto," *Liberal Education*, 54 (October 1968), 423.

One must also ask whether professors are truly equipped to make the practical contributions that Professor Johnson seems to favor. In 1970 a law student exclaimed to me: "Can't you see what it would mean to poor people if the entire law school faculty took a year and addressed itself exclusively to the problems of urban housing in Boston?" I was skeptical then, and I remain so to this day. William Buckley may have gone too far in claiming that he would rather cast his lot with the first hundred names in the Boston phone book than be governed by the Harvard faculty. Nevertheless, even the hardiest optimist has to wonder whether many professors possess the practical knowledge and political skill to make much lasting progress in attacking the problems of urban poverty, deteriorating schools, and hard-core unemployment. These are not the tasks for which most scholars are hired, nor would it seem wise to try to assemble faculties that can effectively combine such disparate qualities as a capacity for teaching and scholarship and a talent for political maneuvering and social action. Teaching and research are demanding tasks that require a high order of ability and dedication. Political action is likewise a difficult enterprise that calls for considerable experience and skill. Thus a university that sought to carry out both activities simultaneously could easily end by doing neither well. If we would truly help the poor and disadvantaged, we will probably go further by trying to improve the agencies specially devoted to such purposes rather than by seeking to divert the energies of teachers and scholars, who will often prove ill-suited for the task of implementing social reform.

One also wonders how many forms of public service Professor Johnson would have the university encourage. Could professors receive credit for advising corporations? the Ford Foundation? the State Department? Or should such special incentives be reserved for services rendered to the poor and disadvantaged? Professor Johnson does not tell us who will make these choices or how the questions should be answered. Nor does he specify how one would evaluate such services in deciding whether professors should receive a merit increase or a promotion. Should faculty members be rewarded for organizing groups of poor white parents to oppose forced busing or for training social workers to detect welfare chiselers? Would sociologists and psychologists be rated as highly for recommending methods of stern discipline as they would be for devising "more compassionate ways to enforce laws"? One suspects that Professor Johnson would not be inclined to treat these cases equally. But a faculty could hardly make such judgments in evaluating colleagues without imposing its values on the work of individual professors in precisely the manner that American universities have traditionally rejected.

In the face of these problems, other activist writers have suggested a different way in which to mobilize the university as an engine of social reform. According to Professor Harold Taylor, presidents and deans have a decisive role to play. "The truth is that the university administrator, although hemmed in by a network of hidden controls, has two major sources of power—the decisions about how to spend the money in his budget and whom to appoint to do what he thinks needs to be done. His actual control over educational policy and the mission of the university . . . lies in what he sets in motion by the persons he appoints." As luck would have it, the means for using this power effectively are readily at hand. "Many of the students involved in the reform movements in the early and middle 1960s have gone on to the graduate schools with no slackening in their enthusiasm for the causes with which they were identified as undergraduates . . . The academic credentials of these new graduate students are usually impeccable. They are among the best students, and their social views, especially on questions of race and poverty, are radical, and at the same time are becoming politically respectable . . . These intellectuals and activists have recruited themselves into the academic profession at exactly the time it needs them most . . . The nature of their commitments then adds to their qualifications for appointment to the universities and colleges."[13]

There is much ambiguity in these remarks. Dr. Taylor may have meant to suggest that larger numbers of radical professors are becoming available and will be appointed to university faculties through normal selection procedures. Once appointed, these individuals can then be counted upon to persuade the university to make a concerted action-oriented attack on such problems as poverty and racial discrimination. If this is the argument, it

13. Harold Taylor, *Students without Teachers: The Crisis in the University* (New York: McGraw-Hill, 1969), pp. 126, 128.

merely reflects the optimism of much activist writing of the early 1970s, overestimating the number of radical reformers and exaggerating their power and persistence to transform the university. But there is a strong implication that academic administrators should actually attempt to use their power to stock the faculty with professors who embrace a particular set of political beliefs and a special determination to engage in political action to reform society. This suggestion is vulnerable on several counts. It proceeds from the doubtful premise that presidents and deans have the power to impose their own appointments on the faculty. It likewise assumes that administrators are entitled to transform the faculty to serve their own political preferences and to subordinate academic values to their own social ends. Although both assumptions are highly controversial, Professor Taylor does not undertake to deal with the difficulties involved.

It is easy to criticize these writers for being naive, unclear, or simply impractical. But it would be wrong to assume that the activist critique has nothing to tell us about the social responsibilities of the university. Enthusiasts of the multiversity were often content merely to proclaim its diverse accomplishments and to explore its administrative challenges and tensions. It remained for the activist critics to expose the moral dangers of marshaling the academic resources of the institution for the benefit of any client who could pay the bill. If we are to make the most of these insights, however, and discover how we can put them to practical use, we will need to lay a more careful foundation by describing the manner in which power is actually distributed in a university and the restraints that limit its exercise.

The Role of Leadership in the University

Unlike armies, corporations, and other hierarchical organizations, universities are communities in which authority is widely shared instead of being concentrated in the hands of a few leaders. Individual professors are largely immune from administrative control over their teaching and research by virtue of the doctrine of academic freedom. Acting collectively, faculties typically have the power to fix the content of the curriculum, set academic requirements, search for new professors, and shape the standards for admission. Students do not have much power to initiate policy directly. Nevertheless, they do exert considerable influence on policy—not so much by collective action but by their ability not to attend institutions they do not like and to force changes in curriculum and teaching methods by the slow, silent pressure of apathy and disapproval. Alumni likewise have considerable power to block developments they oppose by withholding contributions or by voicing their discontent through boards of trustees or in other embarrassing ways. Finally, of course, government agencies can influence institutional policy through their ability to provide subsidies, or to resort to outright regulation, or in the case of state legislatures, to approve or disapprove budgets covering most expenditures made by public universities.

In this environment of shared authority, presidents and deans have limited, though significant, powers. To begin with, they generally have the means to block particular programs or initiatives that they consider unwise or improper—either by refusing to allow the institution to sponsor the activities or award the necessary degrees or, indirectly, by declining to assist in obtaining funds or providing other forms of essential support to the enterprise. There are various reasons for exercising such power. A president or dean may block a program because he believes that it does not meet accepted standards of quality, because it invades the jurisdictional prerogatives of other units in the university, because it permits outside influence over matters of academic policy, or because its administration and financing seem inadequate.

In addition, academic leaders have a responsibility to curb activities and programs that promise to violate generally accepted norms of society or to inflict unwarranted harm on others. This obligation raises difficult issues both in defining the proper ethical standards and in deciding how to reconcile such moral duties with the need to preserve institutional neutrality and academic freedom. These problems will crop up repeatedly in the chapters that follow. Although the conclusions reached will often differ sharply from those of many activists of the late 1960s, these critics were surely correct in insisting that many university programs do raise serious moral issues that are a proper and important concern of the administration.

All the grounds for intervention just described are fully consistent with the traditional and accepted responsibilities of academic leaders. In exercising such authority, of course, presidents and deans must avoid intervening arbitrarily or indiscriminately. In particular, they must refrain from using their authority to impose their private political views on the university. Any attempt to do so would threaten to violate the academic freedom of individuals holding contrary opinions. Such action would also constitute an abuse of office, since academic leaders are appointed to serve the interests of a wide variety of groups who support the university and benefit from its activities. Finally, efforts to use the university for particular ideological goals would jeopardize the independence of the institution by inviting the intervention of outside groups who will respect the university's autonomy only so long as it does not seek to become a mechanism to achieve specific political reforms. It is in this sense that the university administration must be neutral. Any president or dean who ignores that principle not only will violate his trust but will almost certainly be stymied by the opposition of faculty, alumni, and trustees.

In addition to their power to block unwise initiatives, presidents and deans can also exert a positive influence to encourage new ventures, since their position gives them special opportunities to present proposals, have them considered carefully by the faculty, and find the funds and the facilities to carry them out. These advantages are considerable. Yet the extent of a president's influence is limited by the fact that his proposals will succeed only if they command the genuine interest and support of the professors who must put them into practice and the funding agencies that must provide continuing financial support.

In the exercise of this positive influence, the activist critique once again is relevant, though not in precisely the way that its proponents may have intended. Activist critics often exaggerate the monolithic nature of the existing power structure and overstate its effects on the activities of the university. After all, there are many sources of funding in the United States and some are quite hospitable to unconventional proposals. Professors can often write books, give speeches, and offer courses without much need for money. Hence, universities need not be dominated by a single point of view, nor have they been in practice. What *is* true, however, is that no unseen hand exists to ensure that every important opportunity for education and research is automatically recognized and supported by the society. As a result, if universities are to discharge their responsibilities to the public, academic leaders must actively seek to find neglected opportunities and important new initiatives for valuable work. Of course, this responsibility must be exercised with proper regard for the limits and capabilities of the institution and for the maintenance of high academic standards. With more than three thousand colleges and universities in the country, there is no need for each institution to initiate every socially valuable program that comes to its attention. But most presidents and deans can still find room to search for promising new ventures without overburdening their institutions or asking them to take on inappropriate tasks.

We must recognize, of course, that the search for such opportunities has undeniable political overtones. No president can encourage a scholarship program for black South Africans or a preferential admissions policy for minority students or a research center on arms control without making value judgments about the state of the society and the nature of its needs. Nevertheless, we can easily see the difference between this type of assessment and a deliberate effort to promote a particular social reform or to commit the university to a specific ideology. It is one thing to encourage research on poverty and quite another to take an institutional position on appropriate government policies toward the poor. Efforts to stimulate teaching and scholarship on important social problems do not interfere with academic freedom any more than a decision to found a business school infringes on the rights of professors who oppose the free-enterprise system. If each new venture can be debated by the faculty, if participating scholars are chosen purely on their academic merits, if curricula and research projects remain a prerogative of the professors, presidential efforts to launch new initiatives are not likely to evolve into programs that use the institution for predetermined political ends. Nor will such ventures be regarded by the outside world as inappropriate for the university. On the contrary, initiatives of this kind have long exemplified the kind of academic leadership that is essential if the institution is to use its resources to respond creatively to a full range of social needs and opportunities.

In sum, a form of social responsibility exists quite distinct from the vision produced either by traditionalists or by social activists. Those who hold this position recognize that universities have an obligation to serve society by making the contributions they are uniquely able to provide. In carrying out this duty, everyone concerned must try to take account of many different values—the preservation of academic freedom, the maintenance of high intellectual standards, the protection of academic pursuits from outside interference, the rights of individuals affected by the university not to be harmed in their legitimate interests, the needs of those who stand to benefit from the intellectual services that a vigorous university can perform. The difficult task that confronts all academic leaders is to decide how their institution can respond to important social problems in a manner that respects all of these important interests.

Part II

Academic Responses to Social Problems

4

Access to the University and the Problem of Racial Inequality

For generations, blacks and other minority groups have struggled with the burdens of inequality. Although outright discrimination on racial grounds has been prohibited for many years, its effects linger on. Even in the 1980s, the average family income of blacks has reached only 60 percent of the level achieved by whites; unemployment among blacks is still twice the figure for whites; and the percentage of blacks below the poverty line is more than three times the proportion for the rest of the society.[1]

Admitting Students

During the hundred years that followed the close of the Civil War, almost all academic institutions engaged in some form of discrimination against minority groups, and few made any effort to address the racial problems of the nation. After the mid-1960s, however, colleges and universities were pressed with increasing urgency to respond in some fashion to help minority students gain access to the more desirable, influential careers in the society. Although some institutions reacted voluntarily and others in response to pressure, almost all eventually moved in the same direction. In one way or another, colleges and universities began to enroll larger numbers of minority students by admitting blacks, Hispanics, and American Indians with grade averages and ad-

1. *Statistical Abstract of the United States: 1980* (Washington, D.C.: U.S. Bureau of the Census, 1980), pp. 407, 459, 465.

mission test scores well below those of white applicants who were rejected.

Some universities are said to have gone so far in trying to expand minority enrollments that they have actually admitted students who show little promise of being able to pass the regular courses. This practice is very hard to defend. Regardless of their race, students will not benefit in the long run if they cannot graduate; they will only waste their time and take places away from others who could profit much more from the opportunity to enroll. Rather than have such students fail, universities may try to escape the predicament by creating special courses of little academic rigor or by lowering their grading standards. Yet neither alternative can be justified, for each attempts to mislead the public about the true academic accomplishments of the students involved while excluding other applicants who could benefit more from attending the institution. Eventually, the truth is bound to leak out, with the result that most employers will no longer put much weight on the grades received by minority students, and even those blacks and Hispanics who do excel academically will cease to receive due credit for their accomplishments.

Decisions to set fixed quotas for minority students are only slightly less questionable. Quotas are always hard to defend because they commit an institution to accept a certain number of students from a particular group regardless of how their qualifications compare with those of other applicants. This practice can easily cause universities to admit students who are less promising from every point of view than others who must be rejected. If students from the favored category do not apply in sufficient numbers, quotas may also force admissions officers to accept applicants who have little prospect of even meeting the basic academic requirements, and that is a result that cannot be justified on any grounds.

Most universities, however, have not resorted to fixed quotas. Many of them, especially their professional schools, attract a surplus of applicants who can easily pass the regular courses. In such circumstances, admissions officers decide on a case-by-case basis to admit a number of minority students who are qualified to do the work but possess lower grades and test scores than white applicants who are turned away. These policies are not unprecedented. Colleges have extended preferential treatment for years to other groups of students, such as exceptional athletes or children of alumni, and these practices rarely arouse controversy. But efforts to enlarge the enrollment of minority students have provoked an angry outcry from people who feel that universities are acting unfairly by favoring minority applicants.

The debate over preferential admissions has surely contributed one of the murkier chapters in the vast literature on higher education. Some writers display little understanding of how admissions processes actually work, while others reveal biases of one sort or another that lead them repeatedly to overstate their case and to ignore critical arguments from their opponents. Far from illuminating the problem, such authors have succeeded only in misleading readers and confirming their prejudices.

Those who attack preferential admissions generally begin by assuming that the policy represents a well-meaning but misguided attempt by universities to atone for the injustices society has inflicted on blacks and other racial groups. By admitting minority applicants with lower grades and standardized test scores, university officials allegedly sacrifice efficiency and progress by denying superior educational opportunities to white students who are said to be better qualified "on the merits" to receive them. In failing to gain access to the institution of their choice, these students are also made to suffer an injustice, since they are seldom responsible for any past discriminations against minority groups. To make matters worse, leading universities frequently offer preferred treatment to minority students from comfortable middle-class backgrounds and thus are accused of favoring applicants who have suffered the least from discrimination while rejecting white students who often come from poor families and may have had to overcome much greater adversity.

Those who defend preferential admissions usually agree that universities exclude better-qualified whites in an effort to make up for past injustices against minorities. Nevertheless, such writers advance various arguments to justify this practice. Some concede that preferential admissions may inflict a temporary injustice, but argue that this is a price worth paying to achieve greater equality in the long run. Others contend that all whites have profited from the long tradition of keeping down minorities and that all members of minority groups bear the burden and stigma of discrimination. In these circumstances, every black, Hispanic, and American Indian deserves some compensatory advantage in securing better educational opportunities, and every white can be justly asked to bear a part of the cost.

These arguments are not entirely persuasive. It is never easy to insist that deserving individuals be made to suffer a hardship in the hope of someday rectifying an injustice for which they are not directly responsible. Moreover, every attempt to penalize one group to benefit another will produce a number of individual injustices. Few people would assert that *all* white students have benefited from the hardships of discrimination, or that *every* successful minority applicant has suffered greater hardships or disadvantages than *every* white who is turned away.[2] Who is to say that a black student of middle-class parents who has studied at Andover Academy has had to labor under greater handicaps than the son of poor white immigrants who has graduated from an inner-city high school? One also wonders how far we must go and what kind of advantages minority persons must receive in order to make up for prior discrimination. Surely, we would not wish to grant additional votes to all minorities in political elections or require that all blacks on the professional golf tour receive a handicap in competing for prizes. Why, then, should minority students obtain an advantage in competing for admission?

After years of inconclusive debate on these issues, we should accept the fact that critics of preferential admissions cannot be defeated convincingly by accepting their premises and then attempting to refute their arguments on grounds of justice. It is the premises themselves that are vulnerable, and especially the assumptions that preferential admissions are designed to atone for past injustices and that the white applicants who are excluded are somehow superior "on the merits." To test these assumptions, let us begin by considering what an ideal admissions process should seek to achieve in choosing among a large number of applicants.

2. If compensation is to be given for past injustice, it might be better to accomplish this purpose by distributing public funds to needy members of minority groups. This procedure would allocate the burden of compensation more fairly and could be designed to distribute benefits to those who have suffered most.

Only then can we understand what admissions officers are trying to accomplish and decide what types of students are truly preferable "on the merits."

In an ideal world, where admissions officers knew everything, they would presumably try to assemble a class that would allow their university to make the greatest possible contribution to its students and ultimately to the society as a whole. In striving for this goal, admissions committees would certainly wish to select only those students who were qualified intellectually to perform well in their academic work. But suppose that a large surplus of well-qualified applicants remained after this preliminary screening. What would the committee do next? After considering the matter, it would probably not simply select those students with the greatest intelligence or the highest grades. Instead, it would choose candidates who would benefit most from the university by making the greatest progress in improving their powers of analysis, their capacity for legal reasoning, their abilities of self-expression, their capacities for management, or whatever educational goals the institution in question thought important. But even this criterion would not be sufficient in itself; it would have to be modified to reflect two further considerations. Since a university is interested in the progress of *all* its students, and because we know that students learn much from each other, it would prefer to admit applicants who could bring some distinctive talent or special experience that would enhance the education of others. And since the university is ultimately concerned with contributing to society, admissions officers would also favor students who seemed especially likely in later life to use what they learned to benefit their professions and the communities in which they live.

In practice, of course, it is extremely difficult to select students according to these ideal objectives. Admissions officers simply do not know enough to predict with confidence which students will benefit most from their university experience or which will contribute the most to their fellow students or to the society. Nor is there agreement on the appropriate criteria to use in comparing the value of different social contributions or in deciding which forms of diversity will be of greatest benefit to other students.

Hampered by insufficient knowledge, admissions officers in most colleges and professional schools rely heavily on prior grades and standardized test scores in choosing their students. Combined judiciously, these criteria do provide a moderately strong basis for predicting a student's grades in the first year following admission (although they correlate less well with grades in subsequent years).[3] As a result, such measures are the best we have to meet the threshold goal of screening out applicants who are likely to have trouble meeting the academic standards of the institution.

But grades and test scores are much less helpful in deciding whom to admit from a large number of well-qualified applicants. In fact, they are more an index of a certain kind of intellectual capacity than a measure of a student's ability to learn and develop over time. Applicants with exceptional prior grades and scores may enter college with sufficient ability to absorb material of great complexity, and this is a factor to consider in assessing how much they will gain from their studies. Over their entire course of study, however, such students may not improve their powers of analysis and self-expression or even enlarge their store of knowledge to the same extent as classmates with strong but not outstanding talents who work conscientiously throughout their term in the university. In addition, grades and test scores reveal nothing about the progress students will make toward subtler educational goals, such as emotional maturity, ethical sensitivity, creativity, aesthetic appreciation, or a capacity to work effectively with others. For these reasons, in the difficult process of choosing among well-qualified applicants, the standard criteria for admission are clearly relevant, but they are not nearly so useful as many people suppose in helping to identify the students who will benefit most from attending the institution.

Prior grades and tests tell even less about an applicant's ability to make a contribution in later life. Numerous studies reveal that even substantial differences in grades and test scores explain very little of the variations in the success students achieve after gradua-

---

3. Prior grades and test scores can explain approximately 5 to 30 percent of the variance in first-year grades in college or professional school (William H. Angoff, *The College Board Admissions Testing Program* [New York: College Entrance Examination Board, 1971], p. 53). For any single student, this predictive value is not great, but for an entire class, reliance on grades and scores is almost certain to lift the academic performance of the group substantially above the levels that would be achieved if students were admitted randomly.

tion, whether success is measured by salary or status or by more refined criteria of accomplishment. It is true that high grades and scores may have a significant bearing on the ability to succeed in research or a few other callings that make unusual intellectual demands. Since universities are legitimately interested in preparing students for such careers, they may well decide to enroll an ample number of applicants who possess exceptional academic aptitude. Indeed, graduate departments may understandably place primary weight on precisely this quality in selecting candidates for Ph.D. programs. But universities are also interested in preparing students for many occupations, and in most of them a host of other factors play an important role in determining achievement in later life. As a result, an admissions committee in a selective institution can admit a number of students with test scores substantially below the mean without a demonstrable risk that they will accomplish less than their classmates in their subsequent lives.

Grades and test scores are also of limited value in trying to predict an applicant's potential to enhance the education of fellow students. Surveys of graduating classes have repeatedly shown that seniors believe that they have benefited as much from contact with one another as they have from their readings and lectures. Other studies have revealed that students who have the opportunity to interact closely by living together in campus dormitories show greater progress toward important educational goals than students who commute to nonresidential colleges. To maximize these opportunities, an enlightened admissions committee will seek to assemble a class with widely varying backgrounds and talents so that every student can draw on a broad range of values, perspectives, and experiences in the process of developing as a person. From this standpoint, a class admitted solely on the basis of tests and grades might well turn out to be much less interesting and stimulating than a class selected by more diverse criteria. To be sure, one can make a plausible (though unproven) argument that students with outstanding intellectual talents—say, the top 10 to 20 percent of the class—will set a high example that will motivate and stimulate their peers. Whether or not this is true, there will be more than enough room for these exceptional students even if the admissions committee enrolls other applicants with different talents and characteristics that promise to contribute in various ways to the quality of the class as a whole.

One may still argue that grades and scores deserve heavy weight in order to motivate students to work hard in high school and college and to provide them with a just reward for their achievement. But standardized tests do not purport to measure how hard an applicant has worked at his studies. Even high marks may reflect innate intelligence much more than conscientious effort, especially in a period marked by so much grade inflation and so many schools that make limited demands upon their students. As for preserving incentives, it is possible to make special efforts to assemble a class with diverse talents and characteristics and still put more than enough emphasis on grades to motivate students amply—as anyone can attest who has observed high school students competing for places in the best colleges.

What does all this tell us about the arguments for and against preferential admissions? First of all, the evidence suggests that those who oppose such policies have vastly exaggerated the importance of prior grades and standardized test scores. These measures serve a useful purpose in screening out applicants who probably cannot do the work; they also help identify a reasonable number of students with exceptional academic aptitude who seem especially likely to set a high example for their classmates and to excel in careers that make unusual intellectual demands. Nevertheless, in allocating the remaining places in the class among a large number of qualified applicants, grades and scores simply do not correlate well with most of the goals that admissions officers should ideally be seeking to achieve. Thus it is wrong to assume that a white applicant "deserves" to be admitted "on the merits" simply because he happens to have higher grades and scores than a minority applicant—provided, of course, that both clearly have the intellectual qualifications to meet the academic standards of the institution.

The arguments just described also suggest reasons for preferring minority applicants quite apart from a desire to atone for past discrimination. In a country where racial problems and misunderstandings are so prominent, all students stand to benefit from the chance to live and work with classmates of other races who can offer differing attitudes and experiences that will challenge and inform others and increase the understanding and tolerance of everyone concerned. In addition, an admissions committee will make special efforts to enroll minority students because they have exceptional chances to make important contributions to society after they graduate. By any test, talented, well-prepared members of minority groups have greater access to productive careers than ever before.[4] Our national policy of affirmative action reflects the importance society places on providing such opportunities. Whether minority students eventually hold influential positions in corporations, government agencies, hospitals, law firms, and universities or whether they decide to work in disadvantaged communities that lack many kinds of needed services, they will have all the possibilities that any graduate would have to live rewarding, contributing lives. But because there are still so few minority persons in influential posts, they are also likely to have special opportunities to enhance racial understanding and increase the sensitivity of people in power to the needs and problems of disadvantaged racial groups. As they succeed in their endeavors, it is possible that they may also help to lift the aspirations of other blacks and Hispanics and cause them to seek careers and levels of achievement that will eventually establish greater equality throughout the society.

With these ends in mind, we can understand why admissions officers are inclined to prefer the ablest minority applicants they can find, even if they do not come from disadvantaged families. Since universities are not seeking to enroll minority students to make up for past injustices, they have no duty to prefer applicants who have suffered the greatest deprivations. Instead, admissions committees will rationally prefer those minority students, regardless of background, who are best equipped to benefit from the education they receive and most capable of taking full advantage of the opportunities they will have to contribute in later life.

Like any admissions philosophy, the rationale just described is

4. As a result of the keen interest today in finding minority persons to fill more challenging jobs, black college graduates between the ages of twenty-four and twenty-nine currently earn slightly more than their white counterparts (Martin Kilson, "Black Social Classes and Intergenerational Poverty," *The Public Interest*, 64 [Summer 1981], 67–68).

based on informed judgment rather than established fact. It does seem reasonable to suppose that special efforts to assemble a student body composed of different ethnic groups will add to racial understanding and that well-prepared blacks, Hispanics, and American Indians will have unusual opportunities to make important contributions, particularly during the next generation. Indeed, we face a bleak and dispiriting future if these assumptions turn out to be incorrect. Nevertheless, they are still matters of faith—like many basic tenets of an academic community—and have not been demonstrated empirically. For this reason, the theory of preferential admissions remains a plausible but unproven hypothesis and has consequently met opposition on several grounds.

Some writers point out that any differential treatment based on race is likely to create resentment and misunderstanding and that universities do not need to run this risk since blacks and other minority groups could eventually achieve greater opportunities without the benefit of preferential admissions. This argument is highly questionable. To begin with, one wonders how much weight should be placed on any hostility produced by preferential admissions, since these resentments so often result from a faulty perception of the goals of the admissions process and a distorted sense of who "deserves" to be admitted "on the merits." In addition, those who argue that preferential admission is unnecessary seem far too optimistic about the prospective enrollment of minority youth in predominantly white institutions. Although these students might eventually increase their numbers without special help, the data suggest that such progress could have taken an intolerably long time to develop. As late as 1965, just before the advent of preferential admissions, blacks accounted for less than 2 percent of the nation's lawyers and slightly over 1 percent of all law students. In the same year, only 2 percent of the nation's doctors were black, while only a handful of black students were enrolled in predominantly white medical schools.[5] Little or no progress had occurred in increasing these proportions over the preceding generation.

5. See, for example, Allan P. Sindler, *Bakke, DeFunis, and Minority Admissions: The Quest for Equal Opportunity* (New York: Longman, 1978), pp. 31–32, 48.

Although these numbers might conceivably have grown substantially in the natural course of events, the fact remains that such progress did not occur until the new admissions policies came into being. Further studies suggest that even after intense recruiting efforts had encouraged more minority students to apply to professional schools, much of the resulting progress would have been wiped out if admissions officers had been prevented from taking any account of an applicant's race. Thus, studies conducted in the mid-seventies revealed that up to 82 percent of all black law students could not have entered the schools in which they were enrolled without special admissions and that the numbers attending the leading schools would quickly have dropped to a tiny handful.[6] Further studies yielded similar results in the case of minority enrollments in medical schools. In sum, it is probable that the increase in minority lawyers, doctors, and other professionals would have shrunk substantially in the absence of preferential treatment and that their failure to gain admission to the better schools would have significantly impaired their opportunity to have access to the full range of professional opportunities. It is also likely that these obstacles to professional advancement would have produced greater resentment in the minority population than any backlash brought about by current admissions policies. This would be a harsh price to pay for adhering strictly to the traditional criteria of admission, which bear so little relation to professional achievement in later life.

Other writers have assailed the practice of preferential admissions on the ground that it can harm the very people it purports to help. Some observers believe that leading universities, by awarding a heavy preference to minority applicants, may actually sap the incentive of these students, since they will know that they do not need to receive the highest grades in order to gain admis-

6. For those entering law schools in the fall of 1976, only 39 blacks had both Law School Admissions Test scores above 600 and undergraduate grade-point averages above 3.25. In contrast, 13,151 white students had grades and scores above these levels. See Franklin R. Evans, "Applications and Admissions to ABA Accredited Law Schools: An Analysis of National Data for the Class Entering in the Fall of 1976," Report LSAC-77-1 in Law School Admissions Council, *Reports of LSAC Sponsored Research: Volume III, 1975–1977* (Princeton: Law School Admissions Council, 1977), p. 604, Table 16. For a balanced summary of these studies, see Sindler, *Bakke, DeFunis, and Minority Admissions*, pp. 138–145.

sion to the best graduate and professional schools. Others argue that any policy offering special dispensations to minority students stamps them as second rate and thereby lowers their self-confidence and diminishes the respect accorded them by their white peers. According to these critics, this problem becomes particularly acute when leading schools lower their admissions standards so far that minority applicants are academically overmatched and thus feel inferior and insecure. For example, the average admissions test score for black law students at Berkeley in 1975 was 570—or the top 30 percent of those taking the test—while the average score for whites was close to 700—or the top 3 percent.[7] As Professor Thomas Sowell has argued, had these black students gone to somewhat less selective schools, they could have competed on more equal terms and might have proceeded with greater confidence to gain more from their legal training.[8]

Skeptics such as Professor Sowell can point to data that seem to support their concerns. A number of studies have shown that minority students tend to perform below the levels predicted by their prior grades and test scores and that blacks and Hispanics are often densely clustered at the bottom of their class.[9] At present, however, we simply do not know the explanation for these findings. If Professor Sowell is correct, one would expect minorities with the lowest grades and scores to fall furthest below their predicted performance, since these students would presumably feel the most inferior academically. But the evidence fails to bear out this hypothesis and even suggests that the opposite is often true. Hence, other factors would appear to have more to do with the performance of minority students. In today's society, blacks, Hispanics, and American Indians have tended to come from inferior schools and have had to cope with obvious burdens and difficulties in adjusting to predominantly white institutions. Thus the

7. Sindler, *Bakke, DeFunis, and Minority Admissions*, p. 126.

8. "The Plight of Black Students in the United States," *Daedalus*, Spring 1974, pp. 179–196.

9. Findings of overprediction have emerged quite consistently from analyses of standardized tests used for several types of professional schools. Whatever else they may prove, these studies seem effectively to refute earlier claims that standardized admissions tests were culturally biased against disadvantaged minority groups. See, for example, Robert L. Linn, "Fair Test Use in Selection," *Review of Educational Research,* 43 (Spring 1973), 139–161.

failure of many minority students to perform according to expectations may well result from inadequate preparation or from pressures and problems in the university environment that have little to do with lower grades and test scores. If this is true, the proper solution is to improve the environment for minority students or provide them with effective remedial help, not to exclude them from the university.

At most, the available data should caution admissions officers against a policy of awarding excessive preference to minority applicants in an overzealous effort to achieve impressive percentages of black and Hispanic students. Some institutions may have indulged in this practice, either from noble sentiments or to satisfy the demands of vocal minority groups. Regardless of the motive, there is little justification for admitting minority applicants with scores 150 to 200 points below the average for white students. Differences of this magnitude may eventually make a substantial difference in the ability of students to succeed in their profession while threatening to impose handicaps and psychological burdens that will impair academic performance. This point seems particularly telling in the case of professional schools that are already enrolling proportions of blacks or Hispanics greater than the percentage of these minorities in the national applicant pool. Now that so many institutions have adopted preferential admissions, such practices threaten to diminish the number of remaining minority applicants to a point that will force less prestigious schools to run the risk of making even more drastic concessions in the admissions process if they wish to obtain a racially diverse class.

Conceding all this, we must still remember that such arguments merely affect the *degree* of racial preference that should be given and not the existence of the practice itself. Preferential admissions must undoubtedly be exercised with care and judgment. But the traditional criteria for selecting students are so imperfect that substantial differences in prior grades and test scores can be tolerated without a demonstrable risk of interfering either with the academic progress or with the subsequent achievements of black and Hispanic students. Hence there is little to be said for the arguments of purists who insist that *any* preference in admissions will stigmatize minority students or place them at an unfair disadvantage. Unless the preference is so great and so pervasive that most blacks and Hispanics are ranked at the bottom of the class, many of them should do sufficiently well to dispel such crude stereotypes. Moreover, to abandon preferential admissions altogether would almost certainly help to keep the number of minority doctors, lawyers, and other professionals at intolerably low levels. And in the end, that result is likely to retard racial progress and perpetuate racial stereotypes to a degree that will outweigh any harm resulting from a judicious policy of encouraging minority admissions.

Hiring Faculty

In every major research university in this country, minorities make up only a tiny proportion of the regular teaching faculty. Among the ethnic groups recognized as minorities by the federal government, only Asian-Americans have found their way to university faculties in numbers that equal or exceed their percentage in the population as a whole.[10] Blacks, Hispanics, and American Indians are all represented on the faculties of major universities in proportions far lower than their percentages in the total population or in the student bodies of these institutions.

FEDERAL REQUIREMENTS   The scarcity of minority professors in leading universities has aroused much concern, especially now that large numbers of minority students have appeared on these campuses. In an effort to remedy this situation, the federal government currently requires that every university develop and administer elaborate affirmative-action plans. Stripped of the detailed statistical underpinnings and the heavy burdens of

10. Asian-Americans make up a proportion of university faculties several times their proportion of the national population. Why do they fare so much better than other minority groups? Surely not because they receive favored treatment. A principal reason is that they have long considered academic careers to be attractive and have therefore moved into Ph.D. programs in numbers far greater than their proportion in the national population. In contrast, only about 3 percent of the nation's Ph.D.'s are black; the proportion of doctorates held by Hispanics is even lower, and American Indian Ph.D.'s are very few in number. See National Academy of Sciences, *Doctoral Recipients from U.S. Universities, 1973–1979* (Washington, D.C.: National Academy of Sciences, 1980).

paperwork involved, the essential thrust of affirmative action is to ensure that all institutions regularly review their progress in hiring minority professors and make particular efforts to identify and consider possible candidates from these groups whenever a search is made to fill a vacancy in the faculty. Defined in this way, the principles of affirmative action are consistent with the proper goals of a university and would deserve to be retained even if government regulations disappeared. In the last analysis, any procedure that causes a university to enlarge its candidate pool and to search more widely within groups that have been poorly represented in the past will ultimately help to improve the quality of the faculty.

Despite these advantages, affirmative action has provoked great controversy and has often been the victim of unwarranted attacks. Academic critics are particularly fond of suggesting that the program is a faintly disguised method for imposing quotas on unwilling faculties. But the government has not gone this far. Indeed, the regulations expressly forbid preferential hiring. Although they require that goals be set for the hiring of minorities, government officials have not tried to pass judgment on what the goals should be, nor have they declared that universities will violate the rules if they fail to meet their objectives.

At most, affirmative-action requirements have contributed to a feeling of pressure on campuses—an inchoate sense that somehow one had better set substantial goals and at least come close to meeting them. These sentiments may have tipped the balance toward the appointment of minority scholars in questionable cases; on occasion, they may have helped to persuade worried department members and deans to hire individuals whom they plainly would not have chosen on strict academic grounds. But even if this is true, affirmative action is only one of several pressures at work, and the ultimate responsibility must lie with the faculties and administrations that have found it expedient to make appointments they did not legally have to make.

Of course, the government may become much more intrusive at some future point (although the prospects hardly seem likely under the Reagan administration). The critical moment will come if public officials insist on passing judgment on the adequacy of hiring goals and begin to treat the failure to meet these goals as evidence of noncompliance. To adopt such policies would be a great mistake.

It is one thing to estimate goals when an employer is filling routine jobs by hiring people from large pools of candidates possessing the standard minimum qualifications. It is quite another matter to establish goals for university faculties, where the institution seeks the best available candidate for each opening and each position requires a special competence of its very own. The government has tried to meet this problem by making an assumption that universities should eventually succeed in appointing proportions of minority faculty equal to the share of Ph.D.'s held by members of these different groups. But faculties have no way of knowing how far they can move toward this objective in a given number of years. Moreover, the underlying assumption is defective, because universities do not regard the total pool of Ph.D.'s as the relevant source from which to make their tenure appointments. Instead, each faculty and department will typically look only within a tiny group of leading scholars who are located not only in America but throughout the world. A leading history department may seek an expert in European history and identify only a dozen candidates, here and abroad, whom it would seriously consider. Perhaps one will be a minority candidate. But will he be judged the best? And will he accept an offer? And will some other minority scholar appear at some point during the few years in which the appointment must be made? Search committees in other departments will define their candidate pools in markedly different ways, and it would be difficult even to guess at the aggregate proportions of minority scholars within these different groupings. The percentages are bound to vary enormously from one search to another, and there is no reason to believe that the resulting figures will bear a close relation to the national proportions of Ph.D.'s. In view of these uncertainties, we simply lack any reliable measure with which to determine the goals a given institution should expect to achieve, even in the long run.

To complicate matters even further, there are many reasons why a department or a school will fall short of the goals it has set several years before. Several minority candidates may have decided to turn down offers; others may have left the university unexpectedly; budgetary cutbacks may have reduced faculty hiring; or departments may simply have been too optimistic in guessing how many minority scholars would emerge as leading candidates in the constant searches for new appointments.

Under these conditions, it would be hazardous to draw strong inferences of bad faith merely because an institution has not succeeded in meeting its goals. The government would do better to regard such failures simply as signals indicating a need to look more closely to determine whether the university has actually made conscientious efforts to seek out minority scholars. If the government should ever go further and treat a failure to achieve hiring goals as presumptive noncompliance, universities would immediately begin to protect themselves by setting extremely modest objectives. This tactic would eventually force the government to begin passing judgment on the adequacy of the targets themselves. At that point, goals would effectively become quotas.

Quotas are generally disliked in our society, but they are particularly inappropriate for faculty hiring. If universities find it hard to estimate goals, the government would experience even greater difficulty in trying to guess how many minority scholars would emerge as the best available economists, physicists, and philosophers to fill the positions that will open over the next few years. Any effort by federal agencies to perform this function would run grave risks of forcing unmerited appointments and provoking enormous resentment toward the government and toward the candidates hired under such rules.

Until now, at least, the dangers just described have not materialized in acute form. Instead, the basic problems of affirmative action have involved not issues of principle but matters of strategy and practice. From its inception in the mid-sixties, the program was poorly constructed and badly executed. It was poor timing to commence the effort when academic posts were already beginning to dry up, and extending the retirement age for professors has only worsened the problem. The requirement that each institution prepare elaborate plans and statistics proved costly and cumbersome, and Congress appropriated too little money for effective enforcement. As late as 1976, therefore, the government had approved affirmative-action plans for less than 10 percent of the eligible institutions, and by that time the employment prospects had already shrunk appreciably. The burdens placed on universities were also out of proportion to any practical benefits achieved. Volumes of data were required, regulations were unclear and often changed, and several agencies at the federal and state levels entered the fray, only adding to the confusion.

Still more important, it is doubtful whether the government has chosen an effective strategy to achieve its goals. Affirmative action proceeds on the assumption that universities and other organizations should be made to look more carefully for minority applicants because there are many qualified minority candidates who deserve to be hired but who are consistently ignored or overlooked by employers. This premise may be accurate in many fields of employment, but it is clearly inappropriate for university faculties. When the program first began, Asian-Americans were already so well represented in our universities that one may legitimately ask why they needed to be included at all. Other minorities, notably blacks, were clearly underrepresented, but a look at the data would have revealed that only about 3 percent of the nation's Ph.D.'s were black and that they were already commanding higher salaries on the average than their white counterparts with comparable experience and publication records.[11] Hence, it should have been clear that the basic problem was not that qualified blacks were being overlooked for faculty posts but that the supply of potential candidates was far too small.[12] The same would presumably be true of Hispanics and American Indians as well.

11. Richard B. Freeman, "The New Job Market for Black Academicians," *Industrial and Labor Relations Review*, 30 (January 1977), 161.
12. The problem of women faculty is somewhat different, for there were stronger indications of unfair treatment. See, for example, "Opportunities for Women in Higher Education," in *A Digest of Reports of the Carnegie Commission on Higher Education* (New York: McGraw-Hill, 1974), pp. 220–230, and Helen H. Astin and Alan E. Bayer, "Sex Discrimination in Academe," *Educational Record*, 53 (Spring 1972), 101–118. Even so, laws were already on the books forbidding discrimination either in specific cases or as a matter of institutional practice. Affirmative action merely supplemented these laws by imposing costly requirements for elaborate plans, procedural safeguards, and statistical analysis—all of somewhat questionable value. Nothing was done to attack other obstacles of equal seriousness to women, such as having to bear a disproportionate burden of family and child-rearing duties during the years most crucial to academic advancement and tenure.

In these circumstances, Washington officials would have done well to consider other strategies for solving the problem. Instead of insisting on volumes of data and expensive statistical analyses, the government might have restricted itself to a few procedural requirements to encourage the use of minorities on search committees and to insist that these committees regularly ask for the names of candidates to consider from established minority professional groups. By removing much unnecessary paperwork, the government could have achieved widespread compliance more rapidly while avoiding much of the confusion and resentment that have plagued the program from the beginning. At the same time, positive steps could have been taken to increase the number of black, Hispanic, and American Indian candidates by offering graduate fellowships and training grants and by providing funds for summer programs to expose talented minority students to graduate work in research universities.[13] The government might also have made more imaginative use of information as a means of influencing university behavior. Federal officials could have helped to expand employment opportunities by working with groups of minority professionals to disseminate more useful data about prospective candidates. And government agencies could have helped to generate more informed concern within academic communities by publicizing data on minority hiring that compared the progress of each university with the achievement of other institutions of a similar type.

Reasonable people may disagree with these proposals, but it would be hard to argue that the present affirmative-action program is the best way to achieve the government's goals. Universities have been forced to spend many millions of dollars for results that are meager at best, and even these gains have resulted less from federal regulation than from the modest growth in the number of minority Ph.D.'s. At the very least, therefore, affirmative action illustrates the difficulties that arise from moving too quickly to impose industrial models on the university without taking time to analyze the problem carefully and consider alternative methods of intervention.

13. It is not entirely clear that grants limited to minority students would be upheld by the courts, but this doubt merely illustrates the problem of developing an effective regulatory strategy in a fragmented political system where different units of government can impose contradictory policy judgments.

PREFERENTIAL TREATMENT   Since affirmative action has not substantially increased the numbers of minority faculty in research universities, the question endlessly arises, however subtly it is put, whether faculties should not employ some form of preferential treatment to hire minority professors even if more talented white candidates are available. For the most part, faculties have not been receptive to this idea. While favoring preferential *admissions* in selecting students, almost all academic institutions have strongly resisted preferential *hiring* in appointing professors. Yet the two situations have important similarities. In both situations, favoring minority applicants may increase the diversity of views within the university. In each case, preferred treatment can counteract the risk of subtle prejudice and hasten the process of placing blacks, Hispanics, and American Indians in important posts where they can help to overcome racial misunderstanding and act as models to inspirit other members of minority groups.

These parallels are sufficient to warrant the special efforts involved in a sound affirmative-action program. They justify the use of procedural safeguards to diminish the risk of subtle biases that could prejudice the appointment of minority professors. But the process of choosing faculty members differs from the selection of students in ways that caution against any attempt to go further and resort to preferential hiring.

In selecting students, admissions committees must work with crude instruments to make extremely difficult predictions about the ability of different applicants to learn from the institution and to contribute in different ways to their fellow students and, eventually, to their communities and professions. Conventional measures, such as prior grades and standardized test scores, do not afford a reliable means of selecting applicants who are most likely to fulfill these objectives. As we have seen, therefore, admissions committees have chosen to admit minority applicants with somewhat lower grades and scores in the plausible belief that they may benefit as much as other applicants from enrolling in the institution while having special opportunities to enrich the education of their fellow students and to contribute to society in later life. In this sense, a carefully administered program of preferential admissions is entirely consistent with the goals of a sound admissions policy.

The process of hiring faculty presents a very different situation. Since the overriding mission of our major universities is to provide the highest quality of instruction and research, faculty members in these institutions are selected almost entirely for their ability as teachers and scholars. These activities are thoroughly understood by the professors who serve on selection committees. Moreover, most of the candidates they consider will already have done considerable teaching and research and thus will have compiled a record that bears directly on their ability to do the type of work they are being hired to perform. Even applicants for a junior faculty post will normally have completed a thesis and have had some experience as a teaching assistant. In addition, search committees typically devote great care to considering the leading candidates—interviewing them, reading what they have written, and checking with colleagues who have observed their work. For these reasons, universities normally appoint new faculty members with considerable confidence that they are choosing the best available teachers and scholars. If selection committees decide to pass over the ablest candidates in order to appoint a minority scholar, they can scarcely be said to be furthering the primary educational aims of the institution. On the contrary, they will generally be acting with a clear probability of diminishing the quality of teaching and research. Consequently, preferential hiring in the choice of faculty is much more difficult to justify than preferential treatment in the admissions process.

Some writers may dispute this point by insisting that black and Spanish-American professors often deserve an appointment because they possess peculiar qualifications that entitle them to special consideration "on the merits." The most extreme advocates of this position claim that certain subjects, such as Afro-American studies, can only be taught properly by minority professors. But this is a very difficult proposition to defend. Most of the highly regarded minority scholars reject the argument out of hand. Moreover, any list of the leading works on race relations or Afro-American history and culture will include many entries by white as well as black authors.

Others have argued that preferential hiring will enrich the quality of the faculty by adding professors with different backgrounds and values. This claim, however, can easily be overstated. Even the most avid proponent of diversity would be hard put to argue that the special perspective of a minority scholar will contribute much to teaching and research in the natural sciences or in classics, English literature, logic, or many other important fields of study. For certain subjects, such as American history, sociology, or political science, such perspectives can have greater relevance. In these fields, a minority scholar may conceivably have a capacity for unusual insights or a taste for neglected problems that can be linked in some fashion to his race. If these special capacities have already resulted in genuine contributions to teaching and research, the candidate may well deserve an appointment. This is scarcely an example of preferential hiring; it is simply a proper recognition of superior work. But when a candidate has not actually demonstrated qualities of originality and insight, there is no basis for appointing him on the assumption that the mere fact of his belonging to a minority group will automatically add a desired quality of diversity to the faculty.[14]

One can make a stronger case that minority professors render a special service as role models and counselors for minority students. Although this argument has substance, its importance probably depends upon the educational objectives of the institution involved. Black colleges are dedicated to the special educational needs of particular groups of students. In pursuing these goals, they may sincerely believe that the presence of many role models on the faculty is important to lift the aspirations of their students and motivate them to pursue more demanding careers. Although the truth of this argument has yet to be proved, one can scarcely accuse such institutions of sacrificing principle as long as they prefer minority professors in a genuine belief that they are furthering the welfare of their students.

14. In this sense, diversity plays a different role in the appointments process than it does in admitting students. With thousands of applications to deal with and only limited information available, an admissions committee will normally have no way of predicting how much a minority applicant will actually contribute to the understanding of his fellow students. Hence, the committee can only assume that a substantial number of minority students will enhance the racial understanding and awareness of the entire class. But a faculty selection committee need not rely on such assumptions, for it can generally ascertain whether a minority candidate has unusual contributions to make to teaching and research either by personal observation or by examining his published work.

Arguments of this kind are undoubtedly weaker in a research university. And yet they do retain some force, for minority students often feel beleaguered and estranged in traditionally white institutions, and the presence of minority professors may increase their confidence, raise their aspirations, and provide a source of help and understanding that white faculty may be much less equipped to offer. The problem is to decide how much weight to put on considerations of this kind. They are surely important enough to reinforce the need to search vigorously for minority candidates who merit an appointment; they may also justify the selection of minority professors in every case in which the traditional academic qualifications of the leading minority and nonminority applicants are approximately equal. Beyond this point I would be reluctant to go—and for a number of reasons.

Whatever value we ascribe to counseling and role modeling, they are surely less important in a research university than the quality of teaching and scholarship. It is also hard to predict which minority professors will eventually prove to have the skill or desire to play a substantial part in advising students. Moreover, despite impressions to the contrary, we do not know a great deal about the impact of role models, especially on students old enough to go to college. As Jonathan Cole has observed, after a careful review of the research on this subject, "There simply is no strong evidence that gender matching or racial matching between young people and their elders has a significant influence on career choice. We might like to think that there is such an effect; it may have intuitive appeal; but the facts that are assumed to exist simply don't."[15]

Even if universities wished to attract more role models and counselors, efforts to achieve this goal through preferential faculty hiring are unlikely to succeed, at least for higher education as a whole. At present, the numbers of black and Hispanic professors are extremely small. In view of the attractiveness of careers in law, business, and medicine, there is little chance that preferential hiring can expand the supply appreciably under the depressed conditions that promise to afflict the academic job market for another generation. As a result, successful efforts by one university

15. *Fair Science: Women in the Scientific Community* (New York: Free Press, 1979), p. 269.

to increase its minority faculty are only likely to diminish the minority presence at other institutions. For all these reasons, universities would be ill-advised to appoint professors with lesser academic qualifications in an effort to provide needed guidance and support for their students. Instead, they would do better to meet these needs in other ways, such as making greater efforts to appoint minority persons to administrative and counseling posts.

In sum, preferential treatment in faculty hiring cannot be justified on academic grounds. Worse yet, hiring professors on this basis would also be unjust to white candidates of superior ability, for the latter could make a strong claim that they truly deserved the job "on the merits" and that they had done nothing to warrant the loss of the appointment. In view of these objections, can we discover any overriding social reasons that should lead universities to engage in preferential hiring? Some observers may argue that blacks and Hispanics deserve favored treatment to compensate for a long history of discrimination. But past prejudice does not provide a convincing reason for taking jobs from candidates of greater academic promise who bear no responsibility for prior injustices inflicted on minority groups. Nor are minority applicants for faculty posts particularly appealing candidates to receive compensatory benefits. Such persons are among the most privileged of their race, possessing talents and educational attainments that offer them excellent opportunities to compete for rewarding careers. Black professors already receive higher rates of compensation than white professors of comparable age and experience—a condition that exists in almost no other occupational group in the United States. Thus preferential faculty hiring would represent a highly questionable way of trying to atone for our history of racial injustice.

The only remaining argument for favored treatment is that it will produce greater equality for all minorities in the long run, thus justifying any unfairness and loss of academic quality that may occur in the shorter term. But it is always hard to demonstrate that we should impose an injustice on some in the hope of alleviating it for others. In the case of faculty hiring, these difficulties seem particularly severe. Comparative salaries for black and white professors suggest that substantial equality of opportunity already exists for those who seek academic careers. One can argue that preferential hiring may generate even higher rewards for minorities that will draw more blacks and Hispanics into academic life and thereby increase the numbers having access to relatively highly paid careers. And yet, now that universities have largely eliminated racial discrimination in faculty hiring, it is far from clear that they should go so far as to reject more qualified candidates in order to provide still greater opportunities for minorities. Moreover, from a practical standpoint, since it takes a number of years to obtain a Ph.D., such a policy cannot do much in the near term to increase the number of minority faculty; it will simply increase the salary premiums already paid to black and Hispanic professors. Even in the longer run, no one can be certain that preferential hiring will succeed in attracting more minority students away from careers in law, business, or medicine, which provide much higher incomes and offer opportunities and satisfactions entirely different than those of academic life. In these circumstances, the hope of achieving greater justice and equality seems far too speculative and insubstantial to make a convincing case for departing from the normal academic standards in selecting professors.

For all these reasons, preferential hiring is extremely hard to defend on any basis. A judicious policy of encouraging minority admissions can further legitimate educational goals while also helping to promote social ends. It is therefore a policy that every responsible university can support. But the practice of hiring minority professors preferentially cannot be justified on these grounds. On the contrary, it threatens to diminish the academic enterprise by lowering the quality of teaching and research. No university should knowingly take such a step save for the most extreme and compelling reasons. Far from promoting justice, preferential hiring unfairly penalizes candidates of superior ability while holding little promise of achieving greater equality in the society as a whole. Such a policy is not merely unnecessary; it is also wrong.

5

The Moral Development of Students

IF UNIVERSITIES wish to address the many wrongs and injustices of society, they might begin by seeking ways to help their students become more thoughtful and perceptive about these problems. In recent years, we have observed repeated instances of wrongdoing in high places. Surveys reveal a wide belief that ethical standards in the society have been declining and suggest that trust in the integrity of those who guide our major institutions has sunk to disturbingly low levels. If such moral deficiencies exist, however, they have their roots in the actions of individuals, and especially in the decisions of those who occupy positions of influence and power.

In teaching their students, universities have a special opportunity to make a useful contribution. Although families, churches, and schools seem to have declined in influence over the past few decades, higher education has assumed a more important social role, and much larger proportions of the population now come in search of advanced instruction. Indeed, virtually every business executive and lawyer, every public servant and physician, every politician and engineer will now pass through our colleges and probably through our professional schools as well. At a time of such dissatisfaction and concern over the level of ethical behavior in the society, there is every reason for educational institutions to consider how they might use their strategic position to encourage students to think more deeply about ethical issues and strengthen their powers of moral reasoning.

Early Approaches to Moral Education

In the nineteenth century, universities devoted great efforts to the moral development of their students and considered this an integral part of their mission. To emphasize the importance of this task, many college presidents took it upon themselves to present a compulsory series of lectures on moral philosophy to the entire senior class. According to one scholar, this course "was regarded as the capstone of the curriculum. It aimed to pull together, to integrate, and to give meaning and purpose to the students' entire college experience and course of study. In so doing, it even more importantly also sought to equip the graduating seniors with the ethical sensitivity and insight needed if they were to put their newly acquired knowledge to use in ways that would benefit not only themselves and their own personal advancement, but the larger society as well."[1]

This practice may seem quaint and unrealistic today, but in its time it served its purpose reasonably well. In 1850 one could discern a common moral code that could be passed along from one generation to the next. Partly because of their positions of authority and partly because of the force of their personalities, many college presidents seem to have succeeded in expounding this prevailing ethic in a manner that left an abiding impression on the minds and characters of their students.

In addition to these lectures, efforts were also made to surround students with living examples of rectitude and principled behavior. To paraphrase Aristotle: If you would know virtue, behold the virtuous man. Acting on this principle, presidents put great emphasis on the character of candidates in appointing professors to their faculties. In his inaugural address of 1871, Noah Porter of Yale declared: "The most efficient of all moral influences in a college are those which proceed from *the personal characters of the instructors* . . . A noble character becomes light and inspiration, when dignified by intellectual power and attainments."[2] At Harvard,

1. Douglas Sloan, "The Teaching of Ethics in the American Undergraduate Curriculum, 1876–1976," in Donald Callahan and Sissela Bok, eds., *Ethics Teaching in Higher Education* (New York: Plenum Press, 1980), p. 2.
2. Quoted in Lawrence R. Veysey, *The Emergence of the American University* (Chicago: University of Chicago Press, 1965), p. 45.

Charles W. Eliot put these sentiments to practical use. According to his friend Ephraim Emerton:

> As one watched the continuous process of appointments, promotions and failures to promote, one came gradually to understand the often puzzling motive that underlay them. There are, of course, two obvious qualifications for academic success: sound scholarship and ability to teach. But aside from these there is also the quality, for which there is no better word than academic character: No one could for a moment accuse Mr. Eliot of indifference to scholarship or to the teaching gift, but the dominant question in his mind was always this of character ... What distinguished the complete remaking of the Faculties which took place during his long administration was his extraordinary flair for this subtle quality. He could detect its presence under the most misleading disguises of manner or of speech, and he could detect its absence behind what seemed to be the best of qualifications.[3]

In the ensuing years, changes occurred that gradually discredited these efforts. As faculties began to take greater control over the appointments process, it was harder to reach agreement on what good character meant in deciding whom to hire or to promote. With competition for academic excellence becoming ever more demanding and important, appointments committees grew reluctant to pass over promising scholars because of doubts about their personal behavior. More serious still, suspicions were aroused that "character" could easily become an excuse to screen out eccentrics, Jews, or individuals with controversial and unsettling opinions.

The growing skepticism was plainly expressed in 1939 by a distinguished Harvard committee studying the process of faculty appointments: "Qualities such as 'character,' 'leadership,' 'personality,' and 'cooperation' are enumerated among those actually considered by certain departments in recommending appointments. Such qualities are extremely difficult to assess. There is a certain danger, furthermore, in giving them emphasis." Having briefly considered the risks involved, the committee concluded:

3. "Personal Recollections of Charles William Eliot," *Harvard Graduates' Magazine*, 32 (1924), 342, 349–350.

"Personal characteristics should not be considered as primary criteria. A faculty made up wholly of amiable and attractive men, or even of saints, would not as such serve the purposes of a college or university."[4] In this fashion, the earlier emphasis on character was pushed aside, save in exceptional cases, as incompatible with the standards of academic freedom and scholarly excellence that seemed more and more essential to the modern university.

By the end of the nineteenth century, presidential lectures on ethical standards had also fallen victim to changing social conditions. For one thing, the sense of a common moral code began to break down. As early as the 1850s, the president of Oberlin could declare with certitude that slavery was immoral at the very time that his counterpart at Mercer College in Georgia was vigorously upholding the practice on biblical and pragmatic grounds. As social change led to new forms of conflict, educators seemed increasingly arbitrary and doctrinaire when they sought to convey a set of proper ethical precepts. And since their lectures were didactic in style, they also failed to prepare their students to think for themselves in applying these moral precepts to the new controversies and ethical dilemmas that an industrializing society seemed constantly to create.

While the role of college presidents was declining, changes were occurring in the aims and methods of scholarly work that further undermined traditional approaches to moral education. One by one, the social sciences split away from philosophy to form their own separate disciplines. For a time, these new fields retained an interest in philosophic questions. Before long, however, they fell under the leadership of scholars who emphasized the scientific nature of their work and its freedom from normative judgments. Economists searched for the determinants of economic behavior without regard to its moral content. Psychologists looked for theories to explain differing patterns of conduct but expressly declined to pass judgment on whether one pattern was "better" than another. Anthropologists described variations in the ethical standards of different societies as if to suggest that such divergences were simply cultural phenomena of no normative significance. Even moral philosophers eventually began in growing

4. *Report on Some Problems of Personnel in the Faculty of Arts and Sciences* (Cambridge, Mass.: Harvard University Press, 1939), p. 77.

numbers to shift their attention from the ethical dilemmas of public and private life to the analysis of moral language and the study of ethical theory.

To be sure, most colleges continued to provide survey courses on moral philosophy. These offerings acquainted students with a great intellectual tradition in a manner that could scarcely be called doctrinaire. But courses of this kind were normally elective and enrolled only a small fraction of the student body. Since classes were usually devoted to lecturing, they could not engage the students actively enough to develop their powers of moral reasoning. And to the extent that they merely offered a survey of various ethical theories, they did little to help students cope with the practical moral dilemmas they would encounter in their own lives.

Professional schools scarcely improved upon this record. Although discussions on the teaching of professional responsibility took place periodically in faculty meetings, most schools virtually ignored moral education in practice. Some of them did offer elective courses to a tiny portion of their student bodies, but instructors were generally content to review the prevailing codes of professional ethics without exploring the moral adequacy of the codes themselves or the ways in which they were often used as rationalizations to justify self-serving practices. Other faculties sought to address ethical problems by weaving them into a variety of courses in the regular curriculum. This method had the advantage of suggesting to students that such questions were not isolated problems but an integral part of the daily life and experience of the profession. In that sense, the efforts were valuable and deserved encouragement. For several reasons, however, even this approach by itself could have only a limited success in bringing students to reason more carefully about moral issues.

In scattering the responsibility for moral education among a large number of professors, faculties conveniently overlooked the fact that few, if any, among them had a knowledge of ethics that was equal to the task. Lacking properly trained professors, the rest of the faculty had no one whom they could approach to discuss these issues in depth. In practice, therefore, since instructors almost always had more than enough material to cover, they tended to give short shrift to the ethical problems in order to concentrate on other aspects of the course materials that they felt more equipped to teach. The results of this process were revealed all too clearly by the findings of a confidential report issued some years ago by a committee that visited one of Harvard's professional schools. After listing a wide variety of moral issues distributed throughout the curriculum, the report described the reactions of a sample of students and faculty: "Almost without exception, the faculty members indicated that they touch on one or more of these issues frequently . . . but while they were certain they covered the issues, they often had second thoughts about how explicit they had been. Almost equally without exception, students felt the issues are seldom touched on, and when they are, are treated as afterthoughts or digressions."

In sum, by the mid-twentieth century, little remained of the earlier efforts of colleges and universities. Catalogues continued to speak of moral development as a prominent aim of the institution, but there was scant evidence of any serious effort to pursue this objective. In the selection of faculty, the traditional emphasis on character had given way almost completely to the demands for scholarly excellence and academic freedom. Presidential lectures on moral issues had likewise disappeared without any visible replacement, a casualty of the search for value-free learning and the reluctance to engage in any form of teaching that could be criticized as doctrinaire.

The Revival of Moral Education

As so often happens, the pressure for reform came from forces outside the university. The Watergate revelations produced a widespread concern that ethical standards had eroded in high places. Similar episodes called attention to moral issues in many of the professions. Multinational corporations were accused of attracting business by offering bribes to foreign officials. Doctors became embroiled in litigation over such issues as whether they could perform abortions or shorten the lives of hopelessly ill patients. And, as I have already observed, universities themselves were caught up in angry moral debates over the standards of admission for minority students, the holding of stock in corporations doing business in South Africa, and the responsibilities of scientists for the consequences of their research.

In this atmosphere of argument and concern, faculty members and administrators began to search for a different approach to the problem of moral education. New initiatives were not long in coming. As in earlier times, attempts were made to reach students by example as well as by formal instruction. But the methods used took a radically different form in order to satisfy the altered standards and demands of the modern university.

Even with the awakening interest in ethics, no research university could hope to reinstitute character as a basis for appointments. The criterion is simply too susceptible to abuse, too vague, too remote from the primary commitment to learning and discovery. The faculty would quite properly refuse to allow it. Instead of trying to hire professors to set a personal example, therefore, academic leaders sought to provide an *institutional* example by making a serious and open effort to address the moral dilemmas that confronted the university. Student-faculty committees were established to discuss how the institution should vote on shareholder resolutions involving issues of corporate responsibility. Similar groups were formed to consider how to respond to requests to participate in boycotts against suppliers that engaged in questionable labor practices. And university presidents, if they no longer taught formal courses, at least took pen in hand to explain the policies of the institution in response to student demands of an ethical nature.

To many eyes, these efforts doubtless appeared to be little more than an administrative gambit to cope with a difficult political situation. After all, what were student-faculty committees or elaborate policy statements if not an attempt to appeal to moderate elements and thus avoid the escalation of activist demands into a serious campuswide revolt? There is doubtless some truth to this view, but it hardly provides a complete explanation. In most universities, presidents and trustees had spent countless hours debating how the institution should respond to the moral issues raised by students and faculty. Few academic leaders could have overlooked the importance, on educational grounds, of calling these efforts to the attention of their communities and explaining the complexities involved. In the face of protest meetings, student editorials, and picket lines, no educator could be unaware of the corrosive cynicism that would arise in the minds of many students and faculty if the administration seemed indifferent to serious ethical concerns.

In addition to these efforts by the administration, faculty members began to show new interest in devising courses explicitly designed to explore practical moral problems. Over twelve thousand of these offerings are now in existence across the country, most of them created since 1970. In colleges, professors may take up ethical questions facing our social institutions, such as the moral problems of war, government secrecy, or race relations, or they may emphasize issues of deception, breach of promise, and other dilemmas that confront individuals in everyday life. In schools of law, public affairs, business, and medicine, the emphasis is on professional ethics. Medical students will grapple with the moral dilemmas of human experimentation, the limits of confidentiality, the just distribution of scarce medical resources. Students of public administration will discuss whether government officials are ever justified in lying to the public, leaking confidential information to the press, or refusing to carry out the orders of their superiors. In schools of business, such courses may take up any number of issues—corporate bribes abroad, deceptive advertising, the sale of potentially hazardous products, or employment practices in South Africa.

Regardless of the problems considered, classes have generally proceeded by discussion rather than lecturing. Instructors may present their own views, if only to demonstrate how one can proceed to make carefully reasoned choices about ethical dilemmas. But they are typically less concerned with presenting solutions than with engaging the class in an active discussion to encourage students to perceive ethical issues, identify the competing arguments, evaluate these contending views, and ultimately arrive at thoughtfully reasoned conclusions.

What can these efforts hope to accomplish? One object is to help students become more alert in discovering the moral issues that arise in their own lives. Of course, even the hardiest enthusiast will admit that formal education can rarely improve the character of a scoundrel. But many students who are disposed to act morally will often fail to do so because they are simply unaware of the ethical problems that lie hidden in the situations they confront. Others will not discover a moral problem until they have gotten too deeply enmeshed to extricate themselves. Through repeated discussions that seek to identify moral problems and define the issues at stake, courses in applied ethics may help students to avoid these pitfalls by sharpening and refining their powers of moral perception.

Another objective is to foster a capacity to reason carefully about ethical issues. Many students feel that such problems are only matters of personal opinion and are not fruitful subjects for debate. A well-taught course may succeed in showing that this is not true and that moral issues can be discussed as rigorously as many questions taken up in more established courses in the curriculum. With the help of carefully selected readings and well-directed discussions, students may learn to sort out all the arguments that bear upon ethical problems and apply them with care to concrete situations.

A final object of these courses is to help students clarify their moral aspirations and consider why they should take pains to respect the rights of others. Whether in college or in professional school, many young people will be trying to define their identity and to establish the level of integrity at which they will lead their personal and professional lives. They may be encouraged to consider these questions more fully by exploring a series of ethical problems in a setting where no serious personal consequences are at stake. Prospective lawyers, doctors, or business executives will arguably set higher ethical standards for themselves if they have already encountered the moral problems of their calling in the classroom, instead of waiting to confront them at a point in their careers where they are short of time and under pressure to act in morally questionable ways.

Evaluating the New Approaches

How can we appraise these new attempts to come to grips with the problem of moral education? This is a subject that invites hyperbole but requires the most hard-headed analysis. For though the objectives may be laudable, the enterprise itself is beset with the gravest difficulty.

Academic leaders are bound to encounter heavy criticism as they attempt to set an example of care and concern for ethical issues. However well-intentioned presidents and deans may be, their efforts will usually fall far short of satisfying activist students and faculty. The disagreements are not merely a matter of conflicting political philosophies. Activists in the university not only care deeply about social issues; they are often trying to decide how they can justify their privileged position in a world characterized by widespread deprivation and injustice. The moral dilemmas that confront the university offer them an opportunity to demonstrate to others and, most of all, to themselves that they do care about the misfortunes of others and care enough to make sacrifices in behalf of what they believe. In their desire to make a significant contribution, they are likely to exaggerate the influence of the university in combating social injustice and to minimize the resulting costs and burdens to the institution. Since academic administrators are subject to exactly the opposite biases, conflict is bound to ensue over the proper course for the university to follow.

When such differences arise, activist critics will normally seek to discredit the administration, not only because they disagree strongly with official policies but also because they need to arouse the concern of a broader campus community in order to mobilize effective opposition. Since they are strongly motivated and can usually find abundant time for their work, they may spend countless hours trying to impugn the motives of the university leadership. Such efforts often made headway in an era when educational institutions were subject to widespread cynicism and mistrust. The president and trustees might do their best to reply by countering opposing arguments in detail. Even better, they could manifest the seriousness of their concern by trying to identify significant moral issues on their own initiative instead of merely reacting to demands initiated by others. And yet, in the face of determined opposition, the administration frequently found it difficult to establish its good faith, let alone secure agreement with its policies.

Despite these problems, there can be little doubt that such efforts are worth making. Granted, the positive results may be impossible to document. But the consequences of doing nothing are plainly intolerable. A university that refuses to take ethical dilemmas seriously violates its basic obligations to society. And a university that fails to engage its members in debate on these issues and to communicate with care the reasons for its policies gives an impression of moral indifference that is profoundly dispiriting to large numbers of students and professors who share a concern for social issues and a desire to have their institution behave responsibly. Moreover, any administration that fails to discuss such questions openly and in detail will allow the campus debate on serious moral problems to degenerate into slogans and oversimplifications unworthy of an institution dedicated to the rigorous exploration of ideas. Even if only a fraction of the community is aware of the efforts being made by the institution and understands more fully all the arguments involved, the efforts by university leaders will be eminently worthwhile.

Attempts to buttress these administrative initiatives by fostering the teaching of applied ethics have given rise to problems of a different sort. Despite the recent proliferation of these courses, it would be wrong to suppose that such instruction has taken the curriculum by storm. A large number of institutions have undertaken to provide an experimental course or two. But these offerings are very new and are still greeted with indifference and even skepticism by many members of the faculty.

INDOCTRINATION   The liveliest discussions of applied ethics have occurred over the issue of indoctrination. Many professors fear that any course on controversial moral issues will degenerate into a thinly disguised attempt on the part of instructors to impose their personal beliefs on the students. Most of these skeptics probably suspect that such indoctrination will take place at the hands of their radical colleagues. As a result, one might have expected a rebuttal from faculty members of the Left. Curiously enough, however, an opposing argument has been launched, not from radical professors, but from writers of a distinctly conservative persuasion. Far from fearing too much indoctrination, these critics worry that courses in applied ethics will not have *enough*. In their eyes, such classes are all too likely to breed a vacuous form of casuistry and moral relativism in which students learn to make ingenious arguments about bizarre moral dilemmas while never being taught to believe in essential precepts such as not to lie, cheat, or steal. As one of these writers has observed, "The first step to reviving an ethos of public administration is to send the philosophers home . . . and to admit that moral education will take place, much as it always has, through examples and even a bit of 'indoctrination' in the virtues of democracy."[5]

In the face of these conflicting arguments, one must be clear about just what indoctrination is. An instructor does not indoctrinate his students merely by disclosing his own ethical values. The critical line is crossed only when a teacher attempts to force his values on his students by refusing to entertain contrary arguments or by using his power as grader and discussion leader to coerce students into accepting his views. With this definition in mind, it is easier to respond to critics on either side of the debate. In problem-oriented courses, instructors can avoid the danger of indoctrination simply by taking care to expose their students to a variety of readings and to refrain from dictatorial methods in conducting class discussions. The vast majority of university professors understand these pedagogic principles well enough. Granted, an occasional instructor may ignore such restraints. But no sensible person would cite this risk to prohibit all courses in applied ethics, for the same argument could be used with equal force to forbid classes in political economy, social theory, political philosophy, or any other subject touching on controversial issues. It would be a sorry university indeed that had to abandon such courses because it could not rely on its professors to teach objectively or trust its students to have the independence of mind to avoid being influenced unduly by an occasional instructor who overstepped the bounds.

At the same time, instructors need not act as though they are totally neutral on such issues as stealing, lying, or violence. Such extreme neutrality may occur in some of the efforts in "values clarification" carried on in public schools. But the same practice does not occur in most college and professional school courses on

5. Mark T. Lilla, "Ethos, 'Ethics,' and Public Service," *The Public Interest*, 63 (Spring 1981), 17.

applied ethics. Instructors at this level need feel no hesitation in expressing their own position on ethical questions, and this is particularly true when they are defending the merits of moral precepts essential to civilized society. The critical point arises when a student expresses opposition to such precepts or dismisses them cavalierly for superficial reasons. On these occasions, the professor should not simply rule such students out of order or peremptorily mark them down; instead he should try to draw them out in a discussion that will expose the problems and inadequacies of their position.

It is difficult to disagree with this approach if one has a reasonable appreciation of the mentality of most undergraduates. Students will not believe more strongly in telling the truth or keeping their promises merely because professors inform them that contrary arguments are unacceptable. They will develop strong convictions about basic moral precepts only if they comprehend the reasons that underlie these principles—for example, if they stop to think what the world would be like if everyone felt free to lie or break promises. This is precisely what courses in applied ethics seek to achieve by discussing moral issues carefully and applying basic precepts to difficult, borderline cases. Any effort to abandon this process in favor of didactic pronouncements by the professor would merely awaken suspicion and resentment in the minds of students while leaving them ill-prepared to apply their principles to the difficult cases they will encounter in later life.

THE LIMITS OF REASON   Indoctrination is not the only issue raised by courses of this kind. Many observers suspect that most moral dilemmas involve a conflict between competing basic values that cannot be resolved through logical reasoning. They may concede that a conscientious teacher can bring students to appreciate the relevant ethical arguments and to use those arguments with greater skill. But they will argue that this new sophistication may simply leave young people more confused than ever and unable to arrive at satisfactory conclusions. Worse yet, students may simply become more clever in finding reasons to justify their selfish and unethical behavior.

These criticisms are easily exaggerated, for careful reasoning can surely do much to clarify and resolve a number of moral issues. For example, thoughtful arguments can often change the views of individuals who have arrived at incongruous ethical positions through a faulty analysis of the consequences. As newspaper articles report, many young people consider it permissible to steal merchandise because they feel that they are merely reducing the profits of large corporations. Apart from many other counter-arguments that could be made, a few moments of discussion should serve to make the point that theft is not so likely to reduce profits as to increase the price to other consumers. Similarly, students sometimes try to justify cheating on exams by asserting that the very process of grading is destructive and unfair. Once again, a brief debate should lead most participants to realize that cheating is unlikely to lead to basic grading reforms but will merely inflict an injustice on other students.

A much more common error is to consider a moral issue too narrowly by looking only at the immediate consequences involved. For example, the greatest flaw in the rationalizations just described for cheating and stealing is that the students have clearly given too little thought to the problems that would occur if everyone proceeded to engage in similar conduct. If these examples seem too obvious to carry weight, the *Wall Street Journal* reported that in one class at a leading university a majority of the students thought it proper for a government official to lie to a Congressman in order to forestall a regressive piece of legislation. According to the instructor, the students "seem to see things essentially in cost-benefit terms. Is [the lie] for a good policy? What are your chances of getting caught? If you get caught, how much will it hurt you?"[6] This is a very limited view of deception. Surely those students might have revised their position if they had been asked to reconsider the consequences and to imagine what would happen in a society in which *all* public officials felt free to lie whenever they happened to feel that deception would help to avoid a result which they believed was wrong.

Careful discussion can also help expose instances of circular argument, *ad hominem* reasoning, and errors of logic and consistency in drawing conclusions from moral premises. To revert to the problem of preferential admissions, suppose that an angry alumnus argues that all applicants should be admitted "strictly

6. April 11, 1974, p. 12.

on the merits"—that is, on the basis of past grades and standardized test scores. In response, one can ask whether the same principle should be mechanically applied to the admission of football players, outstanding student leaders, and children of loyal graduates. Questions of this kind will often uncover inconsistencies of thinking that will cause the protesting alumnus to reconsider his initial premise and to acknowledge that a sound policy should attempt to achieve several goals embracing qualities beyond prior intellectual achievement. Further discussion can expose the limitations of the standardized test as a predictive device. Once these points have been accepted, the initial premise (that all students should be admitted "on the merits") will have to be refined in ways that can no longer support the simple conclusion that white students should invariably be preferred to blacks with lower grades and test scores. Through this process, the alumnus may eventually come to understand the current admissions policy, or at least agree that existing practices are not so unjust as he initially supposed.

Courses in moral reasoning can also teach students to avoid ethical dilemmas by devising alternate methods of achieving their ends. This is a simple point, but it is often overlooked. For example, researchers in the social sciences sometimes deceive their human subjects in order to carry out an important experiment. Careful study can often help these investigators to see the dangers of deception more fully and to use their imagination to devise experiments that do not require such questionable methods. Even in much more difficult cases—such as deciding who will be saved by receiving a kidney transplant—one can at least make limited progress by learning to turn from the vexing problem of deciding who shall live to the more promising task of devising procedures for making such decisions in a manner that seems reasonable and fair to all concerned.

To be sure, difficult problems will remain for which we can find no answer that will satisfy everyone. In some instances, we may disagree because we have no reliable way of estimating the consequences of alternative courses of action. In the case of voluntary euthanasia, for example, opponents are partly motivated by the fear that such practices will gradually engender an insensitivity to human life that may lead to greater cruelty and suffering. Most of those who support euthanasia believe these fears to be exaggerated. In the face of these conflicting predictions, even reasonable people may be unable to resolve the issue satisfactorily. In other cases, we may agree on the facts but disagree about the underlying values involved. Thus a major issue in the current dispute over abortion is the question of whether respect for life should include the prospect of human existence embodied in a fetus or only extend to those who are already born and capable of experiencing life and feeling pain. This is not a matter we can resolve on logical grounds. As a result, one side will continue to argue that abortion is a fundamental right of women, while the other will doggedly insist that no one can claim the right to commit murder.

Despite these intractable problems, it is better for students to be aware of all the troubling arguments that bear on important moral issues than to act on simplistic generalizations and unexamined premises. Many traditional forms of study are devoted to questions that are not susceptible to definite answers. This is certainly true of philosophy, literature, art, and even many parts of law and business. No one would dream of abandoning these subjects simply because professors must often leave their students in a state of profound indecision. In the last analysis, an important part of becoming an educated person is to comprehend the fundamental problems of human existence in all their complexity and thus engage with life at the highest possible level of awareness.

Some educators may concede that skillful teaching can help students to reason more carefully and productively about ethical issues, but they will argue that moral development has less to do with reasoning than with believing in proper moral values and having the strength of character to put them into practice. Since character and conviction are attributes not easily taught in a classroom, these critics question whether a class on moral reasoning can accomplish anything of real importance. It is this point of view that accounts for the statement of one business school representative in explaining why there were no courses on ethics in the curriculum: "On the subject of ethics, we feel that either you have them or you don't."

There is clearly some force to this argument. But it is one thing to acknowledge the limitations of formal learning and quite another to assert that reading and discussion can have no effect on developing ethical principles and moral character. As I have already pointed out, problem-oriented courses encourage students to define their moral values more carefully and to understand more fully the reasons that underlie and justify these precepts. Unless one is prepared to argue that moral values have no intellectual basis whatsoever, it seems likely that this process of thought will play a useful role in helping students develop a clearer, more consistent set of ethical principles that takes more careful account of the needs and interests of others. And one would also suppose that students who fully understand the reasons that support their ethical standards will be more inclined to put their precepts into practice and more uncomfortable at the thought of sacrificing principle to serve their own private ends.

To be sure, no one would deny that ethical values are profoundly dependent on many forces beyond the college curriculum—family influences, religious experience, and the personal example of friends and public figures. As discussed earlier, the university administration itself can have an effect on students by the way in which it deals with moral issues and by its willingness to grapple openly and conscientiously with the ethical problems that arise in its daily operations. And yet, though we must concede that classroom teaching has only a limited role in building moral character, this is hardly a reason for refusing to develop courses on ethical issues. Lawyers, business executives, and public servants achieve success not only because of the instruction they received as students but because of qualities of leadership, integrity, judgment, and imagination that come from many sources other than formal education. Even so, we still have faith in the value of professional schools because we believe that most students possess these personal qualities in sufficient measure to benefit from a professional training that will help them to use their native abilities to become more effective practitioners. In the same way, we should assume that most students have enough respect for the interests of others that they will profit from instruction that helps them become alert to ethical issues and apply their moral values carefully to the dilemmas they encounter in their professional lives.

QUALIFICATIONS OF INSTRUCTORS Beyond these reservations lies a deeper concern about the qualifications of faculty members who seek to teach these new courses. There is undoubtedly some substance to these suspicions. It is simply a fact that many classes in applied ethics have been taught by persons with little preparation in moral reasoning beyond a strongly developed social conscience. Of all the problems that have been considered, this is the most substantial. Poor instruction can harm any class. But it is devastating to a course on ethics, for it confirms the prejudices of students and faculty who suspect that moral reasoning is almost always inconclusive and that classes on moral issues are either a waste of time or, even worse, a forum for expounding the private prejudices of the instructor.

The qualifications for teaching such courses are quite straightforward. Instructors must have an adequate knowledge of moral philosophy, so that they can select the most useful readings for their students and bring forth the most illuminating theories and arguments that have been devised to cope with recurring ethical dilemmas. Effective teachers must also have a reasonable knowledge of the field of human affairs to which their course is addressed. Otherwise, they will neither seem credible nor succeed in bringing students to understand all the practical implications and consequences of choosing one course of action over another. Finally, instructors must know how to conduct a rigorous class discussion that will elicit a full consideration of the issues without degenerating into a windy exchange of student opinion.

These demands are not insuperable, but they present real difficulties because no single department or professional school is equipped to prepare a fully qualified instructor. Professors of law or business may understand judicial procedures and corporate finance—they may even be masters of the Socratic method—but they will rarely have much background in moral philosophy. Philosophers in turn will usually know virtually nothing about any of the professions and may even lack experience in teaching problem-oriented classes. If moral education is ever to prosper, we will have to find ways of overcoming these deficiencies by creating strong interdisciplinary programs for students seeking careers of teaching and scholarship in this field.

FEW LEADING UNIVERSITIES have succeeded in providing adequate training of this kind. Despite periodic demonstrations of interest by alumni and foundations, faculties have simply not cared enough to surmount their disciplinary barriers and create the kind of program that is needed. Universities being what they are, there is little that presidents can do except to continue to raise the issue and look for interested professors who are willing to take the lead. If experience is any guide, however, such efforts will eventually bear fruit—assuming, of course, that the underlying idea is sound.

In the end, therefore, the issue is not whether competent courses can be taught in applied ethics but whether the effort is worth making. I firmly believe that it is. Even if we take the most skeptical view of the matter, such courses have important contributions to make. There is value to be gained from any form of instruction that acquaints students with a rich literature in moral philosophy and forces them to think carefully and rigorously about enduring human problems. In this regard, there is a great difference between well-conceived courses in applied ethics and attempts to achieve a superficial relevance by teaching classes on topical problems of the day based on readings having only ephemeral significance. Moreover, by providing suitable courses with competent instructors to teach them, universities will encourage more systematic study and thought about a wide range of contemporary moral issues. Now that society is expressing greater concern about ethical standards in the professions and in public life, work of this kind is badly needed, for it is surprising how little serious, informed writing has been devoted, until recently, even to such pervasive moral problems as lying, secrecy, or corruption.

Beyond these advantages, what can we say about the effect of such courses on the lives of students and the moral quality of the society? In candor, we cannot answer with certainty. But certainty has never been the criterion for educational decisions. Every professor knows that much of the material conveyed in the classroom will soon be forgotten. The willingness to continue teaching must always rest upon an act of faith that students will retain a useful conceptual framework, a helpful approach to the subject, a valuable method of analysis, or some other intangible residue of lasting intellectual value. Much the same is true of courses on ethical problems. It does seem plausible to suppose that such classes will help students become more alert in perceiving ethical issues, more aware of the reasons underlying moral principles, and more equipped to reason carefully in applying these principles to concrete cases. Will they behave more ethically? One would suppose so, provided we assume that most students have a desire to lead ethical lives and share the basic moral values common to our society. Granted, we cannot *prove* that such results will be achieved. Even so, the prospects are surely great enough to warrant a determined effort, not only because the subject matter is interesting and the problems intellectually challenging but also because the goal is so important to the quality of the society in which we live.

6

Academic Science and the Quest for Technological Innovation

On a crisp October morning in 1980, I awoke to find my own likeness staring forth from the front page of the *New York Times* under the caption "Harvard Considers Commercial Role in DNA Research." The story went on to declare that the university was about to decide whether "to play a leading role in founding a genetic engineering company" in which Harvard biochemists would use the methods of recombinant DNA to develop commercially profitable products. According to the writer, Harvard's deliberations were being closely watched by other institutions considering similar opportunities. A decision to go forward and join in such an enterprise would constitute a new departure in American higher education that could transform the very nature of research universities.

During the weeks that followed, articles appeared in dozens of newspapers and magazines debating the merits and demerits of entering into commercial ventures of this kind. Scientists and editorial writers quickly volunteered their own opinions, most of them hostile. At the same time, letters poured in from high rollers, big butter-and-eggs men, and other entrepreneurs eager to learn of our plans and to explore ways in which they might participate. Once again, the *Times* had managed to transform Harvard's quiet intramural discussions into a public issue of national proportions.

How did I stumble into this morass? And why did the prospect of a small business venture attract such attention and arouse such concern? To answer these questions, one must start not with Harvard's laboratories or its financial offices but with the nagging economic problems that have beset our society in recent years.

The Problem of Productivity

Throughout the 1970s, the American economy consistently exhibited signs of fatigue and sclerosis. The gross national product grew at rates well below those of other industrialized nations; unemployment remained distressingly high; and the cost of living rose more rapidly than in any previous ten-year period in the nation's history. At the core of these familiar symptoms was a surprising lag in productivity. Indeed, productivity not only began to grow at a slower rate; toward the end of the decade, it actually declined, with the result that inflation increased more rapidly while living standards virtually ceased to advance.

We know surprisingly little about changes in productivity. Although economists can list many factors that may affect its course, they do not know the relative influence of each, nor do they agree on which ones are chiefly responsible for its lack of growth. Nevertheless, experts believe that technological change has an important effect on productivity and that the pace of technological innovation has slipped significantly during the past fifteen years. Certainly, industry is now spending a lower share of its sales revenues on research and development than it did in the mid-1960s. And writers who follow business closely assert that corporate executives have gradually become more cautious, less willing to take a long-range view, more inclined to react defensively by making incremental changes in existing products rather than venturing forth with major innovations.

Amid these concerns, one topic that has received increasing attention is the speed and efficiency with which we are able to translate scientific knowledge into useful products and processes. After all, the United States spends larger sums on scientific research than any other nation, and the overall quality of that research is widely believed to be second to none. Surely, then, one promising way of trying to stimulate innovation, and ultimately productivity, is to find better methods of combing the store of scientific knowledge to find new technological breakthroughs that may result in labor-saving devices or even new products and industries. In short, we must work harder at the process referred to somewhat clumsily as technology transfer.

Universities and Industry

From this point, we need take only a short step further to become concerned with the relationships between industry and universities. In 1980, after reviewing studies of a number of important technological innovations, the chief scientist of Xerox Corporation emphasized to a Congressional committee "the very significant function in the innovative process played by the availability of knowledge and people not just within the innovation organization but outside it as well and most often at universities."[1] It is hard to document impressions of this kind with more specific evidence; the links between basic research and technological change are often subtle and indirect and can occur over extended periods of time. Nevertheless, a well-known review of leading technological breakthroughs from 1950 to 1973 revealed that the critical patents involved relied increasingly on basic university research. In fact, during the last half of the period reviewed, over half of all the citations in these patents referred to knowledge produced through work performed on campuses.[2] A study of important advances in clinical medicine from the early 1940s until 1975 discovered that basic research contributed more than 60 percent of the new knowledge that made these advances possible.[3] Such findings are not surprising. Universities employ outstanding scientists who perform most of the basic research carried on in this country, and any effort to apply scientific knowledge with maximum effect must enlist the cooperation of these investigators if it is to be fully successful.

Unfortunately, students of the subject observe that scientific cooperation between industry and the academy declined significantly after 1965. It is tempting to blame such deterioration on

1. U.S. House of Representatives Subcommittee on Science, Research, and Technology, *Report on Government-University-Industry Relations*, June 1980.
2. National Science Board, *Science Indicators, 1974* (Washington, D.C.: National Science Foundation, 1976).
3. Julius H. Comroe and Robert D. Dripps, "Scientific Basis for the Support of Biomedical Science," *Science*, 192 (1976), 111.

the Vietnam War or on the academy's instinctive skepticism toward big business. But more important forces have apparently been at work.

Corporations began to fund university research long before World War II. Although their contributions were modest and were directed toward work of a practical, applied nature, they represented a significant portion of the meager budgets for campus-based research. After 1950, however, the federal government rapidly increased its support of academic science, and corporate funding quickly declined in relative importance. As this process continued, university scientists gradually shifted their attention from industry to Washington. Large federal grants became available to support academic research and to build new "centers of excellence" on a variety of campuses. With universities expanding, the better graduate students were inclined to enter academic life instead of pursuing industrial careers, except in a few large companies that chose to engage in basic research of high quality. As a result of these trends, fewer and fewer industrial scientists had common interests with their colleagues in academic life. Informal contacts diminished. Scientists came less frequently from the corporations to the campus and felt less at home when they did. As the two worlds drifted farther apart, attitudes subtly changed. Universities began to look down on the forms of applied research often practiced in corporations, while industrial scientists were persuaded that their university colleagues were too impractical and abstract to be genuinely useful.

In the late 1970s, major efforts were begun to remedy this situation and to forge closer links between business and universities. Faced with mounting competition from abroad and flagging productivity at home, business executives began coming to meetings and planning conferences on industry-university relations. They sought out university officials and talked about long-term cooperative ventures to promote new lines of research. More firms showed an interest in industry-associates programs that enabled their scientists to visit universities, consult with faculty members, attend seminars, and receive early notice of interesting research developments.

The government itself started to look for more aggressive ways to encourage cooperative ventures between business and academe. In the past, federal agencies were content to fund research and distribute reports on new experiments and discoveries. Now, public officials took bolder steps. Having long claimed title to most of the patents resulting from federally funded research, the Department of Health, Education, and Welfare began in the 1970s to let universities keep these patents if they agreed to launch vigorous programs to identify and exploit new discoveries. The National Science Foundation began to fund innovation centers where academic and corporate scientists could work on common problems. Start-up funds were given to encourage groups of smaller companies to work with universities to perform applied research in particular industries or fields. Money became available to allow small businesses to engage academic consultants who could help them perform feasibility studies to explore new ventures.

Universities were quick to respond to these initiatives and to explore new ways of creating what Exxon Corporation's Ed David has termed "the industrial connection." Several reasons help to explain this interest. Universities have obviously felt a social responsibility to answer appeals to think about collaborative efforts to increase productivity. Such concern is not entirely selfless, since higher education has a vital stake in the long-term strength of the economy. Moreover, academic officials and scientists are certainly aware that massive federal appropriations for campus-based research are largely based on a conviction that such work will eventually lead to practical results. Hence, it is only prudent for universities to take a serious interest in the process of translating scientific knowledge into commercial uses.

More important still, faculty members and administrators are hard pressed financially and see interesting ways to benefit from efforts to improve their relations with industry. For the faculty, opportunities to consult more frequently with research-minded companies can supplement salaries that have been declining in real terms for more than a decade. Industry-associate programs may produce some unrestricted funds for research without making heavy demands on faculty time. A vigorous program to identify useful discoveries and license the resulting patents could conceivably bring new royalty income to faculty members and the university.

Greater rewards may come from interesting large companies in financing the research of particular professors in return for some form of preferred rights to exploit the discoveries that result from their investigations. For example, the Monsanto Corporation entered into an agreement with Harvard University in 1974 to support the work of two professors in the Faculty of Medicine. In return for an exclusive license on patents growing out of the research, Monsanto contributes critical materials and analytic capabilities while agreeing to pay more than $20 million over a twelve-year period. Although similar arrangements are still uncommon, interest seems to be growing among large corporations, creating possibilities for a major new funding source for campus-based research.

Universities may discover even more lucrative opportunities through helping their own professors launch new businesses. Some hint of these prospects can be gleaned from a source quite outside the natural sciences. In the early 1970s, with relatively little capital, a Harvard economist created a major economic forecasting company, Data Resources, Inc., which was sold a few years later for more than $120 million. Sums of this magnitude stir the blood of every harried administrator struggling to balance an unruly budget. This growing excitement has scarcely been stilled by reports on the stock market successes of new biogenetic companies and by articles describing the glittering promise of recombinant DNA research. With the introduction of these new laboratory techniques, possibilities have arisen for manufacturing insulin more cheaply, for discovering cures for hereditary diseases, for unlocking the secret of nitrogen fixation, which could lead in turn to the development of plants that can grow without the use of oil-based fertilizers. Spurred by these prospects, presidents and deans have started to look for ways in which their institutions might share in some of the gains to be made from ideas developed in their laboratories. Could they at least get patent royalties on the inventions used by professors in their new entrepreneurial ventures? Better yet, might they seek out venture capital and help their professors organize new enterprises in return for a modest share of the stock? Should they invest their endowment funds in these companies and agree to share in their management?

In sum, the field of technology transfer offers all sorts of intriguing possibilities to stimulate technological innovation while reaping rewards with which to strengthen academic research. With hard work and a bit of luck, a university might conceivably contribute to the nation's prosperity in ways that could increase its own resources and thereby strengthen its research effort to make still further contributions to the economy—and so on in an endless synergy.

With this bright promise, why does the prospect of technology transfer arouse anxiety among the faculties of every distinguished research university? A few critics may distrust technology and fear the unexpected problems it creates. A few others may instinctively draw back from closer collaboration with business. But the great majority are concerned that programs to exploit technological development will confuse the university's central commitment to the pursuit of knowledge and learning by introducing into the very heart of the academic enterprise a new and powerful motive—the search for commercial utility and financial gain.

To be sure, professors are used to supplementing their income through various kinds of outside activities. The quest for technological development, however, brings to the campus something more powerful, more closely connected to academic work, and therefore more hazardous to the values of the university. Certainly, the sums involved are much larger than faculty members are used to considering. It is one thing to consult for a few hundred dollars a day or to write a textbook in the hope of receiving a few thousand dollars a year. It is quite another matter to think of becoming a millionaire by exploiting a commercially attractive discovery. With stakes of this size, the nature and direction of academic science could be transmuted into something quite unlike the disinterested search for knowledge that has long been thought to animate university professors. In short, the newfound concern with technology transfer is disturbing not only because it could alter the practice of science in the university but also because it threatens the central values and ideals of academic research.

The State of Academic Science

To assess these dangers, one must first set forth the principal conditions that are needed to maintain the highest quality of fundamental research in science. Among innumerable factors that could be mentioned, the following appear to have the greatest importance.

1. There must be sufficient opportunities for a satisfying career in science, especially university science, to attract the most talented young people.

2. First-rate scientists need proper instrumentation and facilities to permit them to do their best research. Without modern equipment, investigators will not be able to work at the frontiers of science, and the initiative will rapidly shift to other countries where better facilities are available.

3. The working environment should be such as to stimulate research of the highest quality. Specifically, scientists need sufficient time to concentrate fully on their work and able colleagues with whom to interact. And since all scientific discoveries build upon existing knowledge, investigators must have access to the widest body of scientific work by having excellent library facilities, opportunities to attend scientific conferences, and maximum freedom to exchange information concerning work in progress.

4. Able scientists should be allowed to decide for themselves which projects to pursue and what research methods to employ. In particular, they must have sources of funding flexible enough to enable them to pursue the problems of their choice. The need for such freedom must constantly be explained, especially to taxpayers and government officials who wonder why expenditures of public funds should not be carefully planned and directed to specific, useful projects. In arguing against restrictions, either on the use of research funds or on the open exchange of scientific knowledge, no one has been more eloquent than Michael Polanyi. Polanyi asks his readers to imagine that society badly needed to assemble a vast jigsaw puzzle. How should it organize the work? Obviously, efforts would be made to assemble a group of highly capable helpers to participate in the task. But it would be inefficient to give each assistant a copy of the puzzle and ask him to work at the problem in isolation. It would also be unwise to establish a central authority to direct the work of all the participants and to attempt to have that authority plan in advance how the puzzle would be put together. By forcing each helper to wait

for orders from the higher authority, we would lose much of the independent contribution that these creative individuals could make. "The only way to get the job finished quickly would be to get as many helpers as could conveniently work at one and the same set and let them loose on it, each to follow his own initiative. Each helper would then watch the situation as it was affected by the progress made by all the others and would set himself new problems in accordance with the latest outline of the completed part of the puzzle. The tasks undertaken by each would closely dovetail into those performed by the others. And consequently the joint efforts of all would form a closely organized whole, even though each helper would follow entirely his own independent judgment."[4]

5. Even if scientists are given great freedom and ample facilities to carry out their work, some process must be created to assess and maintain the quality of research in order to make sure that it does not become shoddy and unreliable. Such a process typically involves widely accepted mechanisms, such as refereed journals and peer review, as well as the cooperation of eminent scientists who help to set demanding and objective standards and to make sure that they are enforced and preserved.

6. Finally, like other forms of human enterprise, good science requires high morale—the general sense among investigators that scientific work is worth doing, that it is widely respected, and that the conditions under which it is performed are fair and reasonable.

In light of these considerations, let me first review in general terms how well basic science has been faring in the United States without determined efforts to encourage technological development, and then explore what effects such efforts might have on the quality of scientific work.

With respect to opportunities for scientific careers, there is much apprehension today, but probably no real cause for alarm. Because the student population in the United States is likely to decline over the next generation, universities will not be expanding and job opportunities will be less numerous than they were

4. Michael Polanyi, *The Logic of Liberty: Reflections and Rejoinders* (London: Routledge and Kegan Paul, 1951), p. 35.

before the mid-1970s. Even so, the sciences have not been as hard hit as other fields of learning because they never expanded as rapidly as the humanities and social sciences in the 1960s and because graduate students in most scientific fields have opportunities to work in industry or government if suitable openings fail to develop in the universities. To be sure, the nation may periodically encounter temporary manpower shortages in particular fields of science, but that is a different matter. To keep basic science strong, the essential point is that enough career opportunities are still available to attract outstanding, committed young investigators. Throughout the 1970s these conditions still seemed to prevail, except, perhaps, in a few areas of research, such as mathematics, astronomy, and astrophysics.

The situation is much less satisfactory with respect to equipment and facilities. Whereas the costs of equipping a modern laboratory have increased much faster than the cost of living, the government has cut its support for these purposes by more than 80 percent since 1967. As a result, the quality of instrumentation has deteriorated to levels far beneath those of the better industrial laboratories and below the levels achieved in countries such as Germany and Japan. Recent studies estimate that the accumulated shortfall in equipment alone exceeds $300 million in our universities. Unless substantial improvement is made reasonably soon, the progress of American science is bound to be affected, even though the results may not become obvious for a number of years.

The quality of the working environment is more intangible and harder to evaluate. In certain respects, scientists occupy an unusually strong position. Modern methods of travel and communication allow them to stay in close contact with greater numbers of scientists than ever before and to have access to a far larger body of information culled from laboratories around the world. Ironically, however, the growing quantities of data tend to produce an "information overload" that prevents many investigators from keeping up with all of the work in progress in their own field, not to mention related areas of research. In today's world, it is no easy matter even to decide what one should read amid a mass of technical journals and research reports.

More serious still, the mechanics of doing research have clearly become much more complicated and unwieldy than ever before. As a result, scientists are heavily burdened with administrative tasks and assorted other distractions. In part, these problems stem from the elaborate process of administering large sums of research money—a task that consumes vast quantities of time applying for funds, helping the government evaluate proposals for grants to others, and accounting for the expenditure of sums already received. Moreover, the administrative burdens grow heavier simply because science is increasingly practiced by larger teams of people who must be recruited, supervised, encouraged, and cajoled. In addition to these tasks, the university itself has become a more complicated place, demanding more committee work and administrative help from many members of the faculty. James Watson once remarked, apropos of his discovery of the double helix: "It's necessary to be slightly underemployed if you are to do something significant."[5] The number of outstanding scientists who are even slightly underemployed has surely diminished over the past half century.

As for the freedom to do scientific work, government funds seem adequate to permit most established scientists to carry on research of their own choosing. The federal budget for basic research may no longer be rising in real dollars, but it has not declined either. If our total expenditures for research and development do not account for as large a portion of the gross national product as those of several other nations, the United States still spends greater absolute sums on fundamental research than any other country. Nevertheless, appropriations are not increasing as rapidly as the cost of doing research, and the available funds must be shared among a growing number of academic scientists. In these circumstances, someone is bound to feel the pinch, and younger scientists are the most likely victims. For these investigators, time is of the essence, because they have only six or seven years as junior faculty members in which to establish their suitability for tenure. Yet they may consume a year or two of this period simply obtaining the grants to enable them to begin work, and many of them must be tempted to submit "safe," conven-

5. Horace Freeland Judson, *The Eighth Day of Creation: Makers of the Revolution in Biology* (New York: Simon & Schuster, 1979), p. 20.

tional proposals rather than run the risk of having their work go unfunded. In fields that rely on expensive instrumentation, junior faculty members may even have to put aside their own interests and join the project of a tenured colleague in order to carry out research at all.

Apart from the problems of funding, the past decade has brought increasing legal restrictions on the methods of research that investigators can employ. Although many of the new regulations impose added burdens of time and paperwork, most thoughtful people would agree that they are necessary to protect human health and safety. Moreover, American science still remains free of any overt restrictions of a political or ideological nature. All in all, therefore, able academic scientists in this country retain a wide freedom to carry out the type of research they wish by whatever methods they choose.

There is also little reason for concern over the process of quality control. Despite periodic criticism, the system of peer review is still the customary mode of awarding federal research grants, the refereed journals still play their traditional role, and financial pressures have caused most universities to exercise even greater care and rigor in reviewing candidates for promotion. As for the quality of leadership, the principal figures in American science are certainly eminent; by every international standard, they dominate the world today.

Notwithstanding these outward signs of strength, one senses an unease in many scientific circles, a fear that the sheer size, complexity, and expense of modern science may have a corrupting effect on quality. As the Soviet physicist Pyotr Kapitza once declared, "The year that Rutherford died (1938) there disappeared forever the happy days of free scientific work which gave us such delight in our youth. Science has lost her freedom. Science has become a productive force. She has become rich but she has become enslaved and part of her is veiled in secrecy."[6] The causes of this anxiety are not entirely clear. Perhaps there is concern that "big science" can bring undue rewards to people who seem more noted for their entrepreneurial talents than for the quality of their

6. Victor K. McElheny, "Kapitza's Visit to England," *Science*, 153 (1966), 727.

minds. Perhaps scientists fear that there is no longer enough time for referees to read papers with sufficient care or for senior investigators to exercise close supervision over younger associates. Perhaps professors feel that the direction of their work is imperceptibly passing from their hands and that research will increasingly be shaped to conform with restrictions imposed by those who control the funds. Whatever the reason, the concerns do exist, and must be watched with the greatest care, because the maintenance of standards is essential to the quality of the scientific enterprise.

The anxieties just mentioned are closely related to the last prerequisite for first-rate science—the intangible but vastly important ingredient of morale. Here again, the situation seems healthy but not altogether secure. Since the mid-1960s, all fields of intellectual inquiry have been subject to sharp questioning, and even savage attacks, concerning their relevance to important human problems and their own intrinsic morality. In the aftermath of Hiroshima, scientists have hardly been spared such criticism. By any standard, however, they have managed to weather the onslaught with remarkably little loss of *esprit*. Distinguished investigators have been more concerned than they once were with the social implications of their work and more alert to its moral dilemmas. And yet, in no other broad field of academic endeavor have professors remained so motivated and so convinced of the value and importance of their research.

Even so, one cannot be complacent about the morale of American science. The intensity of criticism and self-doubt seems clearly greater today than it was fifty years, or even twenty-five years ago, as the public has become more skeptical about the benefits of science—or more precisely, of technology and innovation. There is nothing necessarily wrong with these attitudes; on balance, they are healthy and serve a constructive purpose, as long as they are conveyed in a thoughtful, balanced fashion. Nevertheless, they remain a source of concern, for if they should be expressed in excessively emotional or irrational ways, they could produce a degree of insecurity and distrust that could erode public confidence in science and eventually have a demoralizing effect upon the spirit of scientific enterprise itself.

The Impact of Technology Transfer on the University

With this brief sketch, one can begin to sort out the implications for academic science of a strong program to encourage technological development. As I have noted, many forms of technology transfer not only benefit the economy but offer opportunities to the university for new sources of income. Such income could make a distinct contribution to the quality of science—by upgrading equipment and renovating facilities, by permitting a few more fellowships for talented students, by maintaining faculty compensation, by helping young investigators get started more quickly on their research, by simply providing a little unrestricted money to encourage more venturesomeness in exploring new lines of inquiry. In the 1960s, government funding was abundant enough that these advantages might have seemed marginal. Today, such incremental support could make a substantial difference. One can argue strongly that the government should provide for these needs as a wise investment for the nation's future. But few observers expect any real increases in support either from government agencies or from private donors, foundations, or any of the other traditional sources. In these circumstances, opportunities for industrial funding and for sharing in the rewards of technological development seem to offer the brightest hope for obtaining added resources. Small wonder, then, that many educators have expressed keen interest in these possibilities.

The dangers of technology transfer to the quality of academic science are equally clear. To begin with, the prospect of reaping financial rewards may subtly influence professors in choosing which problems to investigate. Academic scientists have always feared what Vannevar Bush once termed "the perverse law governing research," that "applied research invariably drives out pure." One can certainly ask whether such concerns are not overdrawn and whether academic scientists are not too much inclined to disdain applied research. But few people would welcome a situation in which academic scientists did not simply consider which potential problems for research were most intellectually challenging and important, but were influenced by powerful extraneous factors, such as the prospect of large financial rewards.

Another concern is that professors may drift away from *any* form of research (and teaching) in order to perform other tasks involved in the process of technological development. Whatever disagreements may exist over the relative value of different forms of scientific inquiry, no one will assert that we will be better off if gifted faculty members begin to neglect their teaching and research in favor of massive consulting with corporations or lengthy forays into entrepreneurship.

Many distinguished investigators are also worried by the risk of introducing secrecy into the process of scientific research. Secrecy, of course, is anathema to scientific progress, since new discoveries must build upon what is already known. Every account of major discoveries shows how much scientists depend on being informed, either by publications or by chance encounters, about current research on the same or related problems. Granted, many scientists have never been completely open about their work. In the eighteenth century, Henry Cavendish did not even deign to publish but conveyed his discoveries by private letters to friends. Today, many investigators will withhold information until they are completely satisfied that their findings are correct; others will keep their work to themselves in the race to be first to announce a new discovery. Yet commercial motives can introduce a greater and more threatening form of secrecy. In order to maintain a competitive advantage that could be worth large sums of money, scientists who engage in business may be tempted to withhold information until their discoveries can be further developed to a patentable state. Because the financial stakes are high, investigators may not merely withhold ideas from publication; they may become close-mouthed and refrain from the free, informal discussions with colleagues that are essential to the process of discovery. On occasion, scientists could conceivably secrete information indefinitely rather than risk disclosure in a patent that might be circumvented by some other enterprising firm.

Beyond these specific concerns lies a final, more intangible threat to the quality of leadership and ultimately to the state of morale within the scientific enterprise. As I have already noted, the traditional ideal of science presupposes a disinterested search for knowledge without ulterior motives of any kind. As an ideal, this conception has great power. It encourages established scientists to be objective in evaluating the quality of scientific work. It elicits trust from other scientists not only toward their colleagues but especially toward the leaders of each field who play a crucial role in maintaining the standards that define good research. Finally, the reputation for disinterested inquiry helps to preserve the confidence and respect of the public—a state of mind that is ever more vital to the progress of academic science as its dependence on external support continues to rise.

It is only fair to point out that the quality of disinterestedness has never been universally achieved in practice. Even Galileo tried to sell his inventions for money. In recent times, it has not been money but the force of competition, the lure of prizes, the snares of vanity and fame that have entered the thoughts of distinguished scientists. Yet these motives at least reinforce the traditional goals of academic science. Carried to excess, they may occasionally lead to cheating and other pathological results. But these episodes are rare. Moreover, the feelings involved are so familiar, so inescapably human that one tends to take them for granted. In contrast, the introduction of a different set of motives, oriented toward private gain, threatens to reduce the credibility of the scientists involved and to diminish their capacity either to elicit complete trust from their colleagues or to secure the unmixed admiration of the public.

Ways of Linking the University with Industry

With this quick *tour d'horizon* of the benefits and risks of technology transfer, what can we say about the various means that are available to forge closer links between industry and the campus?

AVOIDING A DISDAIN FOR USEFUL RESEARCH   It is often said that the highest goal of academic science is to pursue knowledge for its own sake and not for the purpose of achieving specific practical results. This ideal is constantly at risk in a world where scientific research depends on heavy support from public funds, for the public is chiefly interested in discovery not as an end in itself, but as a means to new products, new cures for disease, or new solutions to pressing social problems. Even from a utilitarian standpoint, of course, basic research in universities plays a vital role in producing the store of knowledge from which useful inventions must eventually be derived. Nevertheless, the values of unplanned research are intangible enough and its fruits are sufficiently conjectural and long-term in nature that many campus investigators are concerned lest public funding be gradually shifted more and more toward projects designed to attack immediate problems of concern to the government and the public.

It is fitting that professors should proclaim the values of basic research and understandable that they should do so zealously to resist pressures to channel their work toward excessively practical ends. But it would be unfortunate if academic scientists pressed their case so far as to depreciate the value of applied research or to dismiss any effort to consider the potential applications of scientific work. Such attitudes could lead investigators to neglect important problems of genuine intellectual challenge and might subtly discourage their graduate students from choosing to pursue careers in industrial research.

After World War II, when federal research funds grew plentiful, academic scientists were often accused of harboring prejudices of this kind. But there is evidence that these attitudes are changing and that professors are becoming less inclined to draw a rigid line between pure and applied research. Basic scientific inquiry of a nondirective sort quite properly continues to flourish. As Gerald Holton has observed, however, "an alternative and complementary motivation for certain research scientists is making its appearance. The stimulus comes . . . more and more frequently from perceiving an area of basic scientific ignorance that seems to lie at the heart of a social problem."[7]

These attitudinal changes may have important effects on the link between academic science and practical advances in industry and society. As basic scientists grow more inclined to investigate problems with an eye to their eventual applications in the real world, the process of translating new discoveries into useful results may accelerate. By participating in work of this kind, graduate students may also gain experience that will prepare them better for careers in industry and applied research. If this process devel-

7. "Science, Technology, and the Fourth Discontinuity" (Keynote address delivered at the University of Houston Conference on Psychology and Society: Information Technology in the 1980s, Houston, April 10, 1980), p. 15.

ops spontaneously, without misguided efforts by the government to plan the work of able investigators, we may achieve a closer concordance between the desire of academic scientists to choose their own areas of research and society's wish to obtain practical benefits in return for its generous financial support.

IMPROVING COMMUNICATION   There are several opportunities to strengthen communication between universities and industry that carry little risk of impairing the quality of academic science. For example, industrial scientists can often teach part time as adjunct professors and thereby contribute to the academic program of a department while providing a channel of communication between the university and an industrial laboratory. Similarly, many corporations are interested in arranging postdoctoral programs for some of their scientists who need to take a new direction in their research or strengthen their knowledge of recent developments in fields of basic science related to their work. Such fellowships may bring a new perspective to a department and strengthen ties between pure and applied research without imposing undue burdens on the professors involved.

Industry-associates programs also provide a useful method of improving the exchange of information between business and academic science departments. Properly administered, such programs can bring a modest flow of income to the university while making few demands on the time and energy of faculty members. Moreover, despite the concern expressed by a few critics, there is nothing unfair or discriminatory about these efforts as long as membership is open to all at a price that any corporation can readily afford.

A much more common form of communication between business and the academy is consulting by individual scientists. The public may regard this practice as a slightly illicit way of expanding a scientist's personal income at the expense of teaching and research. But consulting serves a more important function. By traveling periodically to corporations, academic scientists carry ideas, recent developments, and critical judgments from the university to industry and thus encourage the process of technological development. The very fact that senior professors perform this role may help to dispel the feeling among graduate students that applied research is inferior and uninteresting. At the same time, consulting can provide useful information to university scientists concerning sophisticated research methods, new forms of instrumentation, or even employment opportunities for graduate students. More important still, consultants may discover practical problems in industry that lead to challenging issues for basic research, as has occurred in fields such as materials science and solid-state physics.

The principal danger in consulting is that scientists will spend too much time away from their academic work. But comprehensive surveys conducted in 1969 and 1975 revealed that only 6 percent of all respondents consulted more than one day a week and that paid consultants taught as much and published more than their colleagues. These studies also recorded no increase in consulting from 1969 to 1975 and no reduction in teaching or research.[8] With faculty salaries declining, some observers fear that professors may have begun to spend more time advising corporations. Even so, the problem has not reached grave proportions, and universities can do much to contain abuse by working with their faculties to develop reasonable guidelines and restraints.

OBTAINING PATENTS   Patents offer universities an incentive to work harder to identify valuable ideas discovered in their laboratories. By making such efforts, they may speed the translation of knowledge into useful products and processes while eliciting new sources of revenue to strengthen academic science. For many years, the paradigm case has been the Wisconsin Alumni Research Fund, a foundation operated by graduates of the University of Wisconsin to license patents resulting from the work of faculty scientists. Over sixty years, this effort has returned many millions of dollars to support research at the university. Few institutions have come close to matching Wisconsin's record; indeed, only a handful of universities even receive enough royalties to cover the cost of obtaining their patents. Nevertheless, the prospects seem brighter now that Congress has passed legislation allowing universities to hold patents on discoveries made in their laboratories under federally funded research projects. Hence,

8. Carl V. Patton, "Consulting by Faculty Members," *Academe*, 66 (May 1980), 181–185.

many institutions are developing more aggressive programs to identify patentable discoveries and to find suitable mechanisms for licensing them to interested companies. Some universities have proceeded by establishing their own patent offices, while others have turned to firms, such as Battelle and Research Corporation, which act as patent brokers between corporations and the academy. In the future, it is even possible that universities may create organizations to develop patents to a commercially feasible state, since the lack of such development seems to be a critical obstacle in securing attractive license arrangements with corporations that can then bring the results of academic science to the marketplace.

Critics occasionally question whether patents are truly consistent with the ideals of academic science, since they offer the owner exclusive rights to a discovery for a period of seventeen years. But patents do not conflict with the principle of open access to knowledge. The rights acquired extend not to knowledge of a discovery as such, but only to its use for commercial purposes. In fact, the very idea of the patent system is to encourage inventors to make their discoveries known instead of keeping them secret to maintain an advantage over competitors. It is possible that a scientist may postpone publication of an idea for a few months until his work has reached a stage where a patent application can be filed. But past experience does not offer much cause for concern on this score. Moreover, it is difficult to perceive any practical way of avoiding the problem. Even if patents did not exist, professors might be tempted to withhold commercially valuable findings from the public by selling such knowledge to corporations to keep indefinitely as trade secrets.

Other skeptics, including faculty members, have ventured the opinion that scientists and universities should not benefit financially from discoveries made through work financed by the federal government. Yet it is hard to attribute such discoveries entirely to the government; at least part of the rewards can justly be given to the investigator, who supplied the ingenuity required, and to the university, which often pays the cost of the laboratory facilities and may have even contributed the salary of the chief investigator. Moreover, the government's chief concern is not to earn royalty income but to encourage the application of scientific knowledge for socially productive purposes. This is the reason underlying Congress' recent decision to allow universities to own and license patents resulting from discoveries made under government research grants. Before this legislation, federal agencies had little success in licensing such patents or in encouraging serious efforts to identify patentable ideas resulting from campus-based research. By allowing universities and their professors to share in the rewards, Washington is likely to stimulate the development and commercial use of many more patentable discoveries, and any income obtained by the universities will help in turn to strengthen the quality of academic research. Thus both the public and the campuses stand to benefit from the new arrangements.

A further danger that patents may create for academic science is the risk of diverting professors from their normal research activities. Scientists might conceivably do experiments of little intrinsic interest simply because they could lead to patentable devices. Investigators might pursue a line of work beyond the point of maximum intellectual value in order to bring an idea to a sufficient state of development to secure a patent. Although such problems could arise, they have not proved serious in the past. Nor are they likely to materialize in the future, especially if the university shares the royalties with its professors in a manner that ensures that their financial rewards are not extremely large. Most able scientists are likely to consider their normal research too interesting and the income from inventions too uncertain to squander large amounts of their time on projects of no great intellectual importance.[9] If there is a danger, it is more likely to come from the efforts of an overzealous university patent officer who may unwisely press faculty members to pursue their work to the point of patentability in the mistaken belief that they are serving the vital interests of the university. These risks, however, can presumably be minimized through careful administration and proper oversight by a faculty committee. And even if such excesses should occasionally occur, the social value of the inventions may

9. The normal rule of thumb is that it takes one thousand reported discoveries to produce one hundred patents; it takes one hundred patents to produce ten licenses; and only one license in ten will yield more than $25,000 per year. At these odds, few scientists will be seriously diverted from academic work by the lure of patent royalties.

help offset any diversion of effort from more fundamental research.

A final issue in the use of patents is how they are licensed to interested corporations and, in particular, whether they are licensed to several firms or only to a single company. One can argue that nonexclusive arrangements are preferable, even if the university must accept somewhat lower royalties, for academic institutions should not deliberately allow a corporation to engage in monopolistic pricing merely to maximize their income. Quite often, however, no company will agree to invest large sums to bring a new invention to market unless it is given exclusive rights that will provide some assurance of recovering its initial investment before other competitors enter the field. During the years when the federal government held patents to discoveries made under its research grants, it ignored this possibility and offered licenses only on a nonexclusive basis. While that policy remained in effect, the responsible officials managed only to license less than 4 percent of the twenty-eight thousand patents under their control. After reviewing this experience, government representatives themselves admitted that the failure to grant exclusive licenses was a major reason for the lack of success in exploiting their patents. Hence, although a university should begin by trying to grant licenses to all interested parties, it need have no qualms about negotiating an exclusive arrangement for a reasonable period if such an arrangement seems necessary to induce a company to develop the patent. For in the end, the public would clearly prefer to have a useful discovery placed on the market through an exclusive license than never to benefit from the discovery at all.

CONTRACTING WITH PARTICULAR FIRMS   Research agreements with particular companies offer yet another opportunity to encourage technological development in ways that may yield new sources of funding for university-based research. Several highly publicized arrangements of this sort have been made in recent years. Yet the very magnitude of the sums involved—$23 million in the Monsanto-Harvard agreement; $10 million for the contract between Exxon and the Massachusetts Institute of Technology— led a few writers to warn universities that they may be co-opted by industry and gradually lose their independence. What lies behind these expressions of concern? How might such arrangements with industry actually distort the scientific enterprise?

One conceivable distortion might arise if companies could somehow use their funds to induce distinguished scientists to study commercially relevant problems of little intrinsic scientific importance. The straightforward way to accomplish this result would simply be to hire away a professor at a salary that he could not refuse, but there is little evidence that this is occurring to any significant extent. As an alternative, a company could offer a university either funds or laboratory renovations in return for help in inducing one of its faculty members to work on problems of special interest to the company. One of the joys of tenure, however, is the right it gives professors to resist such efforts with impunity, and no sane administrator would dream of making such an attempt. Conceivably, a firm could maneuver more subtly. A professor could somehow become dependent on a particular company for funds and thus be subject to pressure later on to work on the company's problems. But even this possibility seems farfetched, for established scientists can normally find funds from the government if a firm will no longer support the work they wish to do. Moreover, no sensible company is likely to believe that it will obtain the results it seeks by pressuring an able academic scientist to do research that is not of his own choosing.

Despite these considerations, many of the journalists who have commented on the rising interest in corporate research agreements have suggested that universities and their faculty members are making some sort of Faustian bargain that will ultimately place their research under the control of corporations hungering for profit. Such writers seem to prefer having Washington fund all basic research. What they do not recognize is the influence that federal officials have long exerted in hammering out the provisions of government research contracts. In recent years, these restrictions have become more and more detailed and increasingly oriented toward the federal agency's specific practical objectives. Thus one reason that many scientists prefer industrial funding today is that corporations usually offer their support with *less* control and *less* red tape than obtain under federal research agreements. No one can be sure how long this state of affairs will continue. But those who are truly concerned about the freedom of scientific inquiry should understand that real freedom is most likely to occur if able investigators have more than one source to which they can turn for their funding.

Another concern expressed by critics of these arrangements is that they may provide an unfair advantage to the company involved. These worries would be justified if a university elected to give a corporation preferential access to information extending beyond the research actually supported by the firm. But there is no evidence that such arrangements have been made in the corporate agreements to date. Even so, critics continue to express concern on this score. For example, David Noble and Nancy Pfund observed in 1980 that "Monsanto gave Harvard what appears to be quite a lot of money, $23 million. In return, they received access to the facilities of Harvard Medical School, a resource they could not have created with many times that amount. The firm has in essence transformed a part of the public-sector social resource into a private-sector preserve."[10] Such criticisms convey a distorted picture. In fact, Monsanto does not have special access to an entire school or department; it has only a working relationship with the two tenured scientists, and their research teams, who receive support from the company. In addition, the Harvard agreement expressly forbids restrictions on the publication of any discoveries that are made. It is possible that a company might encourage a scientist to delay publication for commercial reasons, but this is a danger that can presumably be contained by providing for publication rights in the basic agreement and by careful administration on the part of the university.

The principal advantage that such agreements bring to a company is the favored treatment it receives on any patents that emerge from the funded research. In the case of Monsanto, for example, the company has exclusive rights to any patents for a period of years sufficient to enable it to market the products involved. This is a special advantage, no doubt, but a firm is surely entitled to some reward for risking large sums of money to finance the research. Of course, universities should not grant greater exclusivity than a firm actually needs to develop and exploit the patent. They would also do well to establish some mechanism to

10. "Business Goes Back to College," *The Nation*, 231 (September 19, 1980), 252.

protect the interests of the public, as Harvard and Monsanto did
in establishing an outside review board with power to compel
Monsanto to sublicense if it is dilatory in making use of the patents. But critics would be ill-advised to condemn favored treatment altogether, for without it there would normally be no incentive to fund the research, and the public might be deprived of the
benefits at any price.

INVESTING IN NEW VENTURES   The most controversial topic that
has emerged in considering the university's role in technology
transfer is whether an institution should assist its own professors
in forming companies to exploit their discoveries. Many lucrative
consulting firms have been formed to apply the methods of social
science research. Many high-technology companies have risen
from modest beginnings to earn millions of dollars. If a university
could own a substantial share of even one or two of these ventures,
it might gain a source of added revenue that could go far to remedy the gaps and deficiencies in the current patterns of funding
for research. At the same time, the willingness of a university to
help assemble capital and organize a company could encourage
professors to launch new ventures that they would not otherwise
undertake. In this fashion, the university might play a role in developing new technology while helping its professors avoid costly
entrepreneurial mistakes.

These opportunities are tempting, especially today, when we
appear to be poised on the edge of a vast biomedical revolution.
Indeed, the prospects seemed all but irresistible when Harvard
officials first heard about the prospect of going into business with
some of the university's ablest biochemists in the venture reported
by the *New York Times*. By the time the newspaper articles began
to appear, Harvard was being offered 10 percent of the stock of
the new company at no cost to the institution. University presidents are not accustomed to turn their backs on offers of this kind.
Even so, as my colleagues and I thought more about the matter,
we slowly came to realize that our pathway to riches would be
marked by every kind of snare and pitfall.

Commercial ventures of this kind are bound to lead an administration into conflicts with several constituencies. For example,
any effort to go into business with professors will expose the ad-

ministration to almost certain disagreements, not only with its faculty partners but also with professors who feel envious or upset that their own cherished schemes have not received comparable support. Such commercial ventures will also impose upon the university unwelcome responsibilities it does not have as merely a tiny shareholder in a large established company. Investors who regard the university's participation as an endorsement of quality may feel aggrieved if it decides to pull out. And protests may be voiced by a public that expects high standards from the university, whether in the pricing of life-sustaining products or in the marketing of potentially hazardous drugs. In this environment, scientists, corporate executives, and academic administrators may not prove the most compatible of partners in trying to manage an effective commercial enterprise.

These burdens are troublesome enough to universities already struggling with severe administrative problems. But they are not the burdens that should concern us most. There are other problems that pose greater dangers for the quality of research and even for the intellectual integrity of the university itself.

One worrisome aspect of these ventures is that they inevitably change and confuse the relationship of the university to its professors. The faculty member who joins with the administration in founding a new company is no longer valued merely as a teacher and a scholar; he becomes a significant source of potential income to the institution. In a certain sense, the same may be true of a scientist who has developed a profitable patent or entered into an agreement with a corporation for large-scale research support. In these cases, however, it is unlikely that the rewards to the university will depend on the continuing entrepreneurial efforts of the professor. When a university collaborates with its faculty in a new company, however, the institution will often stand to gain from the ongoing commercial activities of its professors. This new role immediately casts an aura of ambiguity and doubt on many decisions that the administration regularly makes. Suppose an assistant professor is also working for a university-owned venture on a matter of major commercial importance. How is the administration to judge his qualifications for tenure? How will a president or dean respond to any of the university's faculty partners when they ask for an extra leave, or larger laboratory space, or more graduate students? And how will salaries be affected? If a university is trying to attract a professor from another institution who is capable of doing work of great commercial potential, will higher pay be offered in recognition of that fact? Will promising assistant professors receive a "piece of the action" in return for accepting an appointment? Will universities enter into bidding wars of a kind not heretofore imagined once the financial stakes begin to mount?

Most presidents and deans will promptly respond that commercial considerations should have no place in deciding academic matters of salary, space, promotions, and the like. Enterprising administrators will quickly begin to think of organizational structures to insulate academic officials from the university's new technology ventures so that commercial and academic considerations can be kept strictly separate. My own initial thoughts proceeded along these very lines. But structures cannot always work perfectly in practice. It will be difficult, and possibly unwise, to separate a president from any knowledge of the university's business enterprises. And it will be harder still to convince the outside world, or even the rest of the faculty, that commercial considerations have not subtly begun to infect what have always been regarded as strictly academic decisions. Since the reputation for integrity is essential in matters such as appointments, and since the faculty's confidence in that integrity is important to its morale, even the appearance of impropriety could be extremely damaging.[11]

Several other dangers can arise that are equally serious to the university. These problems will not necessarily occur in every commercial enterprise. But they are bound to materialize if such ventures become commonplace. For example, professors who become large shareholders in a new business may also choose to play a significant role in the affairs of the company. In this event, they may find it difficult to confine their involvement to the single day per week customarily allowed for outside activities. Some profes-

11. It is true that appointments decisions may also be influenced by a candidate's record in obtaining large government research grants. As long as such grants are subject to a rigorous peer review, however, the ability to obtain federal support may reasonably reflect the candidate's abilities as an academic scientist. The same is not necessarily true of an investigator who can secure large rewards from commercial ventures.

sors may succeed in living by this rule, at least for a while. But as
the business grows and problems develop, they will find it hard to
avoid devoting more and more of their time to the affairs of the
company. Once faculty members are deeply involved in such a
venture, they may be powerfully attracted not only by the hope of
making money but by the fascination and pride of creating a successful organization. The combination of financial and entrepreneurial motives can often prove so strong that the company's success will gradually come to dominate the creative thought and
imagination of the scientists involved. At this point, their contributions to teaching and research will almost certainly diminish.

Participation in such a firm will likewise increase the risk of secrecy, for every professor committed to the welfare of a business
will be aware of the need to protect its commercial interests by
avoiding premature disclosures. Graduate students may be influenced by habits of secrecy foreign to academic science and may
likewise be diverted from their normal academic work to join in
projects that may be more useful to the company than educationally valuable. Faced with cutbacks in federal support, even junior
faculty may be vulnerable to attractive offers by a tenured colleague to engage in research relating to the interests of his company. Conscientious professors may succeed in avoiding such
practices. Even so, they may be suspected of compromising academic pursuits for commercial reasons, and these suspicions will
contribute to an erosion of trust and a corresponding decline in
academic standards.

Beyond these problems lie intangible but important issues relating to scientific leadership and morale. In these matters, we
have little experience to guide us. Although scientists have left
universities to start successful companies, few established investigators have sought to participate in commercial ventures while
remaining on the campus as full-time academic scientists. Hence,
one can only ask questions; the answers must remain speculative
for the time being. Will academic entrepreneurs find the time to
serve as editors of journals or referees of manuscripts and thus
contribute to the essential process of leadership and the maintenance of scientific standards? What effect will the example of the
commercially successful academic scientist have on the behavior
of younger investigators? Will anything be lost to the morale of

the scientific enterprise if the ideal of the disinterested scientist recedes before the new image of the wealthy professor-entrepreneur? Obviously, it cannot be helpful to the academy if newspapers and magazines continue to publish articles carrying such titles as "Bacteria Tycoons Start a Real Growth Industry" and "The Biology Business: The Bandwagon Begins to Roll." One cannot read many headlines of this kind without wondering what effects they will have on public support for academic science or on the credibility of universities and their faculty members in debates over controversial questions, such as the regulation of recombinant DNA.

At this point, the reader may ask whether these issues have much relevance to whether the *university* chooses to participate in the business ventures of its faculty. After all, problems such as the diversion of faculty time, or excessive secrecy, or the misuse of graduate students, or even the risks to scientific leadership and morale can all be present when faculty members take a substantial equity position in an outside firm, whether or not the university becomes involved. By acquiring a substantial financial stake in the success of a business venture, a professor will be strongly tempted to do what he can to further its success, not only in his free time but in his daily research as well. The more the commercial interests of the firm diverge from the needs of basic research and instruction, the greater the risk that academic values will be subverted.

In view of these dangers, one might argue that universities should actually seek to participate in these new enterprises in an effort to shape them in ways that will minimize the dangers to academic science. The point is intriguing but probably unsound. To begin with, one wonders whether university administrators can be trusted to take strict precautions to protect the interests of science if proper safeguards threaten to reduce potential profits. Even if these suspicions are unwarranted, it is doubtful that a university could afford to participate in all the ventures created by a resourceful faculty. Nor is it likely that an administration could acquire the knowledge to guard against the dangers of excessive secrecy or undue diversion of faculty effort without involving itself quite deeply in the daily affairs of these companies. This is not a task that academic institutions are well equipped to perform and is hardly the sort of added burden they need at this point in their history.

If academic values are at risk when professors engage in commercial ventures, what can a university do to protect its interests? Surely, it must make every effort to counteract these dangers—by trying to make certain that basic research is not neglected, that graduate students are not misused, that lines of communication remain as open as possible. This process will involve examining the rules that restrict the outside activities of professors, constructing safeguards to govern the use of graduate students, and developing guidelines to ensure that university facilities are not exploited for commercial purposes.

The task of erecting internal safeguards is difficult under the best of circumstances and will require much trust and understanding on the part of the faculty. Whatever the administration does and however hard it tries, it will surely compromise its credibility and its moral authority by agreeing to join faculty members in funding new enterprises and sharing in the commercial rewards. This is no trifling matter. If academic leaders serve any important purpose in the university, apart from raising money, they serve to articulate and preserve its essential intellectual values. How can they possibly discharge this function once they are perceived to have jumped into partnerships with their professors in order to profit from the very enterprises that create the dangers they are seeking to counteract?

Of course, one must weigh these disadvantages against the need to increase innovation and secure an added source of university income. But there are other ways of pursuing these objectives that do not carry the risks resulting from going into business with one's own professors. Both faculty members and administration have an incentive to turn new discoveries into useful innovations by working together to secure patents. If these rewards seem insufficient, the university can always try to capture the gains of technological innovation by making modest investments in capable venture-capital companies. Such concerns make it their business to survey opportunities throughout the economy, including opportunities arising from the work of academic scientists. Educational institutions may do better financially if they ask these firms to decide which fledgling companies to support instead of trying to perform this function themselves by picking members of their own faculties and helping them to launch new ventures.[12] Granted, universities may have special knowledge of the work of their own professors and special opportunities to strike unusually advantageous agreements. But there are also dangers that academic administrators will overvalue the work of their own professors, that familiarity will cloud good judgment, that universities will lack the business acumen to organize new ventures, that participation in such companies will bring political pressures and public relations problems which will impede progress and profitability. All in all, therefore, the financial advantages to the university appear more speculative than heretofore supposed, while the dangers to academic science from participating in these ventures seem real and severe.

THIS BRIEF review has revealed several responsible steps that universities can take to assist in the application of scientific knowledge. Consulting arrangements, industry-associates programs, patent procedures, research agreements with individual firms or groups of companies—all these afford useful opportunities to stimulate technological innovation. Although each can be abused in ways that will harm the university or the public, all can be administered in a manner that will bring the dangers within acceptable levels of risk. Hence, a university should properly pursue these opportunities both for its own self-interest and because every institution that depends on public support should recognize a responsibility to serve society's legitimate needs.

12. Conceivably, a university might establish an independent foundation to finance new enterprises created by its faculty members to develop and market their discoveries. Such a foundation could be funded by the institution or by private donors; in either event, the university would share in the financial rewards. But management of the foundation would be placed in the hands of professionals who would act in complete independence from the institution. In this way, the university would insulate itself from controversies with its professors and avoid the burdens of management and the responsibilities of direct ownership in any new commercial enterprise. Even under such an arrangement, however, the institution would retain a clear financial stake in the entrepreneurial ventures of its faculty and might thus appear to encourage these activities and to incur many of the conflicts of interest earlier described. As a result, independent foundations and similar devices would still seem questionable unless and until the university could be satisfied that it had developed adequate internal safeguards to protect itself from these dangers.

The same cannot be said of efforts to join the university with its professors to launch new entrepreneurial ventures. In such enterprises, the risks are much harder to control and there are few benefits to society or the university that cannot be achieved in other ways. All things considered, the greatest risk to science from the growing interest in technology transfer is not that established corporations will corrupt the scientific enterprise by supporting research. The critical danger is that distinguished investigators will be diverted from their academic work by the prospect of personal gain and will begin to devote themselves to commercial activities in a manner inconsistent with a scholar's proper obligation to the university. Instead of encouraging this process by helping its professors to launch new companies, therefore, the administration should do all that it can to maintain appropriate academic standards.

The natural place to begin is with the creation of proper rules and safeguards. A university can insist that no professor spend more than one day a week on outside activities. It can also forbid faculty members to serve as corporate executives on the ground that such management responsibilities are incompatible with a proper dedication to academic work. In order to remove the incentive to use campus facilities for commercial purposes, the university can even refuse to give exclusive patent licenses to any firm in which the faculty member responsible for the invention has a substantial equity interest. Better yet, it can forbid professors to hold significant blocks of stock in companies with parallel research programs, much as high federal officials are restricted in their investments because of the conflicts of interest that such holdings tend to create.

Despite these possibilities, no academic institution can succeed by simply issuing rules. Take the simplest of problems, the amount of time professors can expend each week on outside pursuits. Although universities can limit these activities to one day per week, what does a day each week really mean? One weekday plus evenings and weekends, or literally one day a week? What are outside activities? Do they include professional meetings? Time spent giving lectures at other universities? Days devoted to the State Department at the urgent request of the White House? Even if these issues are resolved, how can the university be sure that its professors are obeying the rules without imposing reporting requirements of a kind that no group of scholars would accept?

Similar problems may undermine the other rules just described. One can forbid professors to serve as corporate executives, but there is no practical way to prevent them from spending countless hours organizing a new company and giving advice about its operation. One can likewise refuse to grant exclusive licenses to firms in which the inventor holds stock, but such a rule may simply encourage professors to pass promising ideas on to their company instead of disclosing them to the university. An administration can bar the faculty from holding stock in firms with closely related research interests, but this drastic prohibition may simply drive some excellent scientists to leave the university or cause companies to devise subtler incentives for motivating professors to work in their behalf.

My conclusion is surely not that rules are useless. In fact, many of the restrictions earlier described seem rather promising. My point is simply that in an academic community everything will turn on how such rules are regarded by the faculty to whom they apply. Even the most sensible guidelines will succeed only as they gain understanding and support through a process of wise application to individual cases. This is a task that must be carried out with the active help of faculty members who appreciate the institutional problems involved while commanding the respect that professors will accord only to their peers.

No problem better illustrates the true meaning of the university as a community of scholars. In such a community, leadership has an important but distinctly limited role to play. Presidents and deans can avoid industrial entanglements that produce intolerable strains; they can point to dangers and encourage active debate. They can even propose appropriate guidelines for the faculty to consider. But only if professors care enough about their institutions to participate fully in the task of maintaining proper academic standards can universities contribute to the useful application of knowledge without eventually compromising their essential academic values.

7

The Social Responsibilities
of Research

THE DISCOVERY of recombinant DNA offered the prospect of important discoveries and vast commercial rewards, but it also awakened anxieties of a much more troubling nature. Were scientists going too far in tampering with nature when they began to combine different organisms in strange, unprecedented ways? Might their findings open the door to new techniques of genetic engineering that oppressive governments could use in manipulative ways? Worse yet, would some novel hybrid organism—conceived in the laboratory and immune to every known antidote—escape to the outside world and unleash an irreversible epidemic?

It was the last of these fears that caused the greatest worry and distress. During a meeting at Asilomar, California, in 1975, scientists took the unusual step of calling for a moratorium on all recombinant DNA research until the risks could be studied and appropriate safety rules put in place. Yet even this action did not stem the growing public alarm. Newspaper stories appeared in a score of cities describing the fearsome consequences of dread new organisms set loose upon the land. City councils in Cambridge and Ann Arbor launched investigations to assess these dangers and consider the passage of safety ordinances. The National Institutes of Health enacted detailed regulations while Congress held extended hearings and debated various regulatory schemes to ensure strict compliance with the NIH standards.

Eventually, the furor receded, in part because interest began to flag and in part because further inquiry showed that scientists could perform recombinant DNA experiments with much less risk than was originally feared. But the episode did dramatize the growing unease over the effects of science and technology. Much of this concern centered on the methods investigators used to carry out their research. In the natural sciences, people feared that scientists might conduct their experiments with too little heed for the safety of employees or the broader risks of radiation and toxic wastes. In medicine and the social sciences, newspapers carried stories that spoke of efforts to conduct experiments on human beings without their consent or to invade their privacy by stealth and deception to observe their most intimate behavior. Beyond these problems lay even deeper worries over the effects of new discoveries. In a country suddenly aware of the impact of technology on the quality of air, water, soil, and life itself, more and more people began to wonder whether the pace of new discovery had not outstripped the rate at which society could assimilate innovation.

In short, since the mid-1970s the public has become much less inclined to look upon scientific research as an unmixed blessing. What most people today seem to want is a means of regulating the methods of research in order to minimize the risk of harm to participants and innocent bystanders. A few might even elect to bar efforts to explore controversial subjects involving racial differences, cloning, or other issues that could result in knowledge unsettling to the society.

This widespread concern calls for careful thought to decide how best to protect society from the harm that can result from scientific inquiry. The subject has obvious relevance to major universities, since much research takes place on their campuses. Yet one cannot simply ask what these institutions should do to avoid the ill effects that may result from modern science, for the university is only one actor in a much more complicated drama. What obligations should the investigator assume as an ethically responsible person? What part should the government play as the principal guardian of the public interest? Only when we have explored these issues can we determine what role, if any, should remain for the university.

The Responsibilities of the Scientist

The individual scientist has long been subject to certain obligations that are basic to the integrity of his craft. He must conduct his experiments honestly, present his findings and methods fully and openly, and credit the work of others on which his own research has relied. In a general way, investigators have also acknowledged a duty to conduct their experiments without endangering others. Until recently, however, this obligation was not well understood and was often ignored amid the fierce competition to be first in making new discoveries. Thus doctors in Tuskegee, Alabama, withheld penicillin from syphilis patients in order to explore the progress of the disease. Researchers in a Laredo birth control clinic gave sugar pills to indigent mothers to determine whether the placebo effect might prevent conception. Live cancer cells were injected into dying patients in New York, while retarded children were exposed to hepatitis virus in order to test a new vaccine.

In the wake of these disclosures, the scientific community has become more careful in the choice of research methods. With government prodding, investigators understand that they must not conduct their work in a manner that endangers participants or the public and that they should not experiment on human beings without first informing them fully and obtaining their consent. Other aspects of research remain under discussion, especially in the social sciences. For example, opinions are divided over the extent to which researchers should feel free to invade the privacy of others or contrive fake accidents and other ruses to observe reactions to extreme social situations. Yet all sides today seem to recognize that investigators have a responsibility to do the best they can to weigh the need for new knowledge against the injuries and inconveniences that their methods may impose on others.

Over the past few decades, scientists have also been reexamining their obligation to consider the uses to which their discoveries can be put and the harmful results that can sometimes ensue. For a long time, researchers disclaimed any responsibilities of this kind. In their eyes, knowledge was neutral. If a new discovery led to unhappy consequences, the fault lay not with the investigator but with the public officials and corporate executives who chose to apply new knowledge in inappropriate ways.

This traditional view was shattered by the exploding of the atomic bomb. Hiroshima set in motion a long and often anguished debate among scientists that may never come entirely to an end. Although no clear consensus has emerged from these discussions, it is obvious that the old conception will no longer fit, if indeed it ever fitted at all. Researchers cannot consider themselves immune from all responsibility for the consequences of their discoveries. To take an extreme example, the German scientists who served the Nazis by investigating the limits to human endurance of torture could hardly expect to go blameless.

Investigators are bound to interpret this responsibility in widely different ways, depending on the type of research they perform and the nature of their values and beliefs. Some professors will be pacifists and will refuse to engage in war-related research. Most scientists will be unwilling to work on certain weapons, such as biological agents, on the ground that their use would be inhumane even in a just conflict. Others may avoid doing contract research for a particular government body, such as the Central Intelligence Agency, because they fear that it will use their findings in irresponsible ways. For most academic scientists, however, ethical questions of this kind are not likely to arise. Most of these investigators perform research so basic that no one could possibly predict what practical results will ensue. To be sure, subsequent events may occasionally reveal that their discoveries are being used in objectionable ways. But if these consequences could not be reasonably foreseen, scientists will not be accountable for the results. At most, they will have a responsibility to do what they can to avert harmful consequences when the danger arises by taking a strong stand against misguided applications of their discoveries and by trying to alert the public to the hazards involved.

More difficult ethical problems can arise for social scientists. To a much greater extent than in the natural sciences, social science research in our universities is directed at specific practical problems and its findings are used by public officials to justify controversial political decisions. We have seen recent examples in fields such as school busing, Head Start programs, and welfare reform, not to mention monetary and fiscal policy. Moreover, unlike most findings in physics or chemistry, which usually have a short and uneventful life if they are wrong, conclusions reached by social scientists are often hard to disprove and can influence government policy or public attitudes even if they are eventually discredited. Hence, social scientists have special reasons to worry about their responsibilities for the consequences of their work.

These dangers underscore the need for certain precautions that conscientious investigators would presumably wish to observe in any event. For example, in studying controversial public questions, the social scientist should exercise particular care in choosing the appropriate research design, selecting the most powerful research methods, picking appropriate samples and control groups, avoiding loaded questions in surveys, and deciding what conclusions the data will bear. In addition, because of the mischief that can come from misinterpreting their results, investigators working on important social problems will have to take special pains to separate policy judgments from empirical findings and to make clear all the limitations that affect the validity and application of their conclusions.

These safeguards are painfully obvious, but other limitations have been suggested of a more questionable kind. For example, a proposed Code of Ethics for the American Sociological Association declares: "Especially when findings may have direct implications for public policy or for the well-being of subjects, research should not be undertaken unless the requisite skills and resources are available to accomplish the research at the highest possible level of excellence."[1] It is hard to quarrel with this admonition if it is merely intended to exhort investigators to observe particular care in exploring controversial subjects. If taken literally, however, the provision could have a severely inhibiting effect. In studying school busing, welfare, Medicare, and many other social problems, one can always argue that "the highest possible level of excellence" can be achieved only with the aid of huge research teams and vast amounts of money. Since support on this scale is rarely available, a rigid application of the rule could seriously retard the progress of work in many important areas.

1. Ethics Committee of the American Sociological Association, *Code of Ethics: May 1981 Revision for Consideration by the ASA Council* (Washington, D.C.: American Sociological Association, May 3, 1981).

Even more troublesome dilemmas may arise when a social scientist arrives at findings that others can use to justify policies which he considers fundamentally wrong. Imagine, for example, that a historian writing a book on urban riots reaches the conclusion that violent outbreaks of this kind have never been halted quickly except by the immediate application of ruthless force. Or suppose that a sociologist deeply committed to integration finds that busing is a major cause of white flight from the cities. In such cases, the author can go back over his work with the utmost care and take great pains to warn against policy applications that he considers to be wrong. But if his work is published and if politicians seize on it to justify the very measures he deplores, he will be implicated to some extent in the final outcome.

In these circumstances, if he can foresee the possibility of adverse consequences, a social scientist may be unwilling to publish his work at all.[2] And yet, this course of action would raise grave objections. When an investigator embarks on serious research, he will not be sure of his findings until the work is largely completed. If he refuses to publish his findings at this late date, those who have funded the research are not likely to take kindly to a decision to abandon the project. They will understandably retort that they did not spend their funds with the expectation that the grantee would censor the work on the basis of his private moral and policy beliefs. Instead, they may feel that they have a legitimate right to insist on publication of the study, much as a newspaper editor might believe that a reporter is obliged to publish a story even

2. N. J. Block and Gerald Dworkin have proposed that a social scientist should not undertake research if (1) there are no "likely and important beneficial consequences" to be anticipated from the investigation, and (2) if there are "serious and probable harmful consequences which flow from the interpretation likely to be placed" upon the author's findings (*The IQ Controversy* [New York: Pantheon Books, 1976], p. 507). This standard purports to avoid difficult problems of judgment since, by definition, the only likely consequences of the research will be adverse. As such, the proposed criteria neatly explain one's immediate disapproval of the hypothetical scholar who sets out to investigate exotic forms of torture on grounds of their intrinsic intellectual interest. In real life, however, the criteria will very rarely apply because almost every research project will have *some* possible consequences that can be considered beneficial. As a result, moral dilemmas of this kind will almost always involve the much more difficult problem of weighing a variety of possible outcomes and applications, some of which are benign and some of which are harmful.

though he personally feels that the revelations will strengthen prejudice or bring unjustified suffering to particular individuals.

Beyond the interests of the funding agencies lies a deeper question involving the obligations of the social scientist. Certain people in society are thought to have an obligation to reveal the truth without regard to the consequences, save in the most exceptional cases. The reason editors are impatient with a balky reporter is that they believe the public has a right to know the facts and that a paper should not suppress a news story unless the writer obtained information unlawfully or its release seems bound to cause the most serious and unjustified harm. A strong argument can be made that social scientists should recognize a similar obligation.

If investigators began to censor their work in order to minimize the risk of abetting policies that they considered wrong, the credibility of social science would very quickly deteriorate. The public would begin to distrust such research once they understood that particular findings were routinely withheld when they tended to support policy decisions that conflicted with the author's ethical beliefs. In addition, such moral inhibitions could distort the process of research itself. It is difficult enough to avoid personal bias in carrying out investigations of social problems. But such biases could become much more intense once investigators knew that the price of arriving at certain findings might be the abandonment of months of investigative effort. More likely still, conscientious social scientists might simply avoid all research on controversial subjects, such as race and poverty, rather than run the risk of confronting such painful choices. If so, able people would be diverted from important topics, leaving such research to those least sensitive to the moral implications of their work or least likely ideologically to risk encountering awkward ethical dilemmas.

Where does all this leave the scrupulous investigator? In considering this question, scholars should remember that their primary obligation is to search for truth and that only compelling reasons should persuade them to withhold conclusions they believe to be correct. As they ponder this responsibility, they should be realistic enough not to exaggerate the effects of academic writings on specific policy decisions. Politicians may cite research to justify their conclusions, but references of this sort are often little more than window dressing for decisions that would have been made in any event. Hence, it is far from clear how often one can truly regard social science research as a significant causal agent of misguided policies. To be sure, investigators should take particular care in carrying out research on controversial topics and should make efforts to warn against any likely distortions or misapplications of their findings. Having taken these precautions, however, social scientists will have done what they can to avoid injury to others and should not feel morally responsible for later misuse of their research, save in the most exceptional circumstances.[3]

The Responsibilities of Government

Although investigators have become more conscious of their ethical responsibilities, the government can hardly refrain from involving itself in the process of scientific inquiry. However seriously scientists view their social obligations, some will be careless, others will ignore ethical restraints in the rush for success, and the entire scientific community may be at odds with the general public in deciding how to weigh the need for knowledge against the concern for human safety and welfare.

For these reasons, the government has taken a particularly active interest in regulating the methods employed in research. Congress has provided tighter safety requirements for laboratory workers through the passage of the Occupational Safety and Health Act. The Department of Health and Human Services has issued detailed rules to govern research on human fetuses. The same department has also ordered teaching hospitals and scientific institutions to establish ethical review boards that must con-

3. The conclusion just proposed should be distinguished from the situation that arises in deciding whether to do research for a particular client or funding agency. In the latter case, the research is more likely to affect the actions of the funding agency, and the danger of abuse can be estimated more clearly on the basis of the agency's past behavior. Moreover, by refusing to do research for a particular client in the first place, the investigator is not in the position of refusing to publish work that another entity has already paid for. Finally, such refusals do not have the same adverse effect on the integrity of research, because social scientists will not be editing their findings to delete those that they consider morally dangerous. For all these reasons, investigators should feel a greater responsibility to take their own moral and political views into account in deciding whether they should agree to do research for a specific client.

sider all federally funded projects in advance to ensure that experiments on human subjects have a reasonable research design and that all the participants will give their informed consent.

More serious problems arise in considering whether the government should seek to limit research which promises to result in knowledge that will be threatening or destabilizing to the society. Our traditions are clearly hostile to restrictions of this sort. The usual premise has been that scientists should be free to investigate anything and that the government should protect the public only by limiting the application of knowledge in order to avoid harmful results. Ultimately, this view rests on a faith closely akin to our belief in free speech—that truth and progress will emerge from a free exchange of ideas. As the ultimate keeper of public values, the Supreme Court has upheld this faith by consistently rejecting government measures "whose justification rests . . . on the advantages of [people] being kept in ignorance."[4]

Yet scientists and other critics have begun to question this principle and to wonder whether it is not too naive to cope with the risks of modern science. Some writers have opposed efforts to search for ways of prolonging human life, because such inquiries might lead to knowledge that could destabilize society by affecting population trends, retirement practices, and demands on scarce resources. Others have criticized research on behavior modification, arguing that the findings from such work could be used irresponsibly by repressive governments. A few authors have even objected to the search for intelligent beings elsewhere in the universe, fearing that the very knowledge that superior beings exist could prove demoralizing to the human psyche.

Whatever one thinks of these examples, one can sympathize with the underlying concern. Modern science is capable of producing knowledge that can be used to alter society in frightening ways, even to the point of endangering its existence. The atomic bomb is sufficient proof of that. Moreover, the social impact of new discoveries has grown much greater during this century because we can now put knowledge to use so rapidly that society has much less time to prepare for the consequences by adjusting its practices and adapting its institutions.

4. Virginia Board of Pharmacy v. Virginia Citizens' Consumer Council, 425 U.S. 745, 769 (1976).

In rare cases, the fruits of investigation will create such evident risks to human health and safety that the government can justly intervene either to prohibit the research or to restrict dissemination of the results. Suppose, for example, that a scientist sought to discover a method for building a homemade atomic bomb. Once such knowledge became known, officials might be powerless to prevent its use by underworld groups or terrorist organizations. In these circumstances, the risks would be grave and immediate and the government could have little hope of protecting the public except by trying either to proscribe the research itself or to avoid any disclosure of the results. Granted, the authorities might not be able to detect such investigations if someone were determined to carry them out. But an outright ban would at least reduce the risk, and one can hardly fault the government for making the attempt.

Until recently, the list of these forbidden subjects has been narrowly drawn, at least for the vast majority of universities that have refused to engage in classified research. Within the past few years, however, the government has begun to place new limits on knowledge. Under the Arms Export Control Act, the President can prescribe regulations to prevent the export of technical data relating to various classes of weaponry. For many years, the term "technical data" was confined to the sort of information used by defense contractors and did not extend to the more fundamental research carried on in university laboratories. In the late 1970s, however, the government began to expand the term to include unclassified work performed by universities in such fields as integrated circuitry and masers. Armed with this new definition, the Departments of Commerce and Defense started to urge universities not to teach such subjects in classes open to foreign nationals from specified countries. The government has sought to prevent such persons from inspecting designated work or from participating as students and visiting scholars in carrying out such research. Officials have even tried to stop scientific meetings to which foreign nationals were invited. For major universities, where foreign students represent a substantial fraction of graduate enrollments in science, such restrictions promise to be unmanageable. Yet the problem involved seems destined to grow in importance as advanced scientific knowledge becomes more and more vital to the military strength of the country, not to mention our competitive position in vying for business with other industrialized nations.

The legality of these new initiatives is very much in doubt. If the research involved is performed without federal support, the government cannot restrict dissemination unless it can demonstrate by clear and convincing evidence that release of the information will "surely result in direct, immediate and irreparable injury to our nation and its people."[5] This test is so strict that only the most sensitive information could qualify. But the situation is more obscure in the case of work performed under government contract. Federal agencies may decide to write research agreements to include limitations on dissemination to foreign nationals. In this event, the restrictions might conceivably be upheld as reasonable conditions on the award of public funds, although it is possible that judges will require the government to show a more convincing relationship between its restrictions and the interests of national security.

Whatever the legal outcome, the government finds itself in an awkward position. To the academy, restrictions of this kind are squarely in conflict with the basic scholarly commitment to the free dissemination of knowledge. In addition, efforts to keep foreign nationals from attending certain classes or from participating in scientific colloquia are repugnant to the principle that all students and scholars should have equal educational opportunities except insofar as limitations may be justified on academic grounds. As a result, if the government insists on restricting dissemination, most leading universities are likely to give up the work altogether for the same reasons that have led them to refuse to engage in classified research.

If universities were to withdraw from restricted work, federal agencies could attempt to carry on the research in their own facilities. But this policy would force the government to run the risk of severely retarding progress by proceeding without the help of a large proportion of the leading scientists in the fields involved. These consequences would have ramifications extending far be-

5. New York Times v. U.S., 403 U.S. 713 (1971). See more generally Mary M. Cheh, "The *Progressive* Case and the Atomic Energy Act: Waking to the Dangers of Government Information Controls," *The George Washington Law Review*, 48 (January 1980), 163.

yond defense technology, since much of the work involved has an important bearing on computers and other areas of inquiry possessing high commercial importance.

Even if universities could be persuaded to continue the research under government restrictions, the costs could easily outweigh any benefits to national security. Many able scientists might turn to other fields rather than submit to the controls, so that the United States could be placed at a competitive disadvantage vis-à-vis other nations working in the same areas. Worse yet, in view of the practical problems of implementation and the distaste of academic scientists for all restrictions of this kind, the government's selective controls would probably fail to function effectively, at least for any information that other countries were truly eager to possess. As a result, Washington's efforts are likely to achieve the worst of all possible worlds. They will not work well enough to safeguard information that other countries are determined to obtain. But they will be sufficiently onerous to retard scientific progress and eventually handicap the United States in competing with other nations. These problems may grow worse as bureaucrats experience temptations to enlarge the scope of government controls because of political pressure to protect the short-run commercial interests of American firms against competition from abroad. In view of all these drawbacks, Washington would do well to avoid such restrictions and simply classify a few, closely limited areas of work if they are deemed so sensitive that dissemination must be effectively controlled.

Beyond the field of defense, the government has not chosen to interfere with research in order to suppress knowledge that could result in harmful applications. This policy is sound. Circumstances may have changed since the time of Galileo, but there is one lesson from his experience that has remained valid over the intervening centuries. Historians have rarely approved official efforts to protect society by muzzling scientists or suppressing their ideas. And the topics writers have proposed for censorship in recent years hardly inspire confidence either.

There are also political contradictions in trying to protect society by suppressing knowledge. If we do not trust our public officials to place adequate safeguards on the use of knowledge about cloning, genetic manipulation, and other issues, why should we assume that they will do better in deciding what knowledge should be discovered in the first place? And if we prevent research on prolonging human life because the public will insist on putting the knowledge to use, are we not denying the people their democratic right to decide whether longer life is worth the strain on social institutions?

Practical problems would also bedevil any attempt to restrict discovery on these grounds. Much new knowledge is produced unintentionally as a by-product of experiments conducted for different purposes. For example, Alexander Fleming discovered penicillin after he became curious about a strange mold that unexpectedly grew around the edges of his Petri dish. Because of this accidental, unforeseeable element in research, there is no sure way of preventing the discovery and dissemination of potentially harmful knowledge without imposing massive restrictions on broad areas of inquiry. And even if we could tolerate such prohibitions, we would have no way of stopping experiments in other countries, which are increasingly mounting major programs of research. For these reasons, government efforts to block the discovery of knowledge are likely to be ineffective as well as unwise.

Instead of forbidding research and dissemination altogether, public officials can simply refrain from giving funds to certain types of investigation. If the costs of the research are high, such a policy may actually come close to a de facto prohibition. Nevertheless, the government undoubtedly has wider powers to deny funds than it does to place an outright ban on research. For example, federal officials cannot regulate speech (save in very limited cases). But they can plainly consider the quality of programming in the award of a television station and refuse to award franchises to applicants because their program plans are considered unimaginative, unbalanced, or in questionable taste. The reason is obvious. In granting the use of a television channel, the government is allocating a scarce commodity. If awarding a station to one applicant means keeping it from another, the government may as well do its best to consider program plans and try to give the franchise to the group most likely to serve the public's tastes and needs. By the same token, since federal research funds are also limited, the government can presumably consider the social consequences of one project as opposed to another in deciding how to allocate the money at its disposal. After all, if public funds are given to research in order to benefit society, it would hardly seem wise to use the taxpayers' money to support investigations that threatened to produce destabilizing or harmful results.

Yet the government does not have unlimited discretion in allocating research funds. The courts would quickly intervene, for example, if the National Science Foundation suddenly announced that it would no longer entertain applications from blacks or Democrats. How much discretion, then, should officials have in reviewing applications to study cloning, or to probe the existence of superior beings in outer space, or to explore the mysteries of behavior modification, or to develop ways of producing heroin in one's basement?

Although the terrain is still uncharted, the government would seem to be on firm ground in rejecting proposals (however brilliant) to find simpler ways of manufacturing heroin. It is hard to conceive of any useful, legitimate applications that could begin to offset the dangers created by bringing that drug within easy reach of many people. Since the government has prohibited the private use of heroin, public officials should clearly have the right to decide not to spend the taxpayers' money to acquire knowledge that will help individuals evade the law. For similar reasons, officials should presumably be free to reject proposals that do not promise to benefit society either by yielding knowledge of intrinsic importance or by producing applications that have some practical value.

More troublesome issues arise in considering research on methods to clone human beings or to modify behavior by methods such as implanting electrodes in the brain. Research of this kind could easily have beneficial consequences. For example, cloning might allow couples who are sterile or who have serious genetic abnormalities to succeed in having healthy children. Similarly, behavior modification could yield important information about mental disorders and provide the means to calm violent people, avoid epileptic seizures, or even stop the obese from eating to excess. At the same time, such work could also create temptations for the state to engage in dubious schemes to improve the racial stock or to control the behavior of those who are considered to be trouble-makers or deviants. At a deeper level of concern, one author has observed that discoveries of this kind represent "a fundamental threat to the concept and the reality of the human person as a unique and intrinsically valuable entity, conscious of its own being and responsible for its own choices."[6]

In short, both human cloning and behavior modification raise basic questions about society's ability to assimilate and control the fruits of science. In these circumstances, the government would probably have the power to withhold support in order to slow the pace of research, recognizing that the essential discoveries might still be made either abroad or as a result of investigations carried out with private funds. Granted, a decision to withhold support would interfere with the growth of potentially valuable knowledge. But the Supreme Court has recognized a substantial difference between the government's power to forbid public expenditures and its right to prohibit private conduct entirely. As a result, the Court would probably uphold the government's decision to allocate its funds to other projects that would not create the problems of regulation or the dangers of abuse that could result from successful research on human cloning or behavior modification.

Perhaps the most vulnerable exercise of the funding power would occur if the government began to deny research support on the ground that the knowledge produced might itself be unsettling to the public. For example, at least one distinguished scientist, Robert Sinsheimer, has expressed serious reservations about proposals to use electronic technology in an effort to search for and make contact with life on other planets. Sinsheimer's chief concern is that such extraterrestrial beings, if they exist, might be superior to humans in profoundly troubling ways. In his words: "I am concerned about the psychological impact upon humanity of such contact ... To really be number two, or number 37, or in truth to be wholly outclassed, an inferior species, inferior on our own turf of intellect and creativity and imagination, would, I think, be very hard for humanity."[7]

6. Laurence H. Tribe, "Technology Assessment and the Fourth Discontinuity: The Limits of Instrumental Rationality," *Southern California Law Review*, 46 (1973), 648.

7. "The Presumptions of Science," in Gerald Holton and Robert S. Morison, eds., *Limits of Scientific Inquiry* (New York: W. W. Norton, 1979), pp. 29–30.

In reviewing research proposals of this kind, of course, the government can ask legitimate questions about the methodology employed or the likelihood of achieving any concrete results. Yet no one could dispute that the knowledge being sought would be of very great significance. And though one cannot readily imagine just how we would use such knowledge, it seems hard to deny that our responses to extraterrestrial beings could be important, possibly crucial, to the welfare of the human race. Thus one cannot easily argue that the aims of the research would be trivial or the practical applications detrimental. Nor is this Dr. Sinsheimer's point. Instead, he is opposed to funding such research on the ground that the very knowledge being sought might be psychologically disturbing or demoralizing to the human psyche. This argument might conceivably be legally sufficient to deny funding. In that event, however, public officials would be saying, in effect, that it is better to live with the hazards of remaining ignorant rather than risk having to come to terms with an unpalatable truth. As a practical matter, this conclusion seems hard to justify. From a constitutional standpoint, the government would appear to be contradicting a basic tenet of the First Amendment by ignoring the Supreme Court's consistent rejection of government measures designed to keep people in ignorance in order to protect their peace of mind or to preserve established dogmas.

However we choose to draw the constitutional line, one point does seem clear. In areas of research such as human cloning, behavior modification, and extraterrestrial life, the issues at stake are beyond the competence of the regular funding agencies to resolve. The National Science Foundation and the National Institutes of Health are well prepared to assess the scientific merits of a research proposal or to make general decisions about the relative importance of different fields of scientific inquiry. They are not properly equipped to make the judgments that are ultimately involved in deciding whether it is wise to discover how to control human behavior by electrical impulses or whether it would be sound to learn how to reproduce exact copies of a living person. These issues are not matters of technical scientific competence so much as questions touching the most profound human and philosophical values. As a result, whatever the government's powers may be under the First Amendment, the normal funding agencies would be well advised not to claim the power to make decisions of this kind but to wait upon Congress either to create a special tribunal for the purpose or to render its own judgment on the vexing issues involved.

The Role of the University

We have seen that scientists are prepared to accept moral responsibility for the way in which they conduct research and even for the foreseeable effects of their findings on others. We have also noted that the government will halt dissemination of knowledge that presents grave threats to the public and prohibit research methods that are dangerous or intrusive. What role remains for the university? Can it play any part in regulating research on campus without violating academic freedom or invading the proper domain of government?

With respect to academic freedom, it is clear that a university obstructs the search for knowledge by placing prior restraints on the conduct of research just as it does when it penalizes professors after the fact for publishing controversial material. Nevertheless, one might well ask whether the traditional principles of academic freedom fit the contemporary realities of science. When these principles were first announced in 1915, most research was carried out by individual professors working alone in simple laboratories. Universities did little more than provide scientists with rudimentary equipment and pay them their normal salaries. Today, the situation has radically changed. Much scientific research is carried on not by individual professors, but by teams that include technical assistants on the university payroll as well as graduate and postdoctoral students. Such work calls for sophisticated equipment and expensive laboratories often supplied by the institution. And the funds that are necessary for these investigations typically come from government grants that must be processed and administered with the help of campus personnel.

In short, scientific research is no longer the preserve of solitary investigators pursuing their own ideas. Modern science has become a collective undertaking that requires large investments and constant support not only by the government but by the university itself. Now that academic institutions play a prominent role in facilitating research, one can argue that they can no longer escape responsibility for any adverse consequences that result from work carried on in their laboratories.

In considering these arguments, we can quickly see that they extend far beyond scientific investigation to embrace almost every form of research. Only rarely do universities provide expensive laboratories to professors outside the scientific departments. But many projects in the social sciences call for costly computer facilities as well as government grants administered by the campus bureaucracy. Even historians and literary scholars depend on large libraries that require massive investments by the university. As a result, academic institutions play a major role administratively and financially in the work of all their faculty. If such participation were enough to justify collective responsibility for the nature and consequences of research, the scope of academic freedom would be drastically curtailed, and virtually every professor would have to submit his research for institutional review and approval.

Such a policy would be extremely unwise and would reflect a gross misunderstanding of the reasons underlying academic freedom. If professors are allowed great liberty in their work, it is not because universities claim no role or interest in their research. Instead, academic freedom has always been founded on a firm belief that the pursuit of knowledge will proceed most fruitfully if scholars can follow their own convictions without limitation from official orthodoxies of a moral or ideological nature. This rationale applies in full force even if the university participates in the administration of research grants and invests heavily in the libraries and laboratories of its professors.

Although the principle of academic freedom clearly extends to scientific research, it does not give *carte blanche* to scientists to conduct their work in any way they please. Unlike *ideas,* which can be met by opposing ideas in open debate, unsafe or intrusive research *methods* create immediate dangers to others that cannot be countered in any way other than by prohibiting the methods themselves. Thus scientists do not have an unrestricted right to search for truth through the use of techniques that invade the privacy of others or subject the public to the threat of explosions or noxious chemicals. In cases of this sort, a university can forbid such methods without infringing on academic freedom.

One may still ask whether an institution needs to exercise such power now that public agencies have begun to take an active role in regulating the process of research. But a moment's reflection will reveal several responsibilities that universities should recognize. At the very least, academic institutions must do their best to ensure that government requirements are scrupulously enforced. Ethics review boards must be established in accordance with existing regulations. Safety rules must be observed and inspections carried out. Auditing procedures must be developed to make certain that government research funds are spent to conform with the terms of the applicable grant or contract.

In addition, universities have a concern for basic academic values that will lead them to insist on certain rules whether or not they happen to concern public officials. For example, whatever the government chooses to do, a university will wish to penalize an investigator who falsifies data or manipulates the results of his research, and it will likewise encourage its professors to exercise the greatest possible vigilance in detecting and discouraging any form of dishonesty. In some instances, universities will even insist on rules that conflict with the government's objectives. Thus most institutions have refused to accept classified projects or to sponsor work when the source of funds cannot be revealed. Similarly, an administration faithful to basic academic principles will be reluctant to authorize research if the funding agency insists on screening the personnel involved or exercising control over publication of the results.

More troublesome questions arise in deciding whether universities should attempt to institute rules of their own to ensure that experiments are carried out in a manner that respects the less tangible interests of others. What if sociologists seek to install hidden devices in the campus lounges to observe the private behavior of university employees? Or suppose that students complain because they are compelled to participate as subjects in an experiment in order to enroll in a psychology course. In such cases, can the administration intervene in order to protect the privacy of the staff and the freedom of choice of the students?

Some faculty members may resist such efforts on the ground that their experiments are important and their lives already complicated enough by government regulations. They may also protest that attempts by a single university to impose further restrictions will simply cause able investigators to move to other institutions with more permissive environments. Despite these arguments, it would be unwise to relinquish responsibility for regulations of this kind. Universities have special obligations to their students and staff that go beyond the concerns of government agencies. Surely, Harvard University had a right to intervene in the early 1960s when two young professors began to enlist undergraduates in experiments with LSD. Today, an academic institution might well ask whether it is educationally sound to use graduate students in experiments that lead them to practice deception by infiltrating religious sects or by simulating accidents and crimes in order to record the responses of passers-by. One can argue over whether such deception is warranted by the need for new knowledge, but it would be hard to maintain that the university has no legitimate concern in the matter.

Moreover, if scientists share a distaste for arbitrary and restrictive government regulations, they should be willing to work with the university to identify genuine problems and devise appropriate protective rules. Once abuses begin to occur, effective self-regulation is the best way to forestall government intervention. Granted, voluntary restraint may not work consistently enough to avoid public regulation. But even if the effort fails, it will often yield a fund of experience that will be extremely useful to universities in persuading public agencies to fashion more sensible rules. Consequently, it is not only improper but shortsighted to tolerate abuse in the hope that the government will never intervene.

As we have seen, ethical problems arise not only in choosing the *methods* of research but in pondering the *effects* of the new knowledge that may ultimately result. Should a clinical investigator try to develop a cheap and simple technique for carrying out self-administered abortions? Should a psychiatrist participate in experiments that may reveal new methods of behavior modification? It is in matters of this kind that the roles of government and individual scientists diverge most sharply. The investigator has an obligation to decide whether his research, on balance, is likely to lead to harmful results. The government—even if it opposes the uses to which an experiment might be put—will normally be prevented by the First Amendment from trying to prohibit the research. These differences leave the university in a quandary. As sponsor of the research, should it stand in the shoes of the scientist and put a stop to the project if it decides that the ultimate consequences will be adverse? Or should it invoke the principles of free speech and refrain from even trying to make judgments of this kind? Or is there some intermediate course between these two extremes?

One's first reaction to this issue is to come down hard on the side of forbearance and restraint, for universities are instinctively reluctant to interfere with the work of their professors. But extreme cases could arise that would severely test this policy. Suppose that a professor agreed to do research for the Mafia on ways to embezzle funds by manipulating the computerized systems of large corporations. Or imagine that a scientist undertook to develop lethal weapons systems for a tyrannical regime. In these circumstances, the government itself could probably intervene, despite the First Amendment, since the results of such investigations would present an immediate and substantial threat to public welfare and safety. For similar reasons, the projects would also fall outside the scope of academic freedom, and the university should presumably stop the work, if only to protect its reputation and avoid supporting research that could result in injury to others and even violate criminal statutes such as the Atomic Energy Act.

In real life, however, such extreme situations will rarely, if ever, occur. When problems do arise, they will involve more puzzling cases. For example, controversy may spring up over research on weapons systems for the Defense Department during an unpopular war, or studies for the Central Intelligence Agency on the causes of social unrest in Latin America, or policy papers on ways to overcome middle-class inhibitions toward gambling, such as the study the Stanford Research Institute once conducted for a large Nevada casino.

Cases of this kind present difficult problems. Under accepted principles of academic freedom, a university could not interfere with the writings of professors in support of an unpopular war, or the overseas activities of the CIA, or the virtues of the gaming table. Is there any difference between the freedom to express these views and the right to carry on research that could help others act in a manner consistent with such opinions? We can certainly discern *some* difference. Articles in favor of a controversial war can be met by opposing arguments and thus may contribute to a free exchange of views from which a clearer understanding will emerge. But the creation of new weapons adds nothing to the debate over the propriety of a war; it simply provides instruments of destruction for generals to use in killing other people, whether or not the underlying conflict happens to be just. In the former case, therefore, intervention by the university would amount to censorship of the ideas advanced by its professors. In the latter, the administration would not attempt to pass judgment on the conclusions of its professors; it would object only because their work could provide the means to inflict unwarranted harm on others.

On closer analysis, however, this distinction seems more problematic than it appears at first glance. By intervening, the university will interfere with the freedom of its professors to do research, whether their work involves the writing of a book or the development of a weapons system. Moreover, books can help to bring about policies that result in unjust wars just as a weapons system can provide the means for wreaking unwarranted destruction. In both instances, the research in question will represent a link in the causal chain that ultimately leads to indefensible violence.[8] Finally, scholars who help to create new weapons systems presumably support the policies of our government or at least believe that decisions about prosecuting wars are better left to elected officials in Washington. Faculty members who do research on gambling may well believe that the practice is not inherently evil, just as persons who investigate social unrest may feel that they can trust the CIA not to use their findings in inappropriate ways. The university can decide to interfere only because it disagrees with these beliefs. In taking such action, therefore, the administration

---

8. It is possible to argue that weapons systems are a much more proximate cause of violence than a book on foreign policy. At first glance, this distinction seems plausible. But the connection between the development of a weapons system and its *unjust* use—for example, against civilians or in a war of unwarranted aggression—is not so direct and obvious as to distinguish the two cases very clearly.

will be acting on moral or political grounds to limit the freedom of its professors to carry out research, and this is a practice inherently suspect under accepted notions of academic freedom.

Critics will reply that the university should intervene nonetheless on the ground that such projects create an immediate danger to human safety and welfare just as in the case of research to create a homemade atomic bomb. But the two situations differ in one important respect. There is a clear consensus in the nation concerning the critical danger of placing destructive weapons within the reach of criminal elements or terrorist organizations. The same cannot be said of public attitudes toward the Vietnam War, the overseas activities of the CIA, or even the practice of gambling, at least in a number of states.

In such disputed cases, individual scholars have the freedom and the responsibility to decide for themselves how to respond to the moral dilemmas involved. A professor can choose to refrain from doing weapons research, just as a citizen can become a conscientious objector and refuse to perform military service. But it is one thing for individuals to reach such conclusions for themselves and quite another matter for universities to arrive at decisions for them. This is scarcely a job for the academy to perform. In our society, we have chosen to give to government agencies and elected officials the task of making official decisions on controversial national issues. If a university prohibited its faculty from doing research for the CIA or the Defense Department, it would set itself above the government by subjecting its professors to rules based on its own collective views on thorny issues of national policy quite outside its normal academic domain.[9]

9. These cases must be distinguished from situations in which the university promulgates rules on such subjects as deceptive social science research. In these instances, the university is not in conflict with the government but is only trying to protect institutional interests that have not concerned the government sufficiently to call forth regulation. Moreover, in these situations the university acts to preserve its own academic and institutional interests and not to pass judgment on issues, such as defense and foreign affairs, that concern the public as a whole. A closer case has arisen in universities that have prohibited their professors from using research activities abroad as a cover for carrying on clandestine intelligence work for the government. Even here, however, the university is not undertaking to pass judgment on the work of United States intelligence but is merely attempting to safeguard the integrity of its overseas research and to avoid the risk of exposés that would cause foreign governments to impose restrictions on professors working abroad.

To intervene in such cases would force the university to make extremely difficult and controversial judgments. Was the Vietnam War justified? Should gambling be discouraged or is it a practice that individuals should be free to accept or reject for themselves? Will research on abortifacients offer a useful means for helping individuals limit their family size or will it create instruments of murder to snuff out incipient human life? Do investigations to facilitate the growth of nuclear power provide a constructive step to meet our energy needs, or do they represent a baneful effort to push us further into an era of constant danger to human health and survival?

Attempts to resolve such issues will result in all of the dangers that gave rise to the principle of academic freedom. In a democratic society, elected officials are much better equipped to gather the evidence and reach collective decisions on troublesome questions of this kind. By trying to exercise such authority, universities will expend large amounts of time and effort and engender internal struggles of the bitterest and most divisive kind. The judgments reached will resemble official dogmas of the sort that have historically met with the greatest resistance within the academy. They will certainly restrict the scholarly freedom of individual professors; they may also be wrong and thus unwisely impede the search for knowledge.

By assuming these burdens and risks, universities are not likely to accomplish much in furthering human welfare. Defense agencies and intelligence units will usually find ways to secure the research they need even if a number of institutions refuse to allow such work on their campuses. At the same time, by contradicting the policies of elected officials on important issues of national interest, universities will move beyond the sphere of their acknowledged concern into a political arena where their actions may be attacked as illegitimate and provoke retaliation. If the government begins to divert research funds from institutions that prohibit work on political grounds, even the usual allies of higher education may shrug their shoulders and conclude that the universities have overstepped the bounds. For all these reasons, presidents and deans would be well advised to avoid such controversies and to intervene only in the rare case, envisaged by the First Amendment, where research presents an evident threat to human safety and welfare as defined by principles that are widely under-stood and accepted in the society.

There is one situation, however, in which the university can safely depart from this principle. That situation arises when the institution must decide how to allocate *its own* scarce resources among a number of competing research projects. In these circum-stances, the decision to accept certain projects entails a decision to reject certain others. Hence, the university has a greater responsi-bility for the projects it chooses than it does when it simply toler-ates a venture arranged by one of its professors through outside funding agencies. Conversely, the professor—who can expect under principles of academic freedom not to have his work halted for ideological reasons—does not have a right to have his project receive a high priority for financial assistance from the limited supply of discretionary funds. In allocating its own resources, therefore, the university possesses wider powers and responsibil-ities akin to those of the National Science Foundation when it dis-tributes federal grants.

In those circumstances, how far should the university go in tak-ing moral considerations into account? Clearly, academic officials will not wish to review every proposal to assess all the conse-quences that could result if the research happens to be successful. Such efforts would be endless and too speculative to be of much value. If the practical applications seem obvious, however, the university should avoid proposals that threaten adverse conse-quences and shift its support to other projects offering compara-ble scientific promise. In theory, such a policy might appear to raise all the hazards of trying to reach collective judgments on controversial social issues. In practice, however, these difficulties should not prove troublesome. One can assign a low priority to a project to assist a gambling casino without placing a precise moral value on the social consequences of roulette. Moreover, the thorny problems of attempting to judge the propriety of wars or to assess the actions of the CIA will probably never arise, because funds for projects that raise such issues will normally come from public agencies rather than from the university's own resources.

For these reasons, universities will seldom find it necessary to reject proposals on ethical grounds. But opportunities for a more positive form of moral responsibility may arise with greater frequency. In certain fields of inquiry, neither the government nor other outside agencies have seen fit to support research to a degree that bears any relation to the potential benefits that successful work might yield. For example, tropical diseases—such as malaria, trypanosomiasis, schistosomiasis, and filariasis—afflict hundreds of millions of people around the world. Relative to other illnesses, these afflictions are reasonably susceptible to investigation. Nevertheless, since they rarely affect our own population, Washington allocates only $25 million for research each year on tropical diseases as compared with more than $400 million for work on cancer.

In such circumstances, how should a university respond in deciding how to allocate its own research funds? Obviously, the administration will consider a variety of factors apart from the potential social benefits of the work, such as the competence of the investigators involved and the intellectual promise of competing projects. Reasonable people will disagree over the importance that should be attached to these considerations. But at least when competing proposals have approximately equal scientific merit, one can hardly deny that the potential benefits of research for human welfare should be entitled to decisive weight.

In conclusion, then, the university does have a responsibility to consider the social consequences of the projects it supports from its own funds. In administering projects funded by outside sources, it also has obligations to review the methods employed in order to protect the special interests of its students and staff and to preserve standards of inquiry essential to the integrity of its research. But the administration's role in supervising research is much more closely circumscribed than it is in guiding most other university functions. In the end, presidents and deans must walk a narrow path tightly bounded on one side by the requirements of academic freedom and on the other by the overriding responsibilities exercised by the government as the principal source of research funds and the ultimate guardian of the public welfare and safety.

8

Technical Assistance Abroad

In NOVEMBER 1974, a delegation from the government of Iran approached Harvard University to seek its assistance in developing a new institute of science and engineering. Intrigued by this novel venture, a group of faculty members offered their services under the sponsorship of the university. Working in cooperation with local officials, they produced a charter for the institute and an academic plan for its organization and staffing. A governing board was agreed upon and an independent agency established to assist in recruiting faculty members from the United States. Architectural drawings were prepared for the new campus, and work eventually began in Iran to clear the chosen site.

Before these labors could come to fruition, the Shah had fled the country, the Ayatollah Khomeini was in power, and the half-completed campus lay abandoned and forgotten amid the turmoil of a new social order. The hours wasted on the project offer a painful reminder of the hazards of supplying academic assistance to far-off areas of the world. And yet, universities have undertaken countless efforts of this kind over the past generation, and many of them have enjoyed a lasting success. At Harvard alone, the Business School has helped found management schools in places as distant as India, the Philippines, and Central America. Several of these institutions have steadily improved and continue to flourish to this day. In addition, Harvard's Institute of International Development has sent advisers abroad to help other nations to produce five-year plans and, more recently, to assist in training programs for local officials, rural-development projects, urban-planning efforts, school reforms, and many similar initiatives. During the past two decades, the institute has completed projects in a score of countries stretching from Colombia and Venezuela to Mali and Ghana, from Kenya and Tanzania to South Korea, Indonesia, and Pakistan.

Many other universities have also mounted programs of technical assistance to help foreign governments on projects as diverse as health-care planning, the development of educational institutions, and the use of better agricultural methods. As a result of these programs, hundreds of professors have traveled all over the world to offer specialized advice and training to dozens of nations in need of such help. While often criticized, these efforts have been successful enough to persuade many governments throughout the Third World to continue soliciting such assistance.

The Appropriateness of University Assistance Programs

These activities have presented their fair share of problems to universities. It is hard to oversee the multitude of programs on a single campus, let alone keep track of teams of advisers thousands of miles away working on projects that can involve expenditures running into millions of dollars. Presidents and deans must periodically spend many hours of their time reviewing these efforts to ensure competent leadership, maintain their solvency, and cope with the recurrent crises that are bound to occur when university staff are working in remote and often turbulent areas of the world. In view of these difficulties, one might legitimately ask whether it is wise to continue offering such services. After all, universities are not alone in these efforts. Countries can obtain such help from the Agency for International Development, the World Bank, large foundations, private consulting firms, and foreign-aid organizations from several industrial countries. Is it not conceivable that universities should avoid the administrative burdens associated with these efforts and leave the work for other agencies to perform?

In examining this argument, one can readily imagine programs of technical assistance that probably should not be continued. A university may organize its overseas staff in such a way that participants will perform little or no serious teaching or research on the home campus. Much of the actual work abroad may even be performed by professionals who are employed ad hoc and rarely, if ever, make so much as a brief visit to the parent institution. Conversely, members of the regular faculty may have no real contact with the overseas programs except for occasional trips of no great value to their scholarly work. In short, technical assistance may exist at the periphery of the institution, giving little benefit to the university and deriving little stimulation in return. One can still maintain that such activities should continue in order to provide a useful service to countries in need of help. And yet, if the university were to halt its overseas programs, these countries would not be deprived of needed assistance; international agencies and foundations would simply direct their technical assistance funds to other organizations willing to do the work. Consequently, unless a university can honestly claim that it supplies a service of distinctive quality, there is little reason to keep such a venture alive.

Despite these cautionary remarks, one can also imagine a program of campus-based assistance that would have a legitimate place in any academic institution. Properly organized and administered, overseas projects should succeed not only in making a distinctive contribution to developing countries but in helping to improve the quality of teaching and research in the university itself.

Efforts to understand economic and social development require a constant interaction between experience in the field and attempts to construct useful concepts and theories. For this reason, scholars who teach and write about these subjects have much to gain from working overseas. Such experience offers opportunities to test prevailing theories and adapt them to include a broader range of variables. At the same time, in the highly specialized and compartmentalized world of the university, assistance projects attract scholars from separate disciplines in a common enterprise that forces them to integrate their separate perspectives in the search for a deeper understanding of the development process. Thus agricultural specialists who offer suggestions for increasing crop yields and city planners who present ideas for reducing urban congestion and unemployment may both benefit from the help of social psychologists and anthropologists who can convey some sense of the special motivations and cultural forces that can affect the implementation of programs to bring about social change.

The experience gained from work in the field can also help participants improve the quality of university instruction, not only for Americans but for students from developing nations who come to the United States in growing numbers to prepare themselves for careers in their own countries. Programs abroad will often yield cases on national planning and rural development that add greater realism to courses on public finance and agricultural economics. The cumulation of overseas projects may likewise provide comparative data to enrich the discussion of basic problems that emerge and reappear in almost every developing nation. It is not likely that universities could obtain these benefits if they decided to leave all technical assistance to agencies outside the academic world.

At the same time, university programs should be able to offer benefits to developing countries that other organizations cannot easily match. No independent agency is likely to equal the university in its ability to help build educational or research institutions abroad. Even for economic planning or training programs for foreign officials, an academic environment can often attract a quality of staff not available to outside organizations. Moreover, the opportunities given such persons to alternate between service in the field and teaching and research at home can enlarge their understanding of the development process in ways that will continue to renew and enrich the quality of their work. In sum, if a university organizes its overseas activities to take full advantage of the academic setting, the combination of teaching, research, and experience in the field should succeed in creating a mutually reinforcing process that offers qualities of service not readily obtainable in any other way.

Moral Difficulties

Despite these benefits, ethical problems can arise in overseas projects, however adroitly they are administered. University representatives may succeed in escaping the pitfalls of cultural imperialism more often than their counterparts in government agencies, since they seldom have the financial leverage with which to force their ideas on other nations. But it is never obvious how to help people who come from starkly unfamiliar cultural backgrounds and live in circumstances so different from one's own. Nor is it easy for experts used to an academic setting to appreciate the ways in which local officials can co-opt their efforts or turn them to unexpected purposes. The history of assisting other nations is studded with failures and frustrations even when intentions have been exemplary. The most straightforward proposals can give rise to very troublesome moral dilemmas. Should universities ever agree to offer their services to a country laboring under a repressive regime? Is it proper to assist a foreign university plagued by government censorship and corrupt administrative practices? Can academic experts give technical advice on economic policies and programs without embroiling themselves in tortuous issues involving the equitable distribution of resources or the clash of modernization with rural societies and traditional values?

PROTECTING ACADEMIC FREEDOM   Although every organization has to face such issues when it engages in foreign-assistance programs, universities confront a special problem unique to academic institutions. An international agency or a foundation can insist on reviewing all overseas projects and prohibiting those that do not satisfy its ethical standards. When a university tries to exercise such supervision, however, critics may accuse it of infringing on academic freedom by subjecting professors and staff to moral and ideological restrictions. One could try to distinguish overseas programs from normal scholarly work because they are collective activities requiring the help of many people. But much research in the sciences, and even the social sciences, is likewise collaborative in nature, involving teams of professors, graduate students, and associated research personnel. Moreover, if the purpose of academic freedom is to preserve the liberty of scholars and promote the pursuit of knowledge, it is not apparent why a university should have a greater right to censor the work of many people than it has to limit the research of individual scholars.

One could also seek to distinguish overseas projects because they render service to specific clients rather than promote research. True, participating advisers often prepare written documents that analyze policy issues and development problems, but these writings typically serve only a limited clientele. Unlike the scholarly book or article, they may not reach a public audience or stand the test of open discussion that ultimately justifies our faith in free expression.

Although this argument is ingenious, it hardly suffices to justify university intervention. Many professors advise government agencies, yet no president or dean would dream of trying to pass judgment on whether such consulting is ethically permissible. Intervention of this kind would be quickly condemned as an intolerable invasion of the liberty of professors and an unwarranted interference with the right of public officials to seek advice from sources of their own choosing. We have also observed that many overseas projects yield useful material for study and scholarship, and often contain an explicit research component. Indeed, service projects may afford virtually the only means of investigating certain aspects of development at first hand, such as the problems of implementing government policy in the Third World or the actual processes through which important national decisions are made. For this reason, any effort by the university to block such projects on moral or ideological grounds could quickly place the institution in the awkward position of interfering with the acquisition of knowledge.

There remains one characteristic that sets most overseas projects apart from ordinary research in ways that may be said to justify university supervision. Unlike the usual forms of research, overseas programs are typically carried on by a special entity sponsored by the university and often bearing its name. Hence, projects of the organization are not only collective undertakings; like degree programs or admissions procedures, they purport to be *university* ventures and are so regarded by the outside world. In fact, the reputation of the university is often a material factor in obtaining the contract for the project and in lending credibility to the services performed. Thus the integrity of the institution is involved in the work of the organization to a greater degree than it is in consulting carried on by individual faculty members, and the administration may therefore have a stronger stake in seeing to it that proper ethical standards are maintained.

Even this argument is open to question. A university sponsors many research projects by administering the funds and providing support services, yet, as I have observed, no administration can properly forbid such projects on the ground that the resulting knowledge may prove to be harmful. As for the university's reputation, although the institution's name is always associated in the public mind with the writings of its professors, this is hardly a sufficient reason to engage in censorship. An overseas project may carry the university's imprimatur more clearly than a book by one of its professors, but the difference is only a matter of degree.

All in all, there is no clear line to be drawn between the research and private consulting of a professor and the overseas programs of an institute. The fact that the institute is a collective enterprise, that it often provides services to specific clients rather than books and articles available to the public, and, more important still, that it bears the university's name and profits from its sponsorship—these are all matters that take the work progressively further from the efforts of the lonely scholar for whom the concept of academic freedom was originally designed. But the distinctions are shadowy and the authority of the university less than clear.

At the very least, therefore, the administration should monitor its overseas programs with the same circumspection it employs in supervising other corporate undertakings, such as the development of admissions procedures and curricula. As with all official university functions, the administration should ask those in charge to make a conscientious effort to observe certain ethical standards in finally deciding which projects they wish to undertake. In the case of programs abroad, responsible officials should certainly be required to observe the prevailing institutional safeguards governing research projects; for example, they should clearly reject any proposal that would expose participants to undue risk of harm or compromise the university's right to select its own personnel. In addition, the administration should insist that the officials in charge consider the consequences of each project for the local population and the propriety of the methods used in carrying out the work. In the application of these principles, however, a president or dean must leave considerable discretion to the responsible officials and interfere only if the grounds for objection seem reasonably clear.

DECIDING WHETHER TO UNDERTAKE PROJECTS IN REPRESSIVE COUNTRIES   In evaluating each overseas venture, the officials in charge will clearly need to consider the nature of the foreign government involved. If a nation has a stable, democratic administration, the university can help to fashion a five-year development plan, or offer training to the civil service, or try to strengthen a local university in the genuine hope that its aid will contribute something constructive to the general welfare. But regimes in many countries are notoriously authoritarian—suppressing free speech, jailing dissidents, neglecting the poor, and resorting to frequent violence and deception. Such governments can easily subvert programs of technical assistance to achieve unsavory ends. Local officials can manipulate advisers so that they accomplish little save to strengthen the government's case for a foreign loan. Training programs may be used to reward supporters of the ruling party. Local universities can be so corrupted by efforts to stifle dissent that further cooperation is intolerable.

In view of these problems, should universities go so far as to avoid all ventures in countries that labor under repressive administrations? Most persons who work overseas resist this notion and support efforts to benefit the poor and disadvantaged, provided there is little prospect that the project will be subverted by the government for its own immoral purposes. They would therefore approve initiatives to establish rural health clinics, or water-purification projects, or village programs to increase crop yields even in countries with flagrantly authoritarian regimes. According to this view, such efforts may well bring help to needy people; the principal danger is simply that the projects will be terminated arbitrarily. Consequently, there may be something to be gained by such ventures, with little possibility of making matters any worse than they already are.

At first glance, the logic of this position seems unassailable. And yet, efforts to provide technical assistance in authoritarian nations, even for the most humanitarian purposes, have scarcely met with universal applause. Skeptics have warned that such programs may eventually do more harm than good by dampening public opposition and undermining the will to resist. In addition, one often hears that the very willingness of a reputable university to enter into an assistance project may lend prestige to the government in the eyes of the people and thereby help it to maintain its repressive grip.

On reflection, both of these arguments seem questionable. A foreign government may prop up a corrupt regime by massive amounts of economic assistance and military aid. But the help that any university can supply to the poor and underprivileged will rarely have a remotely comparable effect. Moreover, we should not exaggerate the prestige supplied by a far-off university or assume that local people will regard its projects as a gesture of support for the government in power. If academic personnel are not advising high officials but simply working in rural areas to assist with health clinics or agricultural improvements, their presence may not be thought to imply anything other than a sincere desire to improve the welfare of people in need.

Even more dubious is the radical argument that universities should not aid the poor in despotic countries because such assistance may alleviate discontent and thus diminish the chances of revolution. It is presumptuous for anyone in comfortable circumstances to make the judgment that the people of another country "need" the violence and disruption of a revolution, and even more questionable to press this judgment to the point of opposing all attempts to diminish suffering and privation. Such arguments require a greater faith in revolution than any fair observer can derive from studying the effects of past rebellions on the welfare of the populations involved. Moreover, even if one accepts the premise, it hardly follows that efforts to combat hunger and disease will actually help perpetuate a tyrannical regime. History does not suggest that the poorest nations are necessarily the quickest to rebel. Education often promotes enlightened opposition, while adequate health care and better economic opportunities may engender higher expectations and greater willingness to resist. Conversely, authoritarian governments often flourish when their subjects are too apathetic, too hungry, and too ignorant to gather their strength and actively oppose injustice. If genuine opportunities exist to help people in great need, it would be arrogant and inhumane to object on the basis of highly speculative theories about the need to encourage social revolution.

Regardless of their effects, assistance projects in authoritarian countries may also be attacked on the ground that universities will compromise their values and sully their reputations merely by associating with regimes that violate elemental standards of democracy and human rights. In considering this argument, no sensible person can ignore the dangers of being co-opted and manipulated by unscrupulous officials or deny the need to examine such projects with the greatest care. Responsible officials should also recognize the temptations that arise to accept questionable projects in order to balance the budget or keep the institute's staff employed. Since self-serving motives of this kind can so easily bias administrative judgments, those who must make these decisions will do well always to seek impartial review in cases that raise a genuine doubt. But it would be difficult to justify a decision to avoid *all* activities in countries with authoritarian governments. Experience does not show that every program in a repressive country will be corrupted by the authorities. Nor should a university fear for its reputation if it undertakes a project in the genuine belief that it will help the poor and disadvantaged. On the contrary, it would seem excessively precious and self-regarding to insist on institutional purity at the cost of refusing help to those who need it most.[1]

One can make a final argument that academic institutions should ban all projects in countries with particularly repressive regimes in order to put pressure on these governments to cease their wrongful activities. Thus Professor David Frisch has pleaded eloquently that universities should refuse to deal with nations where torture is practiced or bans have been imposed on emigration.[2] (Presumably Dr. Frisch would press the logic of his proposal to deny the admission of students or the exchange of faculty from such countries.) This suggestion is quite different in principle from those already discussed. Professor Frisch is not primarily moved by the fear that projects in such nations will have adverse

1. The ethical problems of withdrawal and engagement can never be finally resolved by logic. Although one's judgment on each matter must be guided by the particular circumstances of the case, my own inclinations lie with Milton: "I cannot praise a fugitive and cloistered virtue, unexercised and unbreathed, that never sallies out and seeks her adversary, but slinks out of the race, where the immortal garland is to be run for, not without dust and heat" (*Areopagitica*, 1644).
2. "Human Rights and University Contracts," *The Bulletin of the Atomic Scientists*, 35 (February 1979), 23.

consequences or corrupt the institution; instead, he believes that universities should take the affirmative step of publicly boycotting certain countries in order to force them into changing their ways.

Since Dr. Frisch would oppose an assistance project in such countries even if it promised to help the poor and disadvantaged, he apparently believes that an embargo by universities will have the more important effect of reducing human rights violations. This is a very difficult argument to sustain. Although international pressure and publicity can sometimes help free particular dissidents or put an end to certain programs of persecution, foreign governments scarcely depend enough on the help of universities to go to great lengths to avoid their displeasure. Moreover, like most international boycotts, sanctions of this kind are rarely effective; it is unlikely that all universities will cooperate or that a regime will be unable to find the expertise it needs from individual advisers or from some other source. For these reasons, it is hard to believe that oppressive rulers will change their emigration laws or cease torturing dissidents simply because a number of academic institutions have refused to enter into assistance projects. There is no solid evidence to support this proposition. Nor are knowledgeable observers of one mind on how best to influence authoritarian regimes. Far from recommending boycotts, many people who have devoted years of effort to the cause of human rights believe that universities can make their most constructive contribution by maintaining a presence in repressive countries that will preserve a link with ideas and influences from the outside world.[3]

3. Boycott proposals are also difficult to apply in a consistent, principled fashion. It is hard enough to decide whether an authoritarian government will be likely to corrupt a particular assistance project. But it is even harder to pass blanket judgments on entire nations. Such decisions involve awkward problems of drawing lines and require extensive information that may not be readily available. Professor Frisch seeks to avoid these pitfalls by proposing that boycotts be limited to two specific practices—torture and emigration restrictions—for which considerable data can be obtained. But guidelines of this sort lead to very strained distinctions. To take but a single example, why should a government that prevents dissidents from leaving the country deserve to be ostracized more than a ruler who has put thousands of dissidents in jail? And how can we be sure that a regime actually allows its opponents to emigrate when there are so many subtle ways of preventing their departure? How many residents must be detained to justify a boycott, and what forms of restraint

In sum, we can all agree that universities should exercise the greatest caution in approving projects in authoritarian countries, recognizing the ways in which local rulers can subvert such efforts for improper ends. But it would be extreme to block every project in such nations as a matter of principle. For example, representatives from Harvard agreed to give advice to the Nicaraguan government on the reconstruction of Managua after the devastating earthquake of 1972. No one would dispute that the Somoza regime was extremely autocratic and cruel. But was it wrong to offer such assistance? Other overseas projects have sought to train rural health workers or to find effective ways of drilling wells in drought-ravaged areas. Surely it would be unjust to bar such projects and forgo any chance one has to help people obtain more food for their children, more protection against disease, or added water for their crops in the vague and uncertain hope that universities can somehow help to topple a repressive regime or induce it to change its ways.

ASSESSING THE IMPACT OF INDIVIDUAL PROJECTS   As the previous discussion makes clear, those who evaluate project proposals must consider who will be helped and how the promised benefits will actually come about. For example, problems may arise from proposals designed to assist only a limited category of persons. Thus a university will undoubtedly refuse to engage in a project to improve the curriculum of white schools in South Africa, since such efforts will only aggravate the injustices and inequalities imposed by the apartheid system. But a university could easily reach a different conclusion in the case of a practical program to improve the education of South African blacks, since such a project might achieve just the opposite effects. Even in less repressive countries, the choice of persons helped may affect the value of the project. Assistance programs may aid the poor directly, as in a rural health program; or they may assist the public indirectly, as in a project to train civil servants; or they may benefit the

---

will suffice to warrant an embargo? Professor Frisch would define systematic torture or emigration restrictions "as involving more than one case a year." Under this definition, one wonders how many countries could actually receive a clean bill of health and whether existing sources of information are sufficient to apply such a standard with reasonable accuracy and consistency.

well-to-do primarily, as in an exchange program to train students from an underdeveloped country as brain surgeons or psychoanalysts. In considering these possibilities, much will again turn on the nature of the government involved.

In countries with strongly authoritarian regimes, no university will wish to train police officials, military officers, or other types of government personnel who are likely to have the unsavory task of carrying out repressive measures. Nevertheless, it may be defensible to work with nurses or sanitation engineers or rural-development workers (especially if the training takes place in universities and not within the government itself), since projects of this kind will often have much greater prospects for helping the needy. More serious problems arise in the case of proposals to educate civil servants in agencies such as the central bank, the planning authority, or the ministry of mines or agriculture. If a government is sufficiently corrupt and autocratic, efforts to improve bureaucratic efficiency will normally create too grave a risk of helping an unscrupulous regime carry out its policies. Yet one must take care in making judgments of this kind. Some authoritarian governments, such as those in China, Korea, and Taiwan, have had determined policies of economic growth combined with programs to redistribute wealth and enhance the living standards of the poorer classes. In such countries, programs to train officials in the economic ministries may hold real promise of assisting those who most need help. Despite the suppression of dissent, therefore, universities may properly decide that the potential benefits are sufficient to warrant their participation.

Many governments present an even more ambiguous picture. While avoiding widespread violence or cruelty, they proceed in one way or another to discourage effective opposition. They tolerate vast disparities in wealth, and their programs for the poor are sporadic, half-hearted, and generally ineffective. Although economic growth may occur, with some increase in the real income of the lower classes, the benefits continue to flow in large measure to the well-to-do.

In countries such as these, projects specifically designed to aid the poor have much to recommend them. More difficult problems arise in thinking about programs to strengthen local universities or to found business schools or to train civil servants for ministries in fields such as planning, finance, or industry. Successful projects of this kind may eventually improve the lot of the people as a whole by speeding the process of development through the preparation of more efficient civil servants, more effective business executives, or more enlightened professionals. But the immediate effects will doubtless be to enhance the careers of those already destined to share disproportionately in the wealth of the country. Since such programs may ultimately help to improve the general welfare, it is difficult to condemn them as immoral and even harder to maintain that the disadvantaged would be better off if the university refused to participate. Yet the benefits are problematic at best.

In these circumstances, a university may do well to look particularly carefully at the possibilities that exist for expanding knowledge. If a project promises to cast new light on aspects of the development process and to yield new insights that may eventually enhance research and teaching, the effort may give results that will carry beyond the particular country involved. In this event, the endeavor may be well worth undertaking. If such benefits seem unlikely, however, the project would not appear to deserve a high place on any agenda of development opportunities. Although the venture may not actually be improper, a university may rightly conclude that its services can be more usefully directed elsewhere.

The considerations just discussed can be brought into sharper focus by returning to the proposal to help create a technical institute in Iran. Those of us who worked on this project hoped that several results might ensue. By helping to provide better scientific and technical education in Iran, we thought that we could assist the process of economic and social development while offering opportunities for useful careers to deserving students. By insisting on high educational standards and a charter that guaranteed independence and academic freedom, we also hoped to provide an example that would influence other educational institutions in that country. And though we perceived the obvious risks in trying to establish such a university in an authoritarian country, we decided to proceed in the faith that better education would be likely, in the long run, to represent a force for enlightenment and progress.

Despite these good intentions, it is easy to mount strong objections to such a project. Scientific knowledge and technically trained personnel are resources that could easily be turned to dubious ends, especially by an authoritarian ruler with ambitions to become a dominant presence in the Middle East. In addition, notwithstanding the proclamations of academic freedom and scholarly independence and despite our stated intention to withdraw if these principles were not respected, such paper guarantees could easily be brushed aside by a cynical regime intent on stifling dissent. In short, while scientific and technical education might eventually have served to strengthen freedom and human dignity, there could be little assurance under authoritarian rule that these prospects would not yield to national ambitions of a darker sort.

Subsequent events made it impossible ever to know whether the institute would have served as a force for good or for evil. Years of effort came to nothing beyond a jumble of half-completed buildings near the shores of the Caspian Sea, deserted monuments to the thwarted ambitions of the Shah. In retrospect, however, was it wrong to have launched the venture? Certainly, those of us who joined the project did not think so. After consulting with our colleagues and with Iranians of differing political persuasions, we concluded that the possibilities for achieving useful results outweighed the risks involved. Though reasonable people may disagree with this assessment, the factors involved seem sufficiently imponderable that few would consider us morally derelict for deciding to proceed.

Yet even if the venture was morally defensible, can one justify it as a wise allocation of our time and effort? Under a different regime, one might be reasonably confident that a university such as Harvard could make a distinctive contribution by improving scientific education and research in a less developed country. Even in Iran, something of value might have resulted if we had helped develop programs to train rural health workers, teachers, or development economists. In contrast under the conditions in that country, the benefits of a technical institute were sufficiently uncertain that one could hardly make a strong 'case for the project on social welfare grounds. The effort might still have been useful had it promised to add to knowledge or improve Harvard's educational programs for those planning to work in development in other areas of the world. But few benefits of this kind were likely to flow from the venture in Iran, for the Harvard scientists who helped plan the institute would scarcely have enhanced their own research and teaching by the kind of work they were called upon to perform. All in all, therefore, although one may not fault the motives of the participants, the project does seem vulnerable to the criticisms of those who charge the modern university with squandering its efforts on ventures that neither provide distinctive benefits to others nor strengthen the essential academic purposes of the institution.

EVALUATING THE METHODS TO BE USED   On some occasions, one may fully support the goals of a project but question the methods employed in carrying out the work. Suppose, for example, that members of the overseas staff begin to offer formal recommendations to foreign governments on the content of an official five-year plan. In this event, university representatives will be presenting opinions on matters that may raise such awkward ethical questions as the proper distribution of income between rich and poor or the use of monetary policies that could increase unemployment in an effort to reduce inflation. If these views are delivered in the form of official reports, the university itself may become embroiled in highly sensitive and controversial matters. For example, a Harvard team in Pakistan was criticized in the 1960s for allegedly making proposals for a five-year plan that slighted the interests of East Pakistan (now Bangladesh). Right or wrong, such allegations illustrate the difficulties in which a university can easily find itself. Even if its representatives were making proposals on the most sensitive issues, the administration would be in no position to review detailed recommendations prepared thousands of miles away to respond to the needs of a remote and distant country. Indeed, the mere attempt to censor such reports would raise serious questions of academic freedom.

Fortunately, such problems need not arise in practice. Few governments desire the views of foreign experts on large political issues. They prefer to make such judgments for themselves and understandably doubt whether anyone from abroad would be competent to help. What advisers normally do is to call upon their technical skill and their experience in different countries to present alternative policy choices and analyze their probable consequences. Ideally, the adviser will choose the options to discuss in light of the goals expressed by local officials, seeking to review each alternative in a manner that takes account of local values and concerns. In practice, of course, even the best-intentioned expert will be influenced to some extent by his own preferences and prejudices in deciding which alternatives to present and how they should be analyzed. Nevertheless, there is a vast difference of degree between making specific recommendations and attempting conscientiously to discuss a series of policy options as objectively as possible. At the very least, if advisers present their alternatives in this fashion, it will be difficult to charge the university with attempting to impose its political views on another nation.

Situations may occasionally arise when local officials ask advisers to give their own opinions on the best course of action for the government agency to pursue. When such requests are made, however, experts can usually offer their views in a private, informal capacity without purporting to speak on behalf of the university. This practice seems clearly desirable. Since a university could not possibly exercise control over the opinions of its overseas staff, the latter should be instructed never to offer advice on significant policy issues without making clear that they are speaking on their own behalf and not for the institution. In this respect, they will merely be observing the same standard that any professor employs in consulting for a government agency, corporation, or foundation.

At times, university representatives abroad may be tempted to act in ways that are not only embarrassing to the institution but plainly unethical as well. Thus it would be highly improper to engage in a covert project to disseminate birth-control devices in a country where such practices were forbidden. There is always a strong presumption in favor of respecting local laws, and any exception should require the most compelling justification. In a matter so dependent on religious traditions and indigenous values, it would be arrogant for university representatives to break the rules in order to further their own strong beliefs on the need to limit population growth. To make matters worse, such transgressions might provoke the local authorities to retaliate by imposing broad restrictions that would foreclose opportunities for visiting scholars and other innocent bystanders.

Even if the methods employed in an overseas project are perfectly lawful and even if they are expressly approved by the foreign government involved, they may still violate the ethical norms of the university itself. For example, most academic institutions will support overseas programs of family planning that supply the public with contraceptives and offer factual information about their use. But should the university participate in a program that relies on compulsory sterilization or makes use of misleading information and other deceptive methods to induce families to practice birth control? The objective in both cases is the same and may be entirely laudable. Nevertheless, one program helps people achieve what they feel is best for themselves—and thereby broadens their options—while the other limits freedom by forcing people to do what their government has concluded to be in their best interests. One can appreciate the effects of rapid population growth on the living standards of the poor and understand why governments might be driven to take stern measures when faced with such a prospect. Even so, universities and their staffs must answer to their own consciences; they cannot simply accept the norms they happen to encounter overseas. Hence, few institutions would wish to associate themselves with deceptive methods or with the use of coercion to dictate individual choices of such great personal importance.

These cases are rather simple, but there are many problems of greater complexity. To continue with birth control, several countries have chosen to offer money or food to parents who elect to limit the size of their families. These programs have provoked sharp controversy. Some observers feel strongly that offers of this kind are reasonable because they allow parents to choose according to their own best interests. Others point out that such inducements are both discriminatory, because they have an effect only on the poor, and coercive, because they are so irresistible to poverty-stricken families as to negate any true choice.

There are countless dilemmas of this kind on which reasonable people can disagree. Even greater vexations can arise in trying to evaluate the long-term consequences of particular projects. In this respect, the technical institute in Iran is only one of many examples. If a university offers its assistance in devising a plan to facilitate economic growth, will it contribute to a process that will ultimately destabilize important cultural values and traditions? Will the introduction of new agricultural methods merely hasten the exodus from the countryside to already swollen cities? Will better rural health care only add to population growth and cause more children to endure the sufferings of malnutrition and starvation?

Such issues are extremely difficult to resolve and the answers must generally turn on the particular facts and circumstances involved. No central administration should attempt to impose its own judgment in such cases and overrule decisions reached by people directly involved in overseas work, who possess much greater experience and judgment in these matters. All that presidents and deans can do is encourage the responsible officials to consider each project and to subject their judgments to review by other knowledgeable persons. If this much is accomplished, the university will have done what it can to act responsibly.

Even the most scrupulous university will occasionally find that its judgments are proved wrong by unforeseen events. In the face of such dangers and imponderables, skeptics will continue to wonder whether it is wise to be involved in programs of this kind. That is certainly the view of many traditionalists who point to these activities as a prime example of exactly what a university should *not* undertake to do. And yet, acknowledging all of the difficulties, I would draw exactly the opposite conclusion. Efforts to help others almost always involve troublesome risks and moral problems, and universities should avoid these hazards when the chances of accomplishing anything useful seem remote. Nevertheless, it hardly follows that academic leaders should abandon all attempts to develop overseas programs. Granted, the problems of doing good work in an alien culture are formidable. No university should think of taking on such a task if it is not prepared to put forth its best effort. Even so, with sufficient care and judgment, it should be possible to develop carefully administered projects that stand a good chance of strengthening teaching and research while simultaneously doing something to improve the lot of those who are demonstrably in need. It is this combination, in the end, that makes the critical difference.

Part III

Addressing Social Problems
by Nonacademic Means

9

The University and the Local Community

ALL UNIVERSITIES are prominent members of their communities by virtue of the vast complex of libraries, laboratories, classrooms, and offices they require to carry on their work. Try as they may, they cannot go unnoticed by their neighbors. With their legions of students and their impressive buildings, they are all too visible to those who live and work nearby. Placed in a small city or town, they are likely to dominate the economy and hence be blamed for most of the social and economic pressures that distress their neighbors. Surrounded by a large city, they are quickly caught up in all the problems of contemporary urban America: the fiscal crises of city government, the anger of landless tenants, the anxieties of local residents fearful that their neighborhood values are disappearing. In city or town, the culture of the university—with its bohemian life-styles and youthful exuberance—is often an irritant, as well as a source of pride, to the surrounding community.

Despite their high visibility, it is not clear that academic institutions have many ethical obligations to the community that other kinds of institutions do not also possess. Although they are periodically involved in heated controversies, their duties to tenants are not unlike those of other large landlords, and their responsibilities as a major employer are not noticeably different from those of a major corporation. But there is one characteristic that universities share with only a limited number of institutions. Unlike householders, landlords, factory and store owners, universities are not legally obliged to pay the property taxes that provide the principal revenue source for most cities and towns. This favored status has often strained relations between town and gown as city fathers and local residents look askance at universities for reaping the benefits of their urban setting without helping to pay the cost.

The exemption from real estate taxes was conferred on charitable and educational institutions generations ago when land was plentiful. At that time, this dispensation seemed an inexpensive way of assisting churches, hospitals, universities, museums—institutions that produced little wealth and performed valuable services for the community. Over the intervening decades, however, cities have struggled under the weight of more and more expenditures. In many of these communities the property tax has been strained beyond its capacity. Faced with mounting demands for services and growing resistance from the taxpayer, local officials have become increasingly concerned by the large proportion of exempt land. In fact, most of this land belongs to governments— federal, state, or local. The holdings of educational and other nonprofit organizations account nationwide for only 4 percent of the total value of taxable property. Even so, municipal authorities have been increasingly inclined to look with covetous eyes on nonprofit institutions as a potential source of added revenue. Among these institutions, the private university is a particularly tempting target in view of its seeming opulence and its large holdings of land.

Until recently, at least, few people have expressed much optimism about the prospects for repealing the tax exemption. Most nonprofit institutions have had serious financial problems of their own, and have enjoyed enough community support to make their tax-free status seem secure. As a result, officials in a number of municipalities have approached private universities informally to persuade them to make voluntary payments "in lieu of taxes." These efforts have met with a measure of success, for more than 30 percent of all private universities now make some form of in-lieu contribution. Often, the amount is simply a rough compromise based on no apparent formula or rationale. In some instances, however, payments have been fixed to cover the direct cost of fire protection, sewerage, and other services that the city provides to the institution. In other cases, universities have agreed to pay the regular taxes on any new property they acquire, at least for a stipulated period of years.

These agreements remain a matter of controversy in many communities across the country. In the minds of city officials, they are simply appropriate arrangements to transfer funds from a large and powerful landholder to help defray the costs of essential services for needy people. To university administrators, beset by concerns about rising tuitions and by faculty complaints over lagging salaries, the situation looks entirely different. In their eyes, the demands of municipal officials for in-lieu payments show too little regard for the financial burdens of the university and scant appreciation for its many contributions to the economic and cultural well-being of the community.

These controversies are bound to persist for some time to come. Consequently, there is good reason to look more deeply into the university's financial obligations to the urban community. In the modern world, does any justification still exist for the property tax exemption? If the exemption is to remain, should universities at least acknowledge a moral obligation to make some sort of voluntary payment to the city? If so, what is the basis for this obligation and what kind of payment should be made?

The Benefits and Burdens of Tax-Exempt Universities

The property tax exemption is only one strand in a larger economic web connecting the university, the city, and the state. Each party to this three-cornered relationship offers certain advantages to the others, and each gains certain benefits in return. Only if we understand these costs and benefits can we evaluate the appropriateness of the exemption and decide whether it confers an unwarranted privilege on the private university.

The state has decided that charitable and educational institutions shall be free of taxes, but this decision costs it nothing. The burdens fall on taxpayers in cities that contain universities and other big blocks of exempt land. Of course, most state governments do appropriate some of their own money to support private universities. Many legislatures have established modest scholarship funds, and a few make substantial per capita payments for local residents attending private institutions. A handful have even provided subsidies to private medical schools. In most cases, however, the total payments from the state represent only a small proportion of the university's operating budget.[1]

In return, the state gains substantial advantages from the presence of private colleges and universities. These institutions educate local residents at little or no government expense. The resulting benefits are significant, especially in states with large numbers of private colleges and universities. In Massachusetts, for example, the Commonwealth would have had to spend an estimated $165 million in 1979 in order to educate residents enrolled in its private institutions.[2] By escaping this burden, Massachusetts manages to rank no higher than forty-ninth among the fifty states in per capita public expenditures on higher education, and the average taxpayer devoted only $56 for these purposes in 1979, compared with $139 in California and $93 in New York.

Aside from providing educational services that reduce the costs of public education, private colleges and universities also generate a substantial amount of economic activity that adds to the sales and income tax revenues collected by the state. During 1979, for example, one careful study has estimated that academic institutions in Massachusetts attracted $500 million in out-of-state research funds, $108 million in revenues from tourists, and approximately $200 million in expenditures by almost 150,000 out-of-state students. During the same year, these institutions employed 72,000 people, paid them $838 million in wages and salaries, spent $782 million on goods and services within the state, and expended $70 million more on capital improvements. All told, with both direct expenditures and indirect multiplier effects taken into account, these activities added $2.3 billion to the state's economy and created 130,000 jobs. In addition, private univer-

1. In fiscal year 1979, private colleges and universities received only 3.9 percent of their revenues from state and local governments, while public institutions received 64 percent of their income from these sources (*The Condition of Education, Statistical Report, 1981* [Hyattsville, Md.: National Center for Education Statistics, 1981]).

2. Lawrence Olson and Zofia Mucha, *The Economic Impact of Independent Higher Education on Massachusetts* (Lexington, Mass.: Data Resources, Inc., 1980).

sities played a major role in the development of new industries, notably those using high technology, which benefit from close proximity to major research institutions.[3]

By relieving the Commonwealth of the cost of educating thousands of its residents and by generating economic activity that produced added tax revenues, independent colleges and universities brought benefits to the state government in the hundreds of millions of dollars. In return, Massachusetts appropriated only $16 million in scholarship funds during 1979 and made no other significant payments to these institutions.

In contrast to the states, cities and towns look on private universities as a mixed blessing, at least from a fiscal point of view. Unlike their counterparts in state government, municipal officials must give up all of the property taxes they might collect if these institutions were not located within their borders. In return, city residents gain two types of benefits. To begin with, local communities receive various direct services from universities, such as access to museums, libraries, and athletic facilities; tutoring and legal services from student volunteers; and medical services from university hospitals and clinics. In addition, universities supply a potent stimulus to the local economy by attracting new businesses, enhancing land values, and thereby increasing property tax receipts.

For example, a study commissioned by my own university found that Harvard students spent nearly $12 million in Cambridge during the 1979–80 academic year.[4] Faculty and staff spent an additional $18 million in the city, while the university itself purchased $19.6 million in local goods and services. Visitors spent approximately $4 million, and employees of businesses attracted to Cambridge because of Harvard expended nearly $8 million. All in all, including both direct and multiplier effects, the university was responsible for adding over $100 million to the Cambridge economy during the course of this single year. The city undoubtedly benefited from this economic activity through increased tax revenues, not to mention the added receipts that re-

3. Ibid.
4. James Dalton and William Jackson, of Putnam, Hayes & Bartlett, "Harvard University's Positive Impacts on the Economy of Cambridge," Cambridge, Mass., June 1981.

sulted from well-to-do homeowners attracted to Cambridge by Harvard's presence.

These figures suggest that a city need not lose money as a result of the presence of a private university. Cambridge has not suffered this fate, and the same is likely to be true of other cities that contain universities. Even so, municipal officials sometimes wonder whether they might have been even better off financially if the university had never existed and its land had been occupied by owners who were not exempt from local taxes.

It is difficult to respond to such speculations, because the answer depends on the type of property owners who would take the university's place. If the campus gave way to low- or middle-income housing, tax revenues would go up, but the cost of education and other municipal services would probably rise even further so that the city would lose financially. Worse yet, the new homeowners would not begin to rival the university in stimulating the local economy, generating new jobs, and raising neighboring land values. If the university were replaced not by low-income housing but by wealthy homes and luxury apartments, tax revenues would rise still further and the cost of services to the city might not be as great. But even well-to-do homeowners would probably not attract as much outside money as a university nor would they provide nearly as many jobs or generate nearly as much spending and commercial activity in the surrounding area. As a result, neighboring property values, and ultimately municipal tax revenues, would not be as high, so that the net effect on municipal budgets might well be less favorable than it would be if the university remained. However, if the area could attract high technology businesses, paying substantial taxes and consuming few municipal services, the overall impact on the city's finances might be better than if the land were occupied by a major educational institution.[5]

In sum, it is impossible to be certain whether a city would be better off or worse off without a university because one cannot

5. According to one study, the taxes hypothetically available to the city on property held by a major university as of 1975–76 ranged from $625 thousand to $7.1 million depending on whether one assumed residential or commercial and industrial use (Diane H. Palmer, "Elements of an Economic Impact Study" [Paper presented at the annual meeting of the Association for Institutional Research, Houston, May 21–25, 1978], p. 3).

predict what the community would look like if such a large institution were not present. Even so, one generalization can be made
with reasonable confidence. Relatively few alternative uses will
benefit a city as much financially as the presence of a university.
Since academic institutions usually maintain their own police
forces and make few demands on the local school system, they do
not represent a heavy burden to the city compared with most
other types of land users.[6] At the same time, universities generate
a great deal of commercial activity for surrounding businesses and
provide cultural advantages that attract prosperous residents to
their neighborhoods. In these ways, they exert a positive force on
property values and enhance the tax base of the city. Taking
everything into consideration, although one can only guess how a
city would fare without its university, few municipalities would
put the matter to a test even if they had an opportunity to do so.

Proposals to Relieve the City's Financial Burden

Among the three principals in the drama just described, the state
clearly plays the favored role. It gains much of the economic benefit from private universities while placing almost all of the burden on the backs of cities and towns by virtue of the property tax
exemption. As a result, many people have argued that state officials should do something to lighten the load carried by municipalities with large amounts of exempt land. Several alternatives
exist to achieve this goal.

REMOVING THE TAX EXEMPTION   Although the state could do
away with the exemption, this alternative can be severely criticized as unrealistic and unfair. Many private colleges and universities are in dire financial straits and could not pay substantial
property taxes and still continue to function effectively. As a
practical matter, therefore, cities might find it impossible to levy
the full tax even if the exemption were removed. Moreover, most
universities already contribute much more in benefits to state

6. It is true that university employees living within the city may send their
children to local schools. But these employees presumably pay taxes on their
own residences. University-owned, tax-exempt property will rarely produce
demands on the school system, as it would if the property were occupied by
residential dwellings.

governments than any subsidies they receive in return. Hence, it would seem unjust to place heavier burdens upon them, especially at a time when they are struggling financially.

One can still argue that private colleges and universities should have to pay taxes to cities and towns despite the benefits they provide to local residents and to the state itself. After all, corporations and businesses are made to shoulder a substantial tax load even though they too generate employment and spending and hence make larger revenues available to state and local governments. But educational institutions differ in significant ways from business firms. Colleges and universities supply many public services that would otherwise have to be performed by government agencies. As noted earlier, merely by educating local residents at no public expense, they save the public treasury many millions of dollars per year. Moreover, universities cannot simply pass along the costs of taxation by raising student charges. Unlike the prices charged by corporations, tuitions often cover only a fraction of the university's total costs. In addition, even the extra revenues derived from tuition increases must be used in part to provide additional scholarship aid. Thus hiking student charges hardly provides a practical way to pay for local taxes. This is particularly true today, when the population of eighteen- to twenty-five-year-olds is declining and many private institutions are hard pressed to attract enough students to balance their budgets. If tuitions cannot be raised, expenses must be cut, and that is no easy matter after several years in which maintenance costs have been deferred and academic salaries have lagged substantially behind the levels achieved in other professions. By taxing universities, therefore, state and local governments might simply hasten a decline in the quality of services offered to the public through education and research.

In addition, however one may judge the property tax exemption as an original proposition, it is now a policy of long standing. Universities have relied for generations on the exemption and have acquired their land and built their facilities on the expectation that they will be free of such levies. To a large extent, these decisions are irreversible, since a university cannot reconstruct and reconfigure its buildings in the event of a sudden change in the fiscal rules. As a result, a decision by the state to amend the law at this late date would seem particularly harsh and unfair, especially when the state is already benefiting so handsomely from the presence of private colleges and universities.

There is a final policy objection to any proposal that would allow cities and towns to tax their universities. Since universities own large amounts of land covered with buildings of highly uncertain value, the power to tax would give municipal officials broad discretion to determine the levels of taxation to impose. Ideally, one would want this power to be exercised with some restraint and with a clear appreciation for the value of academic institutions to society. But the pressures that weigh on city officials do not lend themselves to enlightened judgments of this kind. Unlike most businesses, major universities cannot move out, no matter how high their taxes go. Nor have many of these institutions been successful in mobilizing strong political support in their own communities. In these circumstances, there is no real check on the fiscal ambitions of municipal officials. Moreover, since most of the values derived from advanced education and research are state-wide, national, or even international in scope, municipalities are the least likely of all levels of government to weigh these benefits carefully. Local authorities who considered only their own interests would be well advised to tax a university at the highest rate consistent with its survival, even if the quality of its programs, the amount of its scholarships, and the adequacy of its libraries all substantially diminished. From the standpoint of the nation and the state, it is simply not wise to subject universities to this type of tax environment.

STATE GRANTS TO UNIVERSITIES   Perhaps for these reasons, most proposals to remove the tax exemption are accompanied by a suggestion that the state make appropriations to private universities to repay them for the services they render to the public. This alternative has found favor with several legal scholars. In their eyes, the tax exemption is actually a hidden subsidy that accomplishes the same result as if the state simply appropriated the same amount of money to nonprofit institutions. In contrast to a direct appropriation, however, the exemption gives a financial advantage to these institutions without any chance to debate the subsidy openly through established democratic procedures. Worse yet, the state insists that local communities bear the cost of the subsidy even though many of the services provided in return flow beyond the city to assist the state.

Critics also argue that the subsidies provided by the exemption are arbitrary and quixotic. Charitable organizations may render useful services despite their precarious economic circumstances. Even so, neither the benefits they provide nor their financial needs will be accurately reflected by allowing them a tax subsidy based on the value of the property they happen to hold. A university with huge playing fields does not necessarily do more for the community than another university that lacks such facilities, nor is a wealthy college with a spacious campus likely to need more subsidy than a poor college that carries on in cramped, inadequate quarters.

Because of these shortcomings, critics argue that cities should be allowed to tax universities in the normal way and that the state should give each institution an annual appropriation after considering the benefits it brings and its financial needs along with all the other claims for support from public funds. In this way, all landholders would be treated equally and all benefits contributed by the university would be scrutinized to ensure that every appropriation could be clearly justified and explained.

In evaluating this proposal, one should be careful to avoid theoretical abstractions and take pains to examine how such a system would actually work in practice. In this spirit, imagine the task that would confront a legislature in attempting to assess the value of the services a university renders to the public. In their effort to minimize expenditures, state officials would argue that the university is not entitled to payments for educating state residents because it has already charged them ample tuitions. The university would reply that the cost of educating these students is far in excess of the tuition and that the state should at least contribute the amount it saves by not having to enroll such persons in its public institutions. Much the same argument would take place over the payments due for services rendered by the university's hospitals. Similarly, academic officials would ask for appropriations to cover the benefits conferred on the public by its libraries and museums; the state would reply that it never asked that these institutions be built and that the services they provide are local benefits to be paid for by the municipality. There is no clear answer to these disputes, and the ultimate decision would depend not on logic, but on political judgments based on how much the state could afford and how much the university needed financial help. There is little reason to believe that the results of this exercise would be any less arbitrary than those produced by the property tax exemption.

The most that one can claim is that the payments from the state would emerge through established democratic processes. Although there are virtues in this procedure, there are disadvantages as well. Once the state begins to make large yearly appropriations to private universities, temptations will surely arise to use these funds as leverage to secure larger educational objectives. Legislators may push the university to hold tuitions down, at least for local residents. When the state needs a veterinary school, pressure may be applied on some private institution to create one. If residents cannot be accommodated in the state professional schools, private universities will be urged to reserve more places for local applicants. As time goes on, private institutions may be asked to participate fully in creating master plans to guide their development in conformity with an overall, state-wide pattern.

One can always seek to justify these developments as an extension of the democratic process in which private and public institutions are all subjected to rational planning under the aegis of elected public officials. But just as we have rejected comprehensive government planning for our economy, so also should we resist it for our system of higher education. Although legislators are elected, they are not always equipped to make wise judgments on educational questions such as proper tuition levels, the composition of student bodies, or the creation of new academic programs. When they attempt to make such decisions, they may either make mistakes or respond expediently to political pressures. In either case, the quality of higher education will suffer.

In considering comprehensive planning, one should also remember that part of the genius of American higher education has been its mixture of public and private institutions. Extensive state systems have not only produced some universities of outstanding quality, they have provided the means for making certain that basic public needs are satisfactorily met. Independent institutions have made important contributions as well. In particular, they have offered diversity through the existence of small colleges, denominational and single-sex institutions, and experimental programs of various kinds. For a country with a huge student population of widely differing tastes, abilities, and aspirations, such variety is critically important in providing each individual with educational opportunities appropriate to his needs.

By creating a system with many independent centers of initiative, we have also minimized the costs of policy mistakes and maximized opportunities for experimentation and innovation. These virtues are especially important to the process of education, which is inherently uncertain and intangible and in constant need of new initiatives. In addition, aided by their independent status, private universities have managed, despite their lack of state support, to account for the major share of the nation's highest ranking academic departments and professional schools. Through such achievements, they have not only benefited themselves; they have set examples to which public institutions can point in justifying their budgets to their state legislatures. In this way, private universities protect their public counterparts from unwise political decisions to resist innovation, depress faculty salaries, or inhibit necessary expenditures for libraries and other academic facilities.

In making these arguments, I do not mean to suggest that all the virtues of a mixed system of education would vanish if states began to make large grants to private universities. But such appropriations are bound to invite government intervention in the long run and thus diminish the independence of the private sector. It is especially important today to recognize these dangers, for private universities have already become more vulnerable to regulation by having to depend on large sums from the federal government for student aid and scientific research. In the absence of a compelling need, we should not extend the process to yet another level of government and invite still more intrusions upon an independent sector that has brought much creativity and vigor to the entire process of higher education.

ALTERNATIVE TAXES   Faced with serious financial problems, officials in some municipalities have attempted to bypass the property tax exemption by proposing a per capita levy on universities based on the number of students enrolled. Such a tax would impose a direct burden on educational institutions, forcing them either to curtail services or to raise student charges even more rapidly than inflation already requires. Worse yet, per capita student taxes single out educational institutions from other nonprofit agencies. This is a step that is hard to defend on the merits, especially when these very institutions are among the more prominent of the nonprofit organizations in providing services that benefit a wide range of local residents. City officials may assume that such levies will simply fall on well-to-do parents who can afford to pay. In reality, however, the true burden of the tax is likely to descend in large part on needy students whose financial aid may have to be cut or on secretaries, janitors, dining hall employees, and other low-paid workers who make up the bulk of the university payroll. Moreover, such taxes would again put universities at the mercy of municipal authorities, since there is no prevailing rate to check the amount of the levy imposed. As previously mentioned, this is a serious hazard, for local officials have little incentive to place an adequate value on the benefits that universities provide to the state and nation and hence might not take proper account of the impact of their taxes on the ability of these institutions to carry on their work.

In any event, the fiscal crises of the city will clearly not be solved by imposing special levies on universities and other nonprofit organizations. The funds to be gained by such measures are far too small to meet the needs involved. As a result, most commentators agree that broad new sources of revenue must somehow be made available to City Hall. One of the ways often cited to achieve this end would be to authorize the use of municipal sales or income taxes. Such charges have the advantage of spreading the tax burden over a large number of people, especially those who live in the suburbs but work in the city. At present, such persons reap the commercial benefits of the city and enjoy most of its cultural attractions, yet they contribute no taxes in return. Properly crafted, income and even sales taxes could help to correct this problem in a manner that would be no more regressive, and probably less so, than the current levies on real property.

If a state authorized a municipal sales or income tax, students and faculty would presumably have to pay, for they have no persuasive reason to escape the levies imposed on other people in the city. It is likely that the incidence of these taxes would ultimately fall to some extent on educational institutions. Nevertheless, the impact on the university itself would be indirect and probably not substantial enough to produce serious financial problems.[7]

A final source of new revenue could result from permitting city officials to impose a user fee on services, such as water, sewerage, fire protection, and the like, which are provided directly to urban residents and institutions. Such charges encourage a more efficient use of the services involved while yielding additional revenue to municipalities. By extending such charges to universities and other nonprofit organizations, city officials would also satisfy private property owners who resent having to contribute to the cost of maintaining tax-exempt institutions. Unlike per capita student charges, user fees will fall not only on universities but on other residents as well and will be determined by prevailing citywide rates and by the actual volume of services consumed. As a result, such fees do not expose the university to the discretion of municipal officials in deciding how much it can afford to pay. To be sure, these charges do invade the traditional privilege of nonprofit organizations to be free from local taxes. Nevertheless, now that the value of the property tax exemption has become so much greater than originally anticipated, cities can claim that the size of the current subsidy can justifiably be trimmed to this limited extent.

Universities and other nonprofit organizations will protest that they are too hard pressed financially to pay user fees after relying for so long on being exempt from tax. They may also argue that the new tax could have an unintended disadvantage, since they

7. Somewhat different problems are presented by the prospect of a payroll tax. Unlike a levy on students, the payroll tax would apply not only to universities but to all local employees and would also cover workers residing beyond the city limits. However, such a tax would have a more direct impact on universities. In a large institution, even a 1 percent tax could result in a total cost in excess of $2 million. All in all, therefore, the payroll tax would be less objectionable to a university than a levy specifically aimed at educational or other nonprofit institutions but would not be as desirable as a city-wide income, sales, or user tax.

may be forced to defray the added costs, at least in part, by reducing the services they offer to the community. Despite these points, it is hard to assert that user fees are completely unjustified. The stronger argument is that they are simply less appropriate than other alternatives available to the state. After all, user charges do nothing to spread the cost of municipal services to the suburbanites who work in the city and hence will not provide as much new revenue as sales or income taxes. Moreover, it is not completely fair for state officials to stand by and allow universities to be taxed in view of all the benefits that a state derives from the educational services provided by these institutions and the added revenues that they make possible.

If the value of the property tax exemption has risen over the years, so has the economic value of the university to the state. As a matter of fairness, therefore, it would be preferable for the state to share these gains with cities and towns instead of keeping the benefits and taxing universities at a time of severe economic difficulty. As a practical matter, moreover, the state should hesitate before placing added costs on educational institutions lest it harm its own long-term interests. Because of competitive and financial pressures, such added charges may force universities to curtail employment, cut their scholarships, and suffer a disadvantage in vying for students. In this event, user fees will have the effect of reducing the financial benefits that private universities give to the states while impairing the value of their services to others. These objections seem substantial enough to warrant a look at further alternatives for offering state relief to municipalities.

DIRECT STATE RELIEF TO MUNICIPALITIES   If state governments wish to assist cities and towns that are burdened with tax-exempt property, there is a safer and better way of accomplishing the goal than the options considered thus far. The legislature could simply appropriate funds directly to municipalities to help defray the revenue losses resulting from tax-exempt land. Several legislatures already make such payments for property owned by the state itself. Similar treatment could be extended to land held by private universities, hospitals, and other nonprofit organizations that give substantial services to residents outside the city in which these institutions are located. In 1978, Connecticut actually adopted this approach and distributed $10 million to municipalities in compensation for their hospitals and educational institutions.[8]

Payments of this kind could conceivably be set at a figure corresponding to the tax each institution would pay without the exemption. Perhaps a fairer compromise would be to fix the distribution at a lower level to reflect the services and other advantages that city residents already receive from their neighboring college or university. In either case, the payments would doubtless fall far below the value of the savings achieved by the state from the educational services performed by these institutions.

All things considered, this alternative seems distinctly preferable to the methods previously considered for relieving the burdens of the tax exemption. By undertaking to appropriate its own funds, the legislature would recognize the fact that the state and its taxpayers are the chief beneficiaries of the services and added revenues made possible by private colleges and universities. By allocating its payments to reflect the amount of exempt land situated in each municipality, the state would redistribute the burdens of the exemption so that they no longer fell so unevenly and arbitrarily on the various cities and towns. Better still, this result would be achieved in a manner that would not threaten the viability or the autonomy of academic institutions.

VOLUNTARY PAYMENTS BY THE UNIVERSITY   Despite the arguments just outlined, it is possible, indeed highly probable, that many states will not make direct payments to their municipalities or even allow local sales or income taxes. What then? Between the city and the university, which should bear the burdens resulting from the property tax exemption?

Many cities have concluded that universities should assume at least a portion of the cost. Indeed, municipal officers have often felt strongly enough that they have refused to grant zoning variances or give building permits unless the university first agrees to make some negotiated payment to the city. Such tactics, however,

8. Unfortunately, Connecticut has not seen fit to continue appropriating funds for this purpose. In reviewing the Connecticut plan, other state officials may argue that they already distribute funds to cities and towns under a variety of programs. But these funds are given for other purposes and are not allocated in a manner that recognizes the widely varying proportion of tax-exempt land from one municipality to another.

seem clearly improper and represent an abuse of discretion by the officials involved. Public officials have no more right than private citizens to disregard existing laws with which they happen to disagree. So long as the state continues to exempt universities from taxation, municipal officers have no authority to exert informal pressure to circumvent the law and extract payments they have no legal right to receive. As a result, the proper issue is not whether local officials can insist on being paid but whether universities should recognize a moral obligation to make some sort of financial contribution to the cities in which they reside. There are at least three possible arguments for acknowledging such a duty.

In candid moments, most city officials will concede that their principal reason for asking universities to contribute is simply that they believe these institutions can afford to pay. In other words, officials argue that the salaries, scholarships, or educational services universities would have to cut back in order to make "in-lieu" contributions have a lower social value than the benefits such funds would provide for needy people in the community. According to this reasoning, universities should look upon themselves much as corporations or wealthy landowners and make payments even though they already contribute more to the city than they receive in municipal services.

One can engage in endless debate over the merits of this argument. To city officials, universities could easily finance voluntary payments by increasing their tuition, and the added burdens on the parents would represent a trivial cost compared with the value of essential municipal services to the needy. In return, academic leaders will argue that tuitions are embarrassingly high already and that it would be unfair to raise the cost of education still further to assist municipalities when bureaucratic waste seems widespread and police officers and garbage collectors often receive higher salaries than associate professors.

There is no logical answer to such disputes. Nevertheless, the argument itself does not really help resolve the issue at hand. Even if one were to decide that cities "needed" the funds more acutely than private universities, it would still not follow that a university should recognize a moral obligation to offer voluntary payments. This statement may seem startling at first glance. After all, academic institutions are dedicated to high ideals and should be especially sensitive to the needs of others. Nevertheless, university trustees are obligated to spend institutional resources for academic purposes. They are not at liberty to use these funds to support outside organizations or causes, however worthy they may be. For example, a university could not spend its endowment to house Cambodian refugees, despite their acute privations, for the gifts that formed the endowment were given in trust for educational activities, and trustees would abuse that trust if they diverted the funds to other ends. Similarly, academic officials could not take a portion of the money students pay for board and room and use it to relieve starvation in Bangladesh. Although hungry children in Asia may need a portion of rice much more than undergraduates need cheeseburgers, the funds involved were simply not provided for famine relief, and only the students and their parents can decide whether to contribute their money to such a cause. Of course, if municipal officials believe that universities should be forced to contribute to urban programs, they can address their arguments to the state legislature as a policy reason for depriving universities of their tax exemptions (although I would strongly argue that the proper response is not to lift the exemption but to provide direct relief to the cities). But local needs, like Third World needs, are simply not sufficient in themselves to create a moral obligation on the part of universities to make voluntary contributions to the city.

Although universities have neither a moral duty nor even a legal right to contribute their funds to worthy causes, they cannot insist that others make payments to support their own activities. Consequently, if the university obtains direct services from municipal agencies without providing some equivalent benefit in return, one can argue that it should pay for the value of the benefits it receives. Otherwise, the institution will be accepting a subsidy that the city has been forced to pay by another governmental body. While there is nothing unlawful in receiving such a subsidy, a university might consider the situation sufficiently unfair to city taxpayers to require some sort of voluntary payment.

This argument would be stronger if the university actually consumed substantially more in municipal services than it provides the city in return. But this is probably not the case. Although it is difficult to place a dollar value on the direct services that universities supply to their communities, at least one study, jointly conducted by university and municipal officials, reached the conclusion that the value of the medical, cultural, and other benefits provided by the institution exceeded the cost of the municipal services that it used.[9] In addition, as I have pointed out, the university also stimulates the local economy and thereby increases property values and local tax revenues by an amount far beyond the cost of its municipal services. These revenues do not represent a payment for municipal services, but they do undermine any moral argument that the university is somehow burdening other taxpayers by consuming more than it contributes in return.

A final argument for making payments in lieu of taxes can be advanced on more limited grounds. Since cities and towns are forced to rely so heavily on the property tax, universities should arguably assume an obligation not to make matters worse by continuing to purchase land and remove it from the tax rolls. By agreeing to continue paying the prevailing taxes on newly acquired property, academic institutions will not have to sacrifice existing funds but will simply avoid causing additional tax losses to the city. At the same time, the university will further its own interests by minimizing the risk of provoking local officials to protect their revenues by imposing onerous zoning restrictions that will block all future land purchases by the institution. Such payments would also succeed in addressing another problem identified by many critics of the tax exemption. Because the cost of additional land to the university is held below prevailing market levels by the absence of property taxes, the exemption has the effect of artificially encouraging institutional expansion. Neither the sales nor the income tax nor even the distribution of direct state payments to municipalities would succeed in solving this problem.

In examining these arguments, one must recognize that not every purchase of taxable land will increase the financial woes of the city. Universities will often turn such land to uses that will

9. Robert A. Leone and John R. Meyer, "Tax Exemption and the Local Property Tax," in John R. Meyer and John M. Quigley, eds., *Local Public Finance and the Fiscal Squeeze: A Case Study* (Cambridge, Mass.: Ballinger, 1977), pp. 41–67.

bring new income to local residents and thus eventually result in greater revenues for the city than it would have collected had the property remained in its prior state. Even so, the resulting advantages may not be realized for a number of years, while the tax losses to the city will be certain and immediate. As a result, there is much to be said for some sort of arrangement in which the university agrees to pay taxes on newly acquired property for a stipulated period of years after the date of purchase. Such agreements would seem particularly important in cities already burdened with high proportions of tax-exempt land.

The University's Services to the City

Apart from cash payments, universities can also provide a variety of useful services to the surrounding community. A wise administration will find several reasons to pursue these opportunities. Some services will give pleasure to others at so little cost to the university that they are well worth doing for their own sake. Efforts to help the community can also create a measure of good will to soften the inevitable discontents over student behavior, university expansion, or the tax-exempt status of the institution. Finally, many neighborhood projects can serve the interests of the university and simultaneously benefit the community. Thus student instructors may improve the quality of the public schools while helping to prepare the participants for teaching careers, just as cooperative efforts to design a nearby park further the common interest of the university and local residents in enhancing the surrounding neighborhood.

Spurred by motives of this kind, various services to the community have gradually developed over many years. Universities have long opened their libraries, museums, and gymnasia to neighborhood use. Undergraduates have engaged in tutoring or volunteered to read to the aged and the blind. Students in professional schools have helped provide emergency medical services or served as interns in municipal agencies.

In the mid-1960s, however, universities suddenly began to pay much more attention to the cities after high unemployment and racial tensions resulted in serious riots that awakened public concern for the urban poor. In this atmosphere of crisis, academic administrators began to look for new ways of helping inner-city residents. Almost overnight, a battery of projects, institutes, and programs sprang into being, offering consulting and research on urban problems, continuing education for adults, university-sponsored housing for the poor and elderly, and health and dental clinics in the ghetto.

In the bright dawn of these initiatives, enthusiasts spoke glowingly of the possibilities. According to one urban university president, the "university should be, along with City Hall, the command post of all the operations to reclaim, renew, rebuild, and revitalize the city."[10] After more than a decade, alas, the record of these ventures seems decidedly mixed. A few have survived. Many have languished or disappeared. In the words of an experienced foundation officer, "I would guess that although there have been several mutually satisfying tie-ins between academics and office-holders, the failures outnumber the successes by at least ten to one."[11] In a disturbing number of cases, projects undertaken with high hopes met with failures that actually heightened local suspicions and frustrations rather than improving relations with the university.

Looking back on this experience, one can learn something useful for the future. Community services are often high-risk ventures. They clearly work best when they impose little burden on the university and help some local group without antagonizing others. When either of these characteristics is missing, the program must be scrutinized with considerable care.

If a project promises to affect any community group adversely, trouble is almost bound to arise. Local residents who feel threatened will usually make their opposition known with great intensity. Conversely, those who stand to gain from the project will rarely be organized or feel very strongly about prospective benefits they have not yet come to appreciate. Under these conditions,

10. Warren G. Bennis, president of the University of Cincinnati, "Great Expectations," in Howard E. Mitchell, ed., *The University and the Urban Crisis* (New York: Behavioral Publications, 1974), p. 25.

11. William C. Pendleton, "Urban Studies and the University: The Ford Foundation Experience" (Address to the New Orleans Conference of the Office of Urban Affairs, American Council of Education, New Orleans, April 5, 1974), p. 10.

the project is unlikely to attract much grass-roots support and may be blocked entirely by its opponents. Thus even neighborhood clinics proposed by medical schools have sometimes been halted by determined opposition from local physicians. Unless a university has a clear institutional stake in proceeding with such projects and can muster strong backing from City Hall, such ventures are often not worth undertaking.

Other programs may arouse little opposition but require a major, ongoing commitment of time and effort by the university. In this event, it will be difficult to justify the burdens involved unless the project serves valid academic purposes or brings substantial benefits to the institution. This is particularly true of programs that require a sustained effort on the part of faculty members or students, such as an advisory service by a business school for local merchants or free computer instruction for neighborhood high school students. A university rarely has much control over the extracurricular activities of its professors or its students and lacks any practical means of enlisting their genuine enthusiasm for community work. As a result, unless the project brings continuing educational or professional rewards to the participants, the risks are great that the program will not work well or will actually founder completely after a time, leaving resentments and frustrations in its wake.

Although these limiting principles seem severe, they actually permit a wide variety of community services. Museums, libraries, and athletic facilities can all be opened to public use in ways that do not conflict with the educational programs of the institution. Such access offers the clearest example of a service that imposes little burden on the university, benefits the public, and antagonizes virtually no one. Apart from sharing their facilities, educational institutions can also make special efforts to employ workers from surrounding neighborhoods. With slightly more effort, academic officials can institute training programs that will further the interests of the community in obtaining jobs while helping the institution to recruit a suitable work force.

Many universities have evening extension programs that are open to local residents. To many people, these courses offer an opportunity to pursue cultural interests. More often, they provide the means to learn new skills that open doors to better jobs and new careers. Although the institution may charge a fee for these offerings, tuitions can be kept at a modest level and still cover the incremental costs involved. In this way, a university can provide valuable experiences for many participants while giving its faculty members a chance to earn additional compensation.

In recent years, universities have made greater efforts to work with community groups in planning urban-renewal projects or constructing housing or commercial facilities compatible with local needs. The university can frequently supply badly needed expertise and even invest its own funds in such projects. These ingredients will often make the difference between success and failure for an important project. Of course, undertakings of this kind present much greater risks to the institution. They may arouse resistance among community groups or lead the university into improvident investments. It may be difficult even to discover who can speak authoritatively for the community, and tiny groups of dissenters often have the legal means to tie up projects for many months in litigation. Even so, such efforts may be well worth making, not only to assist the local community but also because the university has a strong stake in halting the process of blight and decay that has brought severe problems to several urban institutions. With careful planning and extensive consultation, several universities have avoided the hazards involved by helping to construct facilities that have served local needs while also fostering good will within the surrounding area.

Students have also rendered valuable and continuing benefits to the local community. In many universities, particularly at the undergraduate level, large programs have been developed to read to the blind, tutor underprivileged children, or provide recreation activities for the poor. Despite the commitments of time required, such efforts have continued to flourish, since student participants are energetic, idealistic, and continuously renewed by fresh recruits. With reasonable supervision, service programs run by professional-school students have also fared well in many institutions, for the work involved not only is valuable to the poor and disadvantaged but also offers practical experience that enhances the students' professional development.

More serious difficulties have arisen when universities have sought to provide research and consultative services to the community. If such projects make available technical expertise of a kind that is welcomed by everyone concerned, the university may succeed in providing a valuable contribution. Thus a team of reading experts may help to overcome the learning disabilities of children in a local school, while a psychiatric counseling clinic can offer valued assistance to the families in a neighborhood. But the prospects for success become much more doubtful when the university undertakes to give advice on more controversial issues that have strong political overtones. Nowhere are these problems more apparent than in university projects to advise city governments on how to organize their bureaucracies or design their urban programs.

Such projects are inherently sensitive and will almost always arouse the antagonism of some faction or group. Moreover, there is often a striking lack of "fit" between the outlook of the academic personnel who offer their services and that of the city officials who seek the university's help. Although professors may volunteer their efforts from public-spirited motives, their work tends to be marked by the habits of their vocation. Professors are conditioned to examine problems in a certain way. They are trained to apply the special methods of their particular discipline and are disposed to search for interesting generalizations or novel insights with which to enliven their research. They often have little interest in the practical details of a specific case except insofar as particulars happen to test a general principle. In addition, few scholars have extensive experience with political struggles and constituency pressures; their natural interest lies in analyzing problems and offering solutions without much concern for the messier details of implementation. These characteristics make them more useful as advisers at the national rather than the local level.

Cities, moreover, are extremely difficult clients. Their officials are not always adept at defining the precise problem they wish to have resolved. They often proceed without the support of their subordinates, who will have to implement changes and can easily obstruct reforms in subtle ways. In addition, elected city leaders are wont to shift their priorities and change policies abruptly to conform to sudden political changes in the communities they serve. In this environment, even a well-executed project will often come to naught and leave the participants frustrated and confused.[12]

These difficulties do not suggest that universities should *never* do research or consulting for city officials or local agencies. But work of this kind has a greater chance of success if it is suggested spontaneously by municipal officials instead of being encouraged and funded by third parties. Narrowly defined problems requiring some special form of technical expertise seem more promising than larger, vaguely worded projects affecting bureaucratic interests or entrenched political groups. Questions that are susceptible to definitive answers should have a higher priority than problems in which any foreseeable solution will require an intricate process of implementation. Above all, research and consulting services should not be undertaken unless the academic participants actually possess a distinctive expertise that is needed to solve the problem at hand. In view of these limitations, universities should be wary of establishing consulting organizations to the city that are peripheral to the institution and may be overly aggressive in generating projects in order to balance their budgets.

Although the consulting efforts of the sixties rarely succeeded, save in narrowly defined circumstances, more promising opportunities for community service have emerged in recent years. In several professional schools, there has been a steady growth of officially sponsored clinical programs that enable students to work in poor communities under close faculty supervision. In many law schools, legal-aid services have been transformed from an extracurricular activity into regular programs of clinical education that offer credit and are integrated with formal instruction under the supervision of full-time faculty members. In order to develop better preparation for careers in primary care, medical schools are also expanding their outreach programs by developing clinics in poor neighborhoods. Even greater opportunities may arise as more schools begin to organize prepaid health plans, not only to provide a service to local residents but to provide a setting for better clinical training for general practitioners. In these varied ways, community programs of higher quality are likely to develop as professional schools see opportunities not only to render service

12. See Peter Szanton, *Not Well Advised* (New York: Russell Sage Foundation and The Ford Foundation, 1981).

but simultaneously to improve the quality of their education through supervised practical experience.

Opportunities of a different sort are also emerging through the rapid growth of midcareer education for officials in the public sector. As the tasks of school superintendents, health planners, hospital administrators, budget directors, and even mayors grow more and more difficult and complex, the demand for education steadily rises. At the same time, professional schools are learning to build sound curricula to teach widely applicable methods of policy analysis and administration and to teach these skills more effectively through the use of problems and discussion. Through the convergence of these capabilities and needs, many new programs are springing up around the country. The best of them have been greeted with great enthusiasm by harried officials eager for a few weeks away from their jobs to learn new ways of approaching recurring problems and to share their experiences with other public servants from different areas and agencies.

Educational programs of these kinds offer more promising possibilities to municipal officials than the prospects for extracting payments in lieu of taxes. Nonprofit institutions do not have the financial strength to make a significant impact on the fiscal problems of the city, nor should they feel morally obliged to offer such assistance. But universities do have a growing ability to help prepare local officials to cope with extraordinarily difficult problems. By trying to assist in these ways, academic institutions can make a useful contribution that cannot be readily supplied by any other source, a contribution fully consistent with their central purposes and intellectually challenging to their faculties. In combination, these ingredients offer the most realistic basis for a stronger and more enduring relationship between the university and the city.

10

Taking Political Positions

THE DISCUSSION of property taxes reminds us that universities are not merely communities devoted to teaching and learning; they are also corporate entities that own land, hold shares of stock, purchase goods, and solicit gifts. In this capacity, they are often asked to respond to social problems by using methods quite outside their normal academic processes. Not only do city fathers ask them to aid local communities by making payments in lieu of taxes; concerned faculty and students frequently urge them to sell the shares they hold in companies doing business in South Africa, to boycott the products of firms accused of unfair labor practices, to refuse a gift from a reprehensible donor, or even to issue an official statement condemning apartheid, the Vietnam War, or some other controversial practice or event. Such demands often provoke very intense feelings among members of the campus community and give rise to the most intractable controversies.

When local officials call on universities to offer payments in lieu of taxes, they often assert, rightly or wrongly, that academic institutions place additional burdens on the city and should agree, therefore, to pay for them. In many other situations, however, it is clear that the university itself has not "caused" the evils it is being asked to combat. It has not bought stock to promote apartheid nor does it choose its suppliers to support improper labor practices. In the usual case, these wrongs will have existed before the university entered into such transactions and would almost certainly persist even if the university sold its stock or ceased its purchases of goods. Consequently, university administrators often insist that their institutions are simply not responsible for these injustices, however regrettable they may be.

This response has some foundation in our established values and traditions. Although many social activists deny the very possibility of neutrality—"you are either part of the solution or you are part of the problem"—there *is* a difference between the obligations of someone who has pushed an innocent child into the river and the responsibilities of the spectators who line the shore. By taking some positive action that inflicts harm on others, we incur duties that do not fall on the mere bystander. This distinction finds expression in the legal system of every civilized nation. Although there are circumstances in which affirmative duties have been placed on the onlooker, they have generally been confined to cases in which the third party has voluntarily assumed a special position of responsibility and trust toward the victim—as a doctor possesses toward a patient—or situations in which it seems probable that bystanders could actually prevent the suffering of another at relatively little cost to themselves. Neither of these exceptions fits the situation of the university when critics ask it to make statements against political injustices or sell the stock of companies doing business in South Africa.

Even so, the principles just described hardly represent more than a minimum ethical standard. Institutions as well as individuals may have higher moral aspirations for their own conduct, asking more of themselves than they can rightfully demand of others. Although we do not insist that innocent bystanders throw themselves into an icy river to save a drowning stranger, we may still resolve to take such risks ourselves in order to rescue human beings in mortal danger.

Critics who feel most keenly about injustice and suffering tend to believe that universities should set high standards for themselves in defining their social responsibilities. Granted, universities have not *caused* apartheid in South Africa or poverty among migrant farm workers. Granted, they will probably not make matters any worse by purchasing produce or stock from companies that tolerate apartheid or exploit their workers. Nevertheless, since universities profess humane ideals, one can argue that they should act whenever possible to oppose injustice and help the oppressed and disadvantaged. And if they cannot always find a positive step to take, they should certainly attempt to avoid all taint of evil by severing the links that connect them with people and organizations that may be guilty of grossly immoral behavior. At the very least, they should take the greatest pains not to allow themselves to profit from evil practices by accepting gifts from unsavory individuals or by pocketing dividends from companies that are guilty of unethical and inhumane behavior.

These arguments raise legitimate and important questions. In thinking about them, however, we must recognize that a university's freedom to act is closely bounded by compelling obligations. As I have already pointed out, the university has received its funds for educational purposes and cannot spend money to assist Cambodian refugees or feed the starving in Bangladesh, however severe their privations. Since this principle is widely understood, those who urge universities to fight against injustice by extra-academic means usually call on them to respond in different ways. They will ask not that the university contribute money for the people of Bangladesh but simply that it refrain from purchasing nonunion lettuce; not that faculty members go to jail to protest the draft but simply that they pass resolutions to denounce an unjust war; not that the trustees spend the endowment but simply that they avoid buying stock in companies that do business in South Africa.

Yet even these actions have their costs. Institutional statements on injustices in the outside world may help to create an official orthodoxy that will inhibit assistant professors and other vulnerable persons in the university from expressing contrary opinions. Every order to divest stock is almost certain to lead to losses of money that could otherwise be used for faculty salaries and scholarships. Decisions to refuse a gift from an unsavory donor may cause the loss of a scholarship or block a new professorship that might enrich an academic program. Efforts to inquire into the ethics of corporate policies or the behavior of questionable donors or the propriety of government actions can likewise be extremely burdensome and absorb large amounts of faculty time that could otherwise go toward writing books or advising students.

Critics are often distressed at the very thought of weighing such matters as foregone income, inconvenience, and faculty time against the moral claims to help overcome injustice. In their eyes, the interests at stake in apartheid and oppression are simply on a different level from the self-regarding concerns of the university to husband its funds and protect the time of its faculty. We cannot dismiss this argument out of hand, for academic institutions do have certain principles that rise above considerations of material gain. No self-respecting university would agree to abandon the teaching of evolution in exchange for a million dollars, nor would it allow a donor to appoint a specific professor to its faculty even for the most generous benefaction.

And yet, we can hardly use similar arguments to define the university's affirmative responsibility to alleviate sufferings and injustices that are not of its own making. Even private individuals are not expected to devote their time and money to worthy causes without any consideration for their own personal needs. Universities have much stronger reasons to worry about potential inroads on their material and intellectual resources. This point is often overlooked by those who seek to discredit educational institutions by accusing them of subordinating humane considerations to material gain. For universities, however, time and money are not private matters; they represent the indispensable means for carrying out academic functions that also have moral content, whether they involve the search for valuable knowledge, the teaching of useful skills, or the effort to provide all deserving students with the opportunity to obtain an education regardless of their financial means.

Money has become much more precious to the university than it was in the affluent years of the 1960s. Private institutions have been ravaged by mounting energy costs, double-digit inflation, federal cutbacks for research and student aid, not to mention the sluggish behavior of the stock market. Public universities have been squeezed by state legislators burdened by the spiraling costs of social programs and buffeted by grass-roots resistance to further increases in the tax rate. Amid these pressures, budget officers have had to cut student assistance and postpone building repairs. Worst of all, faculty salaries in all major universities actually declined by 15–20 percent in real dollars during the 1970s.

Time has also become a scarce resource on the campuses of major research universities. Government agencies and corporations have looked increasingly to the academic community for advice and expertise, and the advent of the jet airplane has greatly expanded the opportunities for travel to distant places for speeches, conferences, and consultations. As faculty salaries have declined in real dollars, professors have turned more and more to lectures, consulting, and outside teaching to pay their mortgages and maintain their living standards. At the same time, the rising tide of government regulation and the increasing demands of campus administration have made further inroads into the time available for teaching and research.

In this period of crowded schedules and pinched resources, a loss of institutional funds or a substantial diversion of faculty energy will impair the academic enterprise by diminishing the university's capacity to provide the scholarships, the attention to students, or the facilities essential to teaching and research. These losses may be outweighed by other moral considerations in a specific case, but they are hardly irrelevant to the decision. Ethical choice involves a conscientious effort to select the course of action that does least harm to legitimate human interests and worthwhile social goals. Any diversion of money and time from academic ends is a matter that deserves consideration because it tends to endanger just such legitimate interests and worthy goals. At the very least, therefore, we should recognize that the academic work of the university is no mere private matter. It is a public undertaking possessing a social significance and a moral value of its own. As a result, no action should be taken which interferes with that work without a convincing demonstration that the inroads are warranted by the prospect of achieving a greater public good.

This principle seems particularly important in considering how universities should respond to social problems. Presidents and deans are sometimes asked to act in costly ways that have only the remotest prospect of achieving any tangible benefit. Such proposals make little sense, however worthy the ultimate objectives may be. In the end, therefore, the proper course for the university is not to embrace every proposal to attack injustice or to disclaim all responsibility in such matters, but to consider how best to weigh the prospective burdens and benefits arising from requests to take a moral stand.

Official Political Statements

In the late sixties, students and faculty members across the country became increasingly concerned about the war in Vietnam. The bombing of the North grew heavier, the number of American troops steadily rose, the casualty lists constantly lengthened, and vivid reports of suffering and brutality appeared in newspapers across the United States. In response, professors began to write strongly worded articles of protest, student activists organized teach-ins against the war, and campus volunteers sallied forth to march in political demonstrations and work for candidates committed to ending the conflict.

In the midst of this swelling protest, concerned professors on many campuses rose to their feet in faculty meetings and asked their colleagues to join in officially condemning the war. These motions typically resulted in a heated and acrimonious debate. Opponents of the resolutions pointed to the long tradition of institutional neutrality that had served universities well for many years. They spoke eloquently about the importance of academic freedom. To illustrate the point, they often cited the travails of politicized campuses in Europe and South America, where faculties had strayed from their academic duties to enter collectively into political combat.

Proponents of the antiwar resolutions freely acknowledged that it was unusual for a faculty to debate political matters extraneous to the university or to issue statements aimed at influencing public officials in Washington. Nevertheless, they argued strenuously that the Vietnam War was an exceptional crisis that called for an unorthodox response. It was a war roundly condemned on most campuses. It was a catastrophe resulting in a massive loss of human life. It was a tragedy almost without precedent in the United States, a conflict that divided the nation and aroused feelings of alienation and hostility on the part of countless young people toward their government.

Despite these arguments, most of the resolutions failed. But the votes were rarely overwhelming, and many professors left the meetings deeply troubled by the tangle of conflicting arguments. A dispassionate observer could not reflect on the debates without concluding that in a matter of great importance the relevant issues had not been clearly sorted out, let alone resolved in a convincing manner. Would political statements really endanger the academy and deflect it from its central mission? Or were these insubstantial fears raised by timid persons to dissuade their colleagues from standing up to be counted at a time of grave national danger?

Reading the debates today, one can readily see how inconclusive they must have seemed. Professors on each side of the issue repeatedly talked past one another. Those who pressed for faculty resolutions frequently belittled the notion of institutional neutrality. After all, how could universities claim to be politically neutral once they had allowed military recruiters on campus and accepted public funds for defense-related research? With equal vehemence, their faculty opponents insisted that any attempt to issue official political statements would violate the neutrality of the institution and ultimately endanger freedom of thought on the campus.

Those who argued strongly against the Vietnam resolutions were invoking principles that extended back at least to the Declaration of 1915. But these professors must have known that the situation they faced was quite unlike anything their predecessors had faced over a half century before. In the late 1960s, members of the faculty, rather than trustees, were suggesting that the university take an official political position. Despite the passions aroused by the Vietnam conflict, few people could have feared that professors would run a serious risk by refusing to join in condemning the war. The institution of tenure was firmly established to protect professors; most faculties would have fiercely resisted any attempt to discipline dissenting members; and boards of trustees would have blocked such an effort in any event.

Even so, many faculty members were clearly worried by the prospect of issuing collective political statements. They may have realized that no one would openly condone taking reprisals against political dissenters. But this was not a policy that could be readily enforced, nor could transgressions be easily detected in a world of mixed motives and undisclosed reasons. If a campus began to take official positions on more and more public issues, heated debates would ensue and passions could easily be aroused to such an extent that a junior faculty member hoping for tenure, a young administrator seeking advancement, a full professor worried over a raise in salary might all feel inhibited, however slightly, from openly dissenting from the official doctrine of the university.

Opponents of the antiwar resolutions also had other objections in mind. They feared the strains and antagonisms that might arise and divide the faculty once their colleagues began to enter in debate over controversial political issues. They resented taking time from important academic matters to discuss public questions that many felt inadequate to address. They were upset by the prospect of having institutional positions adopted that might conflict with their own opinions and give a spurious impression of orthodoxy in an academic community that must and should contain a wide variety of views.

How serious are these dangers? Not negligible, perhaps, yet one can easily exaggerate their significance. Every university must make collective decisions, often on controversial matters that provoke spirited debate. A faculty may vote to institute a new curriculum or agree to new teaching responsibilities over the heated opposition of a minority of its members. A department may reject or promote a highly controversial professor after a sharply divided vote. A board of trustees may vote its shares of stock against a popular environmental resolution, or reject a faculty pay raise that many professors strongly support, or select a commencement speaker whose life reflects a set of values offensive to many scholars. All these actions can take much time away from normal academic pursuits. All of them may provoke divisions within the faculty and even endanger collegial relations. All of them can inhibit dissent on the part of the junior faculty or other persons who may oppose a policy yet still not dare to speak and risk the disapproval of those more powerful than themselves.

Apart from the collective decisions that universities regularly make, presidents also speak publicly on controversial issues. In recent years, for example, Father Theodore Hesburgh of Notre

Dame has been an influential spokesman on matters of racial inequality and world poverty, while Jerome Wiesner of the Massachusetts Institute of Technology has written eloquently on questions of arms control. Although many people have welcomed these expressions of opinion, one could argue that there is little reason to distinguish them from formal university statements since both could have an intimidating effect on faculty members holding contrary points of view. If presidents are free to speak, therefore, why should their institutions shrink from issuing official resolutions on important public issues?

Beyond presidential pronouncements, a modern university also generates a host of other inhibitions that can discourage free expression by cautious and apprehensive souls. Assistant professors may hesitate to contradict their department chairman. Graduate students will often fear to disagree too strongly with their faculty advisers, who supervise their dissertations and may exert a decisive influence over their opportunities for future employment. Even the simple act of circulating a faculty petition may be carried out in ways that put pressure on younger scholars anxious to avoid giving offense to their more powerful senior colleagues. Since the campus is filled with subtle influences that constrain the independence of all but the strongest minds, is it not disingenuous to perceive grave dangers in an occasional faculty vote on some important political issue?

These arguments are persuasive enough to require more than a vague appeal to academic freedom. But there is another distinction that does set official political pronouncements apart from other, more familiar expressions of opinion on the campus. If the university seeks to change its curriculum, or choose a commencement speaker, or appoint a new professor, it must act collectively or it will not act at all. Since decisions of this kind must be made, the university has no choice but to continue making them even at the cost of time, occasional divisiveness, and the danger of inhibiting younger colleagues. In the case of political pronouncements by presidents, department chairmen, or senior professors, the options are similarly limited, for such persons either can speak out on a public issue or must remain silent. If they had to refrain from expressing themselves in order to avoid all risk of inhibiting younger scholars, the cure would be worse than the disease, since the net result would be to diminish academic freedom rather than to encourage it.[1]

The situation is quite different in the case of official resolutions on political questions. If students and faculty wish to speak out on a public issue, they need not obtain a university statement. They can easily communicate their views by circulating a petition among their fellow students and professors, and if their cause is convincing, they can probably attract heavy support. As Professor Fritz Machlup declared in opposing a political statement by the Princeton faculty: "The point is that the institution or its faculty as a body has no brain and no heart, and should have no mouth either; the members of the institution *as individuals* have all these organs and have a moral obligation to use them freely in defense of what they consider right."[2]

If concerned students and faculty can issue their own statements, why do they not do so and avoid the danger of irritating their colleagues? What do they hope to gain by passing a formal university resolution that they could not achieve by circulating a petition?

One advantage of a formal university resolution is that the practice is so unusual that it may attract considerable media attention. The very novelty of such a statement will often convey an aura of importance and intense feeling that will propel the un-

1. Although presidents should be free to speak as individuals, they cannot entirely escape the weight of their office, for anything they say will be linked by the public to the universities they serve so prominently. As a result, presidents would be well advised to take particular care not to speak on public issues about which they are not thoroughly informed. This is a point not always grasped by editorial writers, who often contrast the reticence of the current crop of presidents with the outspokenness of prominent university leaders in the "good old days," who expressed themselves quite freely on a wide range of topics. As so often happens, the "good old days" turn out on close examination not to be as good as one might suppose. Over the past century, presidents of distinguished universities have spoken forcefully in favor of racial segregation and against immigration, labor unions, social legislation, and many other reforms that would be endorsed overwhelmingly today. One cannot help thinking that many of these presidents might have served their institutions better by speaking out on fewer issues and by confining themselves to matters on which they could claim to have considerable knowledge and experience.

2. "Academic Freedom," *The Encyclopedia of Higher Education*, vol. 1 (New York: Macmillan and the Free Press, 1971), p. 9.

derlying message with greater force. Put bluntly, official resolutions may simply have more clout than ordinary petitions. But is this reason enough for agreeing to prepare such statements? Clearly not. One can understand why students concerned over a particular issue might wish to capitalize on the publicity that would follow a university's decision to break tradition and issue a supportive resolution. But the institution must look at the long-range consequences of agreeing to address political issues in this fashion. From this standpoint, the risks are evident and the beneficial consequences very slight. Any novelty that might attach to the first political resolution would dissipate after the third or fourth manifesto appeared, and media interest would quickly dwindle. No sensible university would agree to such a burdensome and controversial practice in exchange for such short-lived results.

Concerned students and faculty may still prefer institutional statements to petitions, hoping the public will conclude that official resolutions represent the entire university, with all its collective wisdom and expertise, rather than simply a collection of individuals who have chosen to sign a manifesto of their own. This argument, however, is not only weak but disingenuous as well, since it tries to capitalize on a misleading impression of what official statements actually mean in a modern university. In some cases, such statements will be issued by a handful of trustees and high officials who cannot hope to hold themselves out as experts or to represent the wide array of views held by members of the campus community. On other occasions, official resolutions will emerge through a process of student petitions, demonstrations, and faculty debates. No one who has observed this process would assert that it is a particularly effective way of tapping the wisdom and objectivity of the institution. Many votes are cast and much debate carried on by persons having no special knowledge of the subject involved. The final product results from a process of rhetoric, pressure, and accommodation quite unlike the careful, expert deliberation that characterizes serious academic work. In sum, whether official resolutions come from boards of trustees or emerge through broader processes of debate, they are likely to be much less substantial than they appear, for they will neither represent the full range of views within the university nor reflect the quality of thought and learning that most people associate with academic institutions. In short, official statements often convey a misleading impression, and that is yet another reason not to issue them.[3]

Shareholder Resolutions

Although universities have seldom agreed to issue institutional statements on political questions, they almost invariably vote on shareholder resolutions that come before them as owners of stock in corporations. These resolutions arise under Rule 14(a) of the Securities and Exchange Commission, which requires companies to give their stockholders an opportunity to vote by proxy on any resolution that a shareholder submits in timely fashion, provided it is reasonably related to the business of the firm and raises policy questions going beyond its daily operating activities. For many years, this rule was used infrequently and almost always for issues involving such matters as offers to buy the company or proper compensation levels for the management. In the 1970s, however, churches and consumer organizations began to introduce resolutions to secure a variety of social ends, such as asking corporations to remove their operations from South Africa, or to cease making covert political contributions to foreign officials, or to appoint directors who could represent the interests of consumers, minorities, or other groups. The number of these "social responsibility" resolutions rose steadily through the early 1970s, with 180 being filed in 1977 alone. If universities have agreed to reach collective decisions in order to vote on questions of this kind, one can legitimately ask why they cannot agree to issue statements on issues such as the Vietnam War.

3. To be sure, a university could take pains to provide a higher quality of statement by establishing a committee of experts from its faculty to consider the issues at length and produce a thoughtful statement on behalf of the institution. But even this procedure leaves vital questions unanswered. Why should the institution have the responsibility to empanel a group of experts, when interested faculty members are free to take this step on their own behalf? And why should the resulting statement be labeled an official university resolution instead of allowing the professors to issue their own signed document and present their handiwork for what it actually is—a statement by several professors rather than a reflection of the views of the entire university and all of its members?

In fact, shareholder resolutions do present many of the same difficulties that have led universities to refrain from other kinds of institutional statements. Certainly, the process of deciding how to vote on these proposals often consumes much time and can arouse bitter controversy on the campus. Even so, although these problems are not trivial, shareholder resolutions differ in important respects from requests to take official positions on other social issues. By choosing to hold stock, the university assumes the normal functions of ownership, and one of these functions, expressly confirmed by federal law, is to vote on proposals that are put before the shareholders. In voting on these resolutions, university trustees do not purport to represent the entire institution or to reflect its accumulated wisdom; they are simply carrying out a duty entrusted to them as fiduciaries legally responsible for the endowment. Moreover, students and faculty have no alternative for expressing their individual preferences on issues that come before the shareholders. If they wish to protest an unjust war or some other government policy, they can draft a petition to express their individual concerns, and if their position commands wide enough support, their views will have an influence that is equivalent to that of an official university statement. In voting on shareholder resolutions, however, no comparable opportunity exists, for it would normally cost a prohibitive sum to acquire a block of shares equivalent to the institution's holdings. As a result, universities could not refrain from voting without conveying the awkward message that it is simply too much trouble to take ethical positions on important issues even when there is no other means that is nearly as effective in expressing an opinion that will have a constructive influence on corporate management.

Despite these reasons, it is still possible to argue that universities should not assume the burdens of voting conscientiously on stockholder resolutions. Experience proves that these proposals almost never gain support from more than 5 percent of the votes. With such a record, would it not be wiser simply to abstain on all shareholder issues rather than take the time and effort to examine the facts and arrive at an institutional position on the merits?

Curiously enough, many resolutions do seem to have an effect on corporate behavior even though they never win more than a small fraction of the vote. They attract management's attention by generating publicity and forcing the company to defend its policies publicly before the shareholders. If a resolution makes a valid point, corporate officials may alter their policies, either because the proposal has led them to think about issues previously overlooked or because of a concern over adverse public opinion and possible government regulation. Whatever the reason, changes do occur. General Motors appointed a black community leader, a woman, and a scientist to its board within a year after a shareholder resolution requiring outside directors had attracted less than 3 percent of the vote. In 1976–77, approximately thirty companies negotiated agreements with the American Jewish Congress concerning the Arab boycott after the AJC had placed appropriate resolutions on the ballot. In 1974, nine of seventeen resolutions seeking disclosure of equal-employment data were withdrawn after the companies involved voluntarily agreed to release the information. And according to a recent study by the Investor Responsibility Research Center (IRRC): "It seems clear that expressions of shareholder concern have played a significant role in encouraging United States corporations to improve their treatment of their black employees in South Africa."[4]

One should not exaggerate the significance of this record. Neither experience nor common sense would suggest that corporate executives will be influenced by proposals with which they clearly disagree, especially if the resolutions would require major changes in operations causing substantial losses to the enterprise. In such cases, the threat of adverse publicity will hardly be enough to induce the management to change its position. Still, the fact remains that enough shareholder proposals have had an effect that universities cannot readily abstain from voting on the ground that the entire exercise is meaningless and ineffective. On the contrary, such resolutions have probably been much more effective than institutional statements could ever hope to be, and this is a further reason for taking them seriously.

At the same time, most boards of trustees have taken care to es-

4. *Labor Practices of U.S. Corporations in South Africa, Special Report 1976-A,* April 1, 1976 (New York: Investor Responsibility Research Center, 1976), p. 98. On the general question of the impact of shareholder resolutions, see David Vogel, *Lobbying the Corporation: Citizen Challenges to Business Authority* (New York: Basic Books, 1979).

tablish procedures for voting on resolutions that will minimize the burdens involved. In 1972, several universities took the lead in establishing the Investor Responsibility Research Center, which prepares for its members impartial analyses of the facts and issues involved in each resolution. Over one hundred academic institutions, foundations, investment firms, and insurance companies now belong to the organization. By this device, member institutions share the cost of investigating the facts and identifying the arguments so that intelligent choices can be made. In addition, boards of trustees have retained power to vote on resolutions (often with the help of an advisory group of students and faculty).[5] They have done so not only because they are entrusted with the legal authority to vote, but also because they have wished to avoid the burden and controversy that could result if all decisions were reached through extensive discussion and vote by the faculties and other constituencies of the university.

If even these procedures should eventually prove to be so divisive, so time-consuming, or so threatening to academic freedom as to impair the normal functions of the university, the administration might be forced to call a halt and simply abstain on all resolutions.[6] Indeed, a few institutions have never agreed to vote in the first place, presumably out of concern for just such dangers. In practice, however, although trustees and advisory groups have devoted many hours to deciding what position to take on resolutions, the total burden has not been great enough to justify uni-

5. A few private institutions have also included alumni on their advisory boards. This practice is justified on the ground that alumni not only share an interest in the university but represent the principal source of funds from which the endowment is derived.
6. One can imagine particular issues, however, that could justifiably lead a university to abstain. For example, consider a resolution asking a utility company to cease building nuclear power plants. The underlying questions are so complex that they would require a protracted examination of a long series of highly technical issues. Experience also suggests that even well-informed individuals will arrive at opposite conclusions on the merits. Moreover, the impact of a university vote is likely to be small, for the issues at stake are so basic and costly to a company that one can scarcely imagine the management abandoning nuclear power simply because a resolution to that effect had come before the shareholders and received a small fraction of the votes. In these circumstances, one could well decide that it would be inappropriate to ask trustees and faculty members to spend the time required to reach a conclusion on the merits of the issue.

versities in refusing to discharge their normal responsibilities as owners of stock.

Since universities are generally prepared to vote on shareholder resolutions, one could argue that they should go further and initiate their own proposals for other stockholders to consider. According to this view, ownership carries an affirmative duty to try to improve the behavior of companies from which one derives a profit. As a result, universities should acknowledge a responsibility to exert such influence because they have the prestige to generate stockholder interest and encourage company executives to pay close attention to the resolutions.

The act of initiating resolutions, however, comes very close to the practice of taking institutional positions on social issues and involves the same disadvantages. Whereas no one but the university can vote its stock, anyone can initiate a shareholder resolution—either by purchasing a share of stock or by persuading a church group or another shareholder to introduce the proposal.

There are practical reasons for insisting that individuals take the initiative to have their proposals placed before the shareholders. When a university sponsors a resolution, it is formally taking issue with the conduct of a corporation, and it does so in a more pronounced and visible way than when it merely votes against management on someone else's resolutions. Such an action carries important responsibilities, especially for an institution dedicated to careful inquiry. In order to preserve its intellectual integrity, the university must take particular care to investigate all the facts and arguments in each case and arrive at a reasoned and responsible position. In contrast to voting on resolutions introduced by others, the university cannot minimize the costs of investigation by calling on the services of a central agency to determine the facts. The Investor Responsibility Research Center exists only to explore proposals already on the ballot, and there is little prospect that any single university could persuade the remaining academic institutions, foundations, insurance companies and other IRRC members to assume the costs of taking on a responsibility to investigate all the possible resolutions that participating institutions might wish to consider introducing.

The burdens of initiating resolutions could be extremely heavy. Virtually all research universities own stock in scores of corporations, most of them large organizations doing business in many locations and product markets. The range of corporate activities involved is almost infinite, and relevant information may be difficult to obtain. As a result, it would be prohibitively expensive for trustees to monitor the performance of all these companies in order to initiate resolutions condemning inappropriate behavior.

To be sure, a university could limit these burdens by simply considering requests for stockholder resolutions put forward by its faculty, students, and alumni. But even this policy could result in a large number of proposals to investigate. Moreover, once a university decides to take the initiative and advance its own proposals for corporate reform, it should proceed in a principled manner and not merely offer resolutions embodying one particular social philosophy or a narrow range of ethical priorities. Yet experience shows that pressures for social activism on most campuses emanate almost entirely from groups that express only a limited range of views. Concerns are often voiced over human rights violations in Chile but rarely over repression in Cuba or Tanzania. Protests are often heard against corporations that do business in South Africa but not a word was ever said about the Folger Company, which purchased most of the coffee crop from Burundi during a period when the minority in power systematically slaughtered thousands upon thousands of the rival majority tribe. My point is not to pass judgment on this record but merely to observe that it falls far short of a balanced, comprehensive concern for social problems and injustices. As a result, no university could restrict itself to resolutions suggested by its own students and faculty without appearing to be biased and inconsistent in its actions.

An institution could also try to reduce the administrative burdens by agreeing to sponsor resolutions only in certain categories of cases of unusual social importance. Depending on the categories chosen, however, even this task might prove very difficult. Moreover, defining the categories would be difficult and controversial since reasonable people disagree so strongly over the importance of different social problems. While some might feel that issues of sex and racial discrimination are particularly urgent, others would attach equal or greater importance to protecting the environment, while others would insist that highest priority be given to charges of exploitation in the Third World.[7] Any attempt to draw such lines would inevitably seem arbitrary and would produce strong pressure to expand the scope of responsibility category by category until the cumulative burden became extremely onerous.

Thoughtful people may suggest some other limited set of circumstances in which a university can advance resolutions without exposing itself to the difficulties just described. For example, a few boards of trustees have agreed to initiate proposals asking companies to provide relevant information on their operations and employment practices in South Africa. Such resolutions would have a reasonable chance of success and might be proposed without having to make lengthy investigations. Even so, could a university offer resolutions for disclosure about the employment practices of South African operations without agreeing to introduce similar proposals concerning strip mining, nuclear power, or the treatment of women? And could it responsibly introduce such resolutions without making enough inquiries to establish a sufficient likelihood of abuse to warrant a demand for information? Perhaps these questions can be resolved satisfactorily. If so, a university might agree to proceed. But trustees should be reluctant to affirm any policy that would subject their institution to the task of conducting a series of expensive, time-consuming investigations into corporate activities. Since individuals have reasonable opportunities of their own to place issues before corporate shareholders, the reasons for asking universities to assume this burden are unlikely to be great enough to justify the costs.

7. Because of the recent campus debates on apartheid, some may argue that South Africa represents a special case and that universities could restrict themselves to initiating resolutions directed at companies doing business in that country. And yet, despite our strong condemnation of apartheid, it is extremely doubtful that a university could properly confine its resolutions to the single case of South Africa. To persons deeply concerned with the environment or with the rights of workers, it would be hard to explain why trustees could initiate a resolution asking a shoe company to withdraw a single retail outlet in Pretoria while refusing to make a proposal to stop a major corporation from engaging in massive strip mining in Wyoming or resorting to flagrant antiunion tactics in the South. To put the matter more precisely, even if one regards apartheid as the most flagrant and massive abuse of human rights in the world, it does not follow that each instance of corporate involvement in South Africa is more reprehensible than any other form of questionable corporate behavior.

Political Lobbying

Now that the federal government has come to play a much more active role in regulating universities and giving them financial support, presidents and their staffs have begun to make determined efforts to influence government officials on a variety of matters affecting higher education. Some institutions filed briefs before the Supreme Court to defend their right to give preference to minority applicants seeking admission. Many administrations employ full-time staff members to press for higher appropriations for research, larger federal subsidies for scholarships, and less onerous regulations governing DNA research.

If universities are prepared to act officially to protect *these* interests, why did they balk at expressing their opposition to a war that distracted their students and engulfed their campuses in bitter protest and conflict? After all, unlike many injustices in the outside world, the Vietnam conflict had a major impact on the life of our universities. Faced with the prospect of having to serve in a war they bitterly opposed, many students became so emotionally aroused that their studies were seriously affected. Their bitterness and disillusion led them to organize in protest not only against the war but against their universities as well. In the turbulence that followed, learning and scholarship were major casualties on many campuses. Were these consequences not sufficient to provoke some response by institutions that were prepared to work officially in behalf of so many other academic interests?

In fact, there are several differences between the Vietnam War and the normal lobbying efforts of universities and their associations. One distinction is particularly crucial. In pressing for government funds or arguing against federal intrusions into academic affairs, university officials speak primarily for the purpose of protecting the interests of higher education. In the case of Vietnam, however, even ardent activists would not have urged their universities to oppose the war on the ground that it interfered with the learning processes of students. The overriding reason for speaking out was to protest the cruelty and violence of the war, especially to the Vietnamese, and it would have been grotesque for academic leaders to assert that the conflict should be ended in order to restore peace to their campuses.

In addition, when universities address the government to protect the interests of higher education, their officials are the natural representatives to carry out the task. No one else can be counted upon to have the knowledge and the motivation to inform public officials how their actions will affect the welfare of academic institutions. If a brief must be filed before the Supreme Court, the university's lawyers are the obvious candidates to undertake the assignment. If Congress is debating complex issues of research support or financial aid, the university's government relations staff must work with scientists or financial officers to develop detailed information and convey it to the appropriate government officials at the proper time. In cases of this kind, it would hardly be possible to rely on individual faculty members and students to take the initiative and communicate to Washington by petition. The issues involved are technical and specialized, and it would be hopelessly inefficient and ineffective to hope that individual faculty members could assume the burden of protecting the university's interests. By relying on such spontaneous initiatives, therefore, the university would fail to protect its vital interests and would also slight the legislative process by withholding information that might help lawmakers reach enlightened decisions. However, in cases such as Vietnam—where the central issue involves not the concerns of higher education but the interests of civilians and others engulfed by a cruel war—university administrators have no special knowledge and no special standing to speak. The basic moral problem affects all individuals as citizens, and it is therefore appropriate for each person to decide what opinions to hold about the war and how to act on those beliefs.

In the future, the line between permissible and inappropriate political activity may become much harder to draw as presidents are tempted to enlarge the scope of their political activities to embrace even broader efforts to protect institutional interests. For example, academic leaders are now beginning to meet with business executives to discuss matters of common concern. In time, the participants could easily come to consider expressions of support for specific programs to reduce inflation, increase capital formation, or otherwise improve the nation's economic performance. Such initiatives would probably not produce a public outcry. Faculty members would not need to discuss the matter. If a professor objected, the president could claim that he gave the university's support to such policy measures in the conviction that they would help bring about a healthy, growing economy which in turn would benefit higher education.

Despite these temptations, there are grave dangers in traveling very far down this road. In contrast to federal programs of financial aid or basic research, the government's economic policies do not bear specifically on the interests of higher education or affect these interests in special ways. At best, lowering inflation or encouraging capital formation will benefit universities incidentally or indirectly along with an infinite number of other people and institutions. If this nexus is sufficient to induce presidents to act, the scope of their government relations programs will be vastly enlarged, because all manner of policies can affect higher education in one way or another.

Such an ambitious agenda would have terrified the venerable professors who framed the Declaration of 1915, since it would permit universities to take official stands on many of the same kinds of issues that originally gave rise to the doctrine of institutional neutrality. On most of these subjects, university officials cannot claim to offer a unique perspective to enlighten the legislative process, for the issues at stake in matters such as capital formation or inflation have little to do with the special needs or circumstances of academic institutions. There may be economists on the faculty who do have important contributions to make on the merits. Even so, they will presumably testify as individuals, rather than representatives of their university, and they will speak with greater credibility by appearing in their private capacity. For these reasons, it is doubtful that academic leaders should even attempt to take an official stand on controversial questions of this kind. Once universities begin to stray beyond the domain of their immediate institutional interests into the larger pastures of public policy, they are likely to make mistakes, display a self-interested bias, and thereby speak to national issues in a manner unbecoming an institution supposedly dedicated to objective analysis of the highest quality. At the same time, they will commit their institution publicly on a growing range of subjects without compelling justification. Indeed, how could universities ever hope to justify their silence on questions such as the Vietnam War if their presidents insisted on taking institutional positions on such a broad agenda of controversial public issues?

These considerations suggest two guiding principles to define the situations in which universities can properly take official action to influence government policy. In the first place, universities should not intervene unless their primary motive is to protect the legitimate academic interests of the institution. If a public issue does not affect students and faculty primarily as learners and scholars (but concerns them rather as individuals and citizens), the university should not act officially but should leave the matter for members of the campus community to pursue individually according to their own consciences. In the second place, universities should minimize their government activities by acting only when they are directly affected by the policies in question and when their interests represent an important part of the political result they are seeking to achieve. Thus universities could properly oppose efforts to repeal the charitable exemption provisions of the Internal Revenue Code, since such a repeal would affect them directly and drastically impair their financial well-being. But it would be highly inappropriate for universities to endorse a particular candidate for President on the ground that his policies toward higher education were more favorable than those of his opponent. As educational institutions, universities have larger responsibilities than ordinary interest groups; they would set a sorry example for their students if they placed their own special concerns above the many more important considerations that should properly determine the choice of the nation's chief executive.

Although these principles offer reasonable guidance for ordinary times, one can conceive of situations in which the nation would be so threatened by demagoguery and despotic rule as to require universities to foreswear their political neutrality. Even so, it is hard to imagine that much could be accomplished in such desperate times by issuing formal statements of protest. Instead, the university would presumably refuse to cooperate with the forces responsible for the breakdown of normal democratic safeguards—especially if cooperation entailed a violation of essential academic values. This was the situation that confronted the German universities in the 1930s, and their response left much to be desired. In the midst of the Vietnam War, some of those who urged universities to protest may have believed that very similar dangers were at hand. If so, their fears seem greatly exaggerated. However tragic the war may have been, one could not discern a major threat to free speech or other basic constitutional safeguards nor was there much risk that the machinery of democratic government was in the process of breaking down. Nevertheless, we should not forget that the welfare of universities in the United States is ultimately dependent on the preservation of a free and democratic society. If that form of society is in jeopardy, academic leaders cannot afford to draw their battle lines too closely. Except in these extraordinary circumstances, however, the guidelines just described seem adequate for the occasion.

11

Accepting Gifts

ALL UNIVERSITIES benefit from the generosity of individuals, foundations, corporations, and even foreign governments. Only rarely do these benefactions present a moral problem. But critics sometimes protest, either because donors make a gift to achieve improper objectives or because their prior conduct makes it awkward or unseemly for the university to accept their donations. Although controversies about gifts have occurred for many decades, little effort has been made to consider the subject with care. As a result, the terrain is unfamiliar and the issues encumbered by intangible and symbolic considerations that are often weighed differently by concerned individuals who approach the subject from widely divergent perspectives. No problems more clearly reveal the tensions that can afflict an institution that honors transcendent values while attempting to maintain itself in a vastly imperfect world.

Gifts That Endanger Academic Values

Amid these difficulties, there is one group of cases in which the lines seem reasonably clear. In some situations, donors seek to attach conditions to their gifts that invade Justice Frankfurter's "four essential freedoms of the university"—"to determine for itself on academic grounds who may teach, what may be taught, how it shall be taught, and who may be admitted to study." Since these freedoms are central to the university, a president or dean must constantly work to protect them against encroachments, whether the incursions come in the form of government regulations or in the more seductive guise of restricted gifts. Accordingly, an institution must reject donations that would require it to deviate from the normal standards of admissions, or give a donor the power to appoint a professor or restrict a chair to persons advocating a particular set of values or beliefs.

Some years ago I received a telegram asking whether Harvard would appoint a professor to be chosen and funded by the Libyan government. Needless to say, no self-respecting university would respond affirmatively to such an inquiry. In another instance, the board of trustees of a prominent university was severely criticized when it solicited for the dean of the business school a chair restricted to "promoting the values of the free-enterprise system." This case seems relatively harmless, since it is hard to conceive of a business school dean who would *not* promote the free-enterprise system. Nevertheless, it is so important to resist every attempt to direct the beliefs of a professor that the trustees were undoubtedly wise in eventually taking steps to remove the restriction. In a university, even the divinity school should refrain from accepting a professorship in Christian ethics if the gift requires the incumbent to expound a predetermined set of beliefs or to refrain from criticizing some prescribed dogma.

Yet universities have traditionally accepted donations limited to special purposes or fields of study. Thus a donor may restrict his gift to research in French history, or to scholarships for the law school, or to the construction of a hockey arena. A university, of course, may decide to refuse such funds if they do not fit its plans and capabilities. The institution may feel that it cannot afford to maintain a new facility that a donor wants to construct or that it lacks the personnel and library resources to enter a new field of study that a benefactor wishes to establish. Such calculations may be difficult, but they are not thought to raise an issue of principle so long as the donor does not seek to impose restrictions that bind the institution in selecting students and faculty or inhibit its members in expressing their opinions.

Since donors can decide which activities they will support, universities are bound to be influenced in important ways by the outside world. Business schools will be better endowed than schools of education, while medical research will expand more rapidly than philosophy departments. Such influences are troubling, but they are inevitable and often quite understandable as well. Private benefactors will sometimes act in whimsical or eccentric ways, but few of us would deny them a right to determine how their money will be used. In any event, universities have little choice in the matter. Corporations, foundations, and individual donors will all be much less inclined to give if the only opportunity they have is to contribute funds for the institution to spend as it wishes. As a result, a university that insisted on complete discretion in the use of all donations would not enhance its academic functions but severely inhibit them instead.

On some occasions, however, a gift designated for a specific project may create ethical problems for the university. For example, a professor may receive a grant to investigate the risks of a potentially toxic substance commonly used in preserving food, or he may be offered funds to write the history of a government agency during a particularly critical era. Both subjects are clearly worthy of inquiry. But suppose that the first study is financed by annual grants from a leading food company and the second by a gift from a major benefactor to the university who happened to head the government agency during the period in question.

By using such funds, professors may experience a subtle pressure to compromise the objectivity of their research in order not to offend the donor and thereby risk cutting off further support. In such circumstances, it will not actually be unethical to accept the money, provided that the institution and the investigator are genuinely convinced that they can perform the work with complete impartiality. But even if they are correct, the credibility of the research may suffer, along with the reputation of the institution. As a result, universities often do what they can to avoid accepting gifts in support of research when the donor has an obvious stake in the results of the work and the investigator has an evident interest in retaining the donor's continuing support.

It is difficult to frame a rule to cover every situation of this kind. A medical school could safely accept a gift from a chemical firm to investigate a toxic substance if it received the entire sum in advance with no strings attached and did not consider the company a likely source of significant continuing support. A business school might accept corporate funds to study the behavior of multinational companies if much of the support came not from interested firms but from other sources. In all such cases, the university should take account of the importance of the research findings to the donor, the degree of judgment or discretion involved in the study, and the extent to which the investigator's future support and the financial well-being of the institution depend on the donor's continued good will.

If a university is reluctant to accept a gift of this kind, it must decide how it can proceed without violating the academic freedom of the scholars involved. Certainly, the administration can talk to its professors and try to dissuade them from accepting the donation. Even better, a dean or president can try to make other funding arrangements that will allow the project to go forward without any threat to its credibility. But in the event that these measures fail, can a university go so far as to reject the gift altogether? One can argue for such a policy on the ground that the university is not seeking to prohibit its faculty from undertaking a project but merely regulating the source of funds. And one can add that the administration is not acting on ideological grounds but merely attempting to uphold its reputation for objective research. But neither of these arguments is convincing. If other sources of funds are unavailable, as is often the case, refusing the gift will be tantamount to barring the project altogether. As for the university's reputation, it is well established that an administration may not interfere with a professor's research even if his writings are unpopular enough to provoke resentment toward the institution.

The means of funding is only one of many reasons for criticizing the way in which an investigator carries out his work. Under accepted principles of academic freedom, a scholar must enjoy wide latitude in choosing his methods of research so long as they do not threaten to injure other people or to violate fundamental canons of the academy, such as the obligation not to doctor evidence or to permit any censorship of the results. Universities would run grave risks if they sought to go beyond these principles and enforce detailed rules to guard against attacks upon the objectivity or reliability of scholarly findings. Faculty members are likely to maintain reasonable standards without interference from the administration, since they have a far greater stake than any president or dean in upholding the integrity of their research. In the end, therefore, a university should depend on the judgment of its professors even if they insist on proceeding with projects that threaten to be controversial or to provoke criticisms of the methodology or disinterestedness with which the work is carried out.

Because universities and their professors may be influenced by the interests and priorities of outside donors and funding agencies, critics sometimes argue that all talk of institutional autonomy and academic freedom is ultimately misleading and illusory. But arguments of this kind cannot be taken seriously. There is an obvious difference between accepting a chair in American history and allowing the donor to name the occupant, or between receiving a corporate grant to study antitrust policies and permitting the firm to censor the results. Despite the subtle pressures that may accompany outside funds, the "four essential freedoms" offer an intellectual environment for the pursuit of learning quite unlike the situation in countries where these safeguards do not exist. As a result, although universities will never be wholly free of outside influence, they retain a vital stake in refusing any gift that would explicitly limit their freedom to make important academic decisions.

Gifts from Questionable Sources

Difficult issues arise when gifts arrive from donors who have allegedly earned their money by immoral means or acted in ways that conflict with strongly held values in the community. Many critics would urge the rejection of these "tainted" funds. Yet there is little evidence that universities have been reluctant to accept such donations. In fact, one president years ago is said to have refused to shun a benefactor who had repeatedly violated the law, arguing that his institution had never assumed that accepting a gift was an affirmation of the donor's good character. Whatever the rationale, few universities have shown much inclination to reach a different result.

Proposals to depart from this policy raise many of the objections discussed in earlier chapters. Severe problems would arise in trying to establish principles and apply them consistently. Should a university disqualify a donor for committing some particularly unpleasant act or should it consider his life as a whole and attempt to weigh the good qualities against the bad? The latter course seems more appropriate and just. But how objectionable must a donor be before the university refuses his donations and by what yardstick will the institution make such calculations? It is often hard to know how to vote on shareholder resolutions even though they typically involve only a single corporate practice. It is much more difficult to judge the entire life of a donor, with its inevitable ambiguities, its noble and ignoble moments, its blemishes and redeeming virtues, its obscurities and half-secreted truths. In these circumstances, the risk of arbitrary, inconsistent decisions looms very large.

It is also difficult to put such standards into practice, for academic officials often know very little about the lives of their benefactors or how they amassed their fortunes. Since the university will often be unaware of any questionable behavior when it accepts the gift, it will be urged to undo agreements entered into in good faith. At this stage, rejecting such donations will constitute a public rebuke that may cause great resentment and inflict pain on relatives and other persons who bear no responsibility for the donor's conduct. One can always argue that the institution should avoid these problems by taking care to discover them in advance, but it would be extraordinarily difficult to investigate the hundreds of benefactors who make donations each year to a university. Imagine how a development officer would react if he were instructed to inform potential donors that the institution would accept their gifts only if they agreed to undergo an investigation or answer questions about their past activities and financial dealings. As a practical matter, even respectable donors would refuse to run the risk of inviting public inquiry into the moral quality of their lives. By insisting on such prior investigations, the university would needlessly deprive itself of substantial amounts of money that could be put to good use in providing scholarships, chairs, and buildings for educational purposes.

Although these problems are forbidding, there will be times when the administration is well aware that a donor has been convicted of serious crimes or has engaged in behavior that flagrantly offends widely accepted values in the community. On such occasions, some people will claim that the university should simply refuse the donation rather than associate itself with someone so prominently linked with unsavory activities. In response to these objections, one can certainly agree that the institution should refrain from celebrating the gift in a manner that appears to honor the life of the donor. Such actions would convey a message that is false and unworthy of a university. But if no gestures of this kind need to be made, it is not at all clear that the administration has any ethical obligation to reject such gifts.

In and of itself, the act of accepting a donation does not imply an endorsement of the views and actions of the benefactor. If the donor has not earned his fortune by unethical means, the university will not profit from evil by accepting his gift nor will it actively encourage immorality. On the contrary, an institution will doubtless do more good by using such funds constructively than by forcing the donor to keep his money. History offers many examples. Few people would argue that universities should refuse gifts from the Ford Foundation because Henry Ford expressed anti-Semitic views or that libraries should have rejected Andrew Carnegie's donations because he resorted to strong-arm tactics to stop unionization. If all charitable and educational institutions felt obliged to reject the gifts of every person who had engaged in improper behavior or expressed objectionable views, the world would be deprived of many valuable works while receiving few, if any, tangible benefits in exchange.

In certain cases, however, the university may find not only that the donor has acted reprehensibly but that the gift itself is designed to achieve some devious end or to advance the donor's interests in questionable ways. For example, Harvard University once turned down the offer of a professorship in modern Greek studies from the Colonel Papadopoulos regime after inquiries suggested that the gift was probably designed to gain the good will of Greek-Americans, who traditionally send large amounts of money to their mother country. A generation earlier, President James Bryant Conant rejected a named scholarship proffered by a confidant of Hitler, in part because he feared that the gift had been proposed and specially publicized "to use Harvard as an

American base to spread approval of the Nazi regime."[1] On both these occasions, the university could not accept the gift without helping to carry out the purposes of a repressive government.

More difficult problems can arise if the university discovers that a donor has gained his fortune by unethical means. In some cases, of course, the taint will be too slight to warrant serious concern. For example, one would surely not object to gifts merely because a tiny, indeterminate fraction of a donor's wealth could be traced to some prior misdeed or to investments in American firms with minor outlets in a totalitarian country. One could argue, of course, that the ethical university should attempt to achieve the utmost purity by striving to avoid every link that might associate it with immoral practices. But efforts to go to this extreme would be highly impractical. In order to sever all connections with injustice, the administration would have to assume an immense investigatory burden extending far beyond the receipt of gifts. The trustees would presumably have to consider selling massive amounts of corporate stock, since many companies do business in countries with unjust and repressive regimes or engage in practices from time to time that might conceivably provoke strong objection. Suppliers would have to be investigated and cut off if they were found to engage in reprehensible practices. Universities might even feel obliged to reject tuitions from parents whose fortunes could be traced to ethically questionable activities.

Few individuals make a serious effort to achieve such purity in their own lives, and universities could hardly do so either without making sacrifices far out of proportion to any benefits achieved. George Bernard Shaw made the point most succinctly when he commented on the clergyman who decided to accept donations only from kindly old ladies: "He has only to follow up the income of the sweet ladies to its industrial source, and there he will find Mrs. Warren's profession and the poisonous canned meat and all

---

1. At that time the President and Fellows also felt that Harvard should not accept a named gift from someone whom it knew to be prominently associated with a political party that had "inflicted damage on the universities of Germany through measures which have struck at principles we believe to be fundamental to universities throughout the world." See James Bryant Conant, *My Several Lives* (New York: Harper, 1970), p. 144.

274 Addressing Social Problems by Nonacademic Means

the rest of it. His own stipend has the same root. He must either share the world's guilt or go to another planet."[2]

One should likewise be willing to accept gifts paid for by funds lawfully earned even if the donor's fortune can be traced back to unsavory practices by members of an earlier generation. For example, Harvard once accepted a chair from the Krupp Foundation even though the foundation might never have existed had it not been for the work of an earlier Krupp in supplying arms to Nazi Germany. Despite its clouded origins, the foundation currently earns its funds from normal business activities, distributes its money to worthy causes, and is even headed by a man honored by the government of Israel for his actions during World War II. In these circumstances, the gift seemed entirely proper. Surely, there must come a point where the acts of one's predecessors cease to be relevant and any stain that may have existed grows too remote to warrant further concern. Were this not so, the descendants of evil men might never be allowed to make amends by directing their inherited funds to charitable ends. So long as they do not seek to use their gifts to honor a maleficent ancestor, it is hard to perceive any useful purpose in refusing such donations.

But how should a university react if it receives a bequest from a known criminal or an unpublicized gift from a prominent official in a corrupt, totalitarian government? Taking such donations could place the institution in the awkward position of accepting funds derived primarily from immoral activity. One can certainly argue that receiving "tainted" money is ignoble and unworthy of the ideals of an academic institution. Yet this policy runs headlong into several awkward problems. Should a university accept tuitions from a Mafia father or treat his children as if they had no means of support and thus qualified for full financial aid? I know of no university that would return the father's check, yet if the university is seeking to avoid tainted funds, it is hard to explain why it can accept tuition but not receive a gift from the same questionable source. Should civil rights organizations, community action agencies, and other social welfare groups have the same obligation to refuse gifts from controversial donors? Many people would argue that such worthy organizations can accept

2. *Major Barbara* (New York: Penguin Books, 1957), p. 26.

such gifts because their needs are pressing and their purposes highly beneficial. But it is difficult to find a principled basis for upholding such donations while denying the university's right to take similar funds to help discover a cure for a debilitating disease or assist a needy student to obtain a college education.

These problems cast doubt on any simple rule that would reject such gifts as "unworthy" of an academic institution. Even so, apart from compromising the university's reputation, it is still troubling to accept funds that were extracted from others by wrongful means, for in an ideal world, one would prefer to return the money to those from whom it was improperly taken. Yet there is rarely a practical means to carry out such restitution. The only way in which a university can approximate this result is by devoting resources equivalent to the gift to benefit the class of persons who have been wronged by the donor. Thus, upon receiving money from a repressive despot, an administration could make added scholarships available to needy students from the nation involved. (A somewhat analogous course has been taken by universities that have offered full scholarships to black students from South Africa, a decision partially motivated by a desire to offset the tiny fraction of endowment income attributable to corporate operations in that country.) By directing its funds in this manner, the institution may succeed in reaching a result more beneficial and more just than it could achieve by either rejecting a controversial gift or simply using it for normal academic purposes.[3]

More serious problems arise when a university undertakes to name a building, a professorship, or a scholarship for a donor who has engaged in immoral behavior or earned his fortune in reprehensible ways. Recognizing a benefactor in this fashion goes be-

3. This question has long given rise to differences of opinion. In the fifth century, for example, a wealthy Roman couple, Pinianus and Melania, agreed to liquidate their large inherited estates, which had been originally secured through force and maintained by repression. Under the influence of Pelagius, who counseled an austere perfection, they first agreed to distribute this property to the poor. Eventually, however, Saint Augustine persuaded them to change their minds and use their lands to endow Catholic monasteries. Alas, we are no closer to a consensus on this issue today than we were centuries ago.

yond the mere acceptance of a gift, since the administration can be accused of honoring immorality and legitimating unethical conduct. Once again, however, the issue is not clear-cut. To name a building for a donor, or for one of his relatives, is not the same as awarding an honorary degree; its meaning is much more ambiguous.

In practice, recipients of gifts and awards have regarded the use of a benefactor's name more as a way of acknowledging the source of the donation than as an affirmation of his moral character.[4] Certainly, universities that name a professorship do so because the donor gave the necessary funds and not because they admire his worldly achievements. Similarly, students who accept the designation of Rhodes scholar (and universities that help to administer these awards) do not believe that they are endorsing the racial and colonial views of Cecil Rhodes. Young men and women who become Fulbright scholars do not thereby condone the votes of Senator J. William Fulbright in support of racial segregation, nor did the universities that named their buildings after celebrated entrepreneurs of the nineteenth century ever intend to affirm the business methods of men whom Theodore Roosevelt once described as "malefactors of great wealth."

Even so, reasonable people may argue that though the naming of a program or a building is not a certificate of good character, it does invest the benefactor with a certain respectability. If not an honor, such designations at least convey an implication that the donor's life and works are not demonstrably at war with the values of the institution. Those who wish to drive the point home can easily conjure up arresting cases to support their position. No university could accept a Hitler Collection of Judaica or a Vorster Center for Racial Justice or a Capone Institute of Criminology. Such titles would devalue the academic enterprise and mock the very programs they purport to designate.

Although these examples seem far-fetched, they do make clear

4. A different situation may arise when a donor wishes to name a chair or a building for an unrelated person. In such a case, the use of the name is not intended to record the source of the funds but to provide a form of honorific recognition. Hence, naming the chair or building more clearly implies an affirmation of good character by the university and thus should require more careful scrutiny.

that a university must draw the line at some point in seeking to recognize its donors. Yet formidable problems could arise if institutions had to regard each named gift as a certificate of good character. As previously mentioned, the university is not equipped to investigate the lives of dozens of benefactors who offer each year to make named gifts, and efforts to conduct such inquiries would only result in dissuading even the worthiest donors from making their contributions. In the face of this dilemma, we can all agree that the administration should exercise good judgment in refusing to memorialize the names of donors whenever it has reason to know in advance that their lives and conduct are plainly offensive to the ideals of the university. This practice by itself should avoid most of the cases that could result in controversy and compromise the values of the institution. But it is doubtful that a university could go further and inquire into the lives of prospective donors without incurring burdens and sacrifices out of all proportion to any lasting benefits to be achieved.

A final group of troublesome cases can be illustrated by the donor who offers a scholarship restricted to a particular class of students. If the funds are limited to "worthy applicants from Kansas," one can accept the gift in good conscience as a harmless personal preference reflecting the donor's affection for his place of origin or his appreciation for the state in which he made his fortune. Similarly, a scholarship limited to "deserving black students" may represent a donor's laudable concern for increasing the number of minority students in our colleges and universities. But what if the scholarship is given for "white students only" or for "young men and women of the Caucasian race"? At some point, such restrictions cease to be harmless preferences *for* particular groups and appear to represent a prejudice *against* the excluded categories.

The problem in such cases is not that the university will be forced to discriminate. Since almost all institutions devote substantial amounts of their unrestricted funds to scholarships, it is an easy matter to make sure that all groups of students receive financial aid on a principled, equitable basis. Ironically, then, a scholarship restricted to whites will often have the effect of increasing the assistance available to black and Hispanic students as well.[5] Nevertheless, by accepting such a gift, the university will associate itself in some fashion with a prejudice deeply contrary to its ideals.

Unlike the named buildings, the restrictive wording of the scholarship need never be publicized; it can remain unnoticed, buried in the fine print of the terms of gift. Yet this is small consolation to a principled university. Whether or not the issue is made public, the administration must still decide how it can balance a distaste for linking itself with prejudice against the opportunity to offer greater support to needy students.

This dilemma lies at the heart of many of the vexing issues that arise from questionable gifts. A donor may restrict his scholarships in racially obnoxious ways. A repressive government may give a chair with no ulterior motive in mind. A notorious slumlord may seek to establish a library fund to purchase volumes that will bear a bookplate in his name. In none of these cases need the university actually honor the donor or help him to achieve an immoral end. Still, the administration will be torn between the desire to gain material support and the reluctance to have the institution associated with individuals or patterns of conduct that are inconsistent with the university's values. Faced with these conflicts, presidents and deans will be inclined to stress the practical value of accepting such gifts in order to provide better programs and needed scholarships. Idealists who have no responsibility for balancing the budget will see the issue as an opportunity for the university to affirm its values even at the cost of some tangible sacrifice to its own well-being.

Both sides of the argument have their merits. In a time of pervasive cynicism, no sensitive person can fail to applaud an institution that is willing to proclaim its ideals in a vivid and convincing manner by refusing a gift from a questionable source. And yet, in an era of retrenchment, when many universities are struggling to maintain a decent level of financial aid and to avoid se-

5. This result does not do violence to the donor's intent. It is common knowledge that gifts to support professors or programs already in existence will have the effect of freeing unrestricted funds for other uses. A donor who adds to scholarship funds for some specified category of students wishes to know that *his* money is being used to help certain recipients. He does not intend that his gift have the effect of creating inequities in the entire scholarship program of the institution.

vere cutbacks in their faculty and staff, it is difficult to condemn a hard-pressed administration that decides to accept such a gift for the good of the institution. Faced with such difficult choices, conscientious trustees will wish to ask how flagrantly the gift departs from the values of the institution and how deeply the university must implicate itself by agreeing to go forward. It is possible to accept a loan fund limited to Jewish students and out of the question to accept a chair with a stipulation that it cannot be awarded to a woman. It is more defensible simply to receive an endowed scholarship from a notorious bigot than it is to implement his prejudices by taking pains each year to allocate the income only to members of the Caucasian race. Although these distinctions seem reasonably clear, intermediate cases will arise that present much greater difficulty. The answers will depend on the circumstances of each case, but they will not be easy, much less persuasive to all concerned. In the face of such dilemmas, one can only hope that each side will have the tolerance to accept opposing arguments with a measure of understanding and good grace, recognizing that there is no compelling logic that can resolve the underlying problem.

12

Boycotts and Other Efforts
to Avoid Outside Relationships

WHEN OPPOSITION to the Vietnam conflict started to mount on the nation's campuses, activists seized upon the relationships that linked universities with corporations and government agencies and exploited these connections to attack organizations that were prominently involved in the war effort. Rallies and demonstrations were held to put an end to ROTC programs. Protesters barricaded doors and sat in corridors to keep recruiters from the armed services and defense industries from holding interviews in university facilities. After the fighting ended in Vietnam, students turned their attention to other causes. Some joined coalitions to picket and petition the administration to boycott firms that were said to engage in unfair labor practices. In response to the injustices of apartheid, other groups held mass meetings and marched by candlelight to press trustees to sell the university's stock in American corporations doing business in South Africa. Although these protests embraced a wide variety of causes, the fundamental questions were the same. Should an educational institution cut its ties with an outside organization in order to pressure it into changing its behavior? And quite apart from trying to influence others, were there goods and services whose origins or purposes were so objectionable that a university should avoid having any traffic with them whatsoever?

Avoiding Undesirable Relationships

Some commercial transactions are so plainly wrong that a university should never agree to be a party. The clearest examples involve transactions that are actually illegal. Surely, universities have an obligation to uphold the law and not sell liquor to students under the statutory age or dispense drugs without observing the requirement for a doctor's prescription. Academic institutions should likewise avoid buying items of property to which the vendor has no legal title. Although such instances may be rare, academic museums have had offers to purchase works of art unlawfully smuggled out of foreign countries, and several universities, along with many public museums, now wisely insist that their curators take pains to inquire into the provenance of any objects they purchase to make sure that each item has been properly acquired by the vendor.

In other cases, a university may refuse to enter into relationships that would subject its members to treatment in conflict with its own basic principles. For example, few universities would agree to hold an alumni event in a club that discriminated against blacks or women. To use such facilities would prevent the institution from inviting all its alumni and thus would keep it from fully achieving its purposes. But the objection runs much deeper. By making such an arrangement, the university would be actively cooperating in a venture that would subject its graduates to discrimination, just as it would if it held a segregated reception for alumni on its own premises. In either case, the institution could not proceed without violating its basic commitment to extend equal treatment to all members of its community. For much the same reasons, a university should not permit a company to use its facilities to interview students for employment when it knows that the firm engages in sex discrimination.

In some instances, students have objected to purchases or commercial arrangements that do not violate the law or directly threaten academic values but do link the university to companies heavily engaged in activities that are unjust or injurious to human welfare. Such issues arise most often in the acquisition of stock. Thus many universities refuse to buy the shares of South African corporations or to invest in companies that manufacture cigarettes.

Although such policies seem enlightened, they raise more troublesome problems than might appear on first glance. There is an elusive quality to arguments opposing an association between the university and organizations that engage in questionable practices. One has to ask what kinds of associations raise ethical problems, and for what reasons. From this perspective, the mere decision to acquire shares or purchase goods does not represent an affirmation of all the policies and practices of the companies involved any more than the hiring of a professor implies support for his political views or his private behavior. Certainly, the university does not intend to make such an affirmation nor can it be held to have done so without saddling the institution with impossible administrative burdens. Moreover, it is often unclear just what a company has done that should be considered unethical. For example, however much one may deplore apartheid, South African mining companies provide a source of livelihood essential to the welfare of black employees. As a result, one cannot easily condemn their very existence. Granted, their labor policies are discriminatory and unjust, but even so, the fault may lie predominantly with the government that imposed the apartheid system rather than with the firms that have to operate within this framework. Similarly, it is not self-evident that a company has done wrong to manufacture cigarettes for the use of those who choose to smoke despite the dangers to their health and well-being.

To avoid these difficulties, a university may seek to justify its policies on a different ground. It may refrain from finding fault with individual companies but simply decide that it does not wish to profit from activities that it considers to be dangerous or wrong. Without presuming to pass judgment on a particular management, it may conclude that it will not receive dividends attributable to the apartheid system or share in the profits derived from activities, such as smoking, that are injurious to human health.

Institutions that decide to adhere to standards of this kind must limit such restrictions carefully or they will soon become unnecessarily burdensome. It is one thing to avoid holding stock in firms selling products that are inherently dangerous to health or safety. But it is quite another matter to refrain from investing in the countless products that are generally safe yet susceptible to misuse by particular consumers. Thus a university may refuse to buy tobacco stocks, but it will probably stop short of barring investments in companies that produce alcoholic beverages, since the consumption of these beverages is not necessarily wrong or harmful even though a minority may regrettably drink to excess.

It is likewise doubtful whether institutions should refuse to hold the shares of a company merely because they disapprove of particular practices or policies that do not contribute significantly to the dividends paid by the firm. Many American companies do business in South Africa, but such operations normally account for only a tiny portion of their overall profits. Similarly, a firm may allegedly engage in unfair labor practices, but it is usually impossible to determine whether such activities are responsible to any appreciable extent for the dividends paid to the shareholders.[1] No academic institution could attempt to eradicate these faint traces of "tainted money" without assuming impossible burdens. To this limited extent, as with decisions to accept gifts, the university must join Shaw's clergyman and "either share the world's guilt or go to another planet."

Cases involving the purchase of stock have no direct or tangible effect on those who live and work in universities. For this reason, unless a company is engaged in practices that give rise to wide political controversy, such decisions rarely attract much notice, let alone provoke a serious dispute. But other types of purchases or commercial dealings can touch the lives of students and faculty in more direct and controversial ways. For example, what if Catholics objected to the university purchasing abortion services for its students from a neighboring clinic? Suppose that vegetarians pro-

---

1. Similar considerations generally apply in cases where the university purchases goods from a firm alleged to be keeping out a union by threats and intimidation. Its prices may be somewhat below those of many unionized competitors. Even so, it will often pay lower wages than some of its competitors, but not others. Its lower prices may be primarily attributable to lower wages, but they may also be the result of greater efficiency or lesser transportation costs. The company may have kept the union out by unfair means, but this is rarely clear, and management will often claim that the union has resorted to dubious practices of its own. It is even conceivable that the employees prefer somewhat lower wages in order to maximize their employment opportunities and avoid paying union dues. It seems unreasonable to expect any university to attempt to investigate matters of this kind in order to avoid all risk of profiting even to a small degree from the reprehensible practices of its suppliers.

tested against serving meat in the dining hall or that blacks or women tried to block the showing of a film on campus because they consider it racist or sexist in character.

Protests of this kind could undoubtedly give rise to serious disagreement. Feminists, blacks, Right-to-Life advocates, and even vegetarians can all feel passionately about such issues. Yet many thoughtful people who dislike cruelty and condemn murder are quite prepared to eat meat or defend a woman's right to have an abortion. And even though students may unite in opposing sexism and racism, many will feel that they can attend *Deep Throat* or *Birth of a Nation* and still not compromise their beliefs.

In almost all situations of this kind, universities can find a way to respect the personal convictions of everyone concerned. Students opposed to abortion can be offered refunds to make sure that they are not forced to contribute to practices they consider immoral. Those who disapprove of *Deep Throat* do not have to attend, while persons who object to eating meat can be given vegetarian dishes so that they will suffer no inconvenience in abiding by their principles.

It seems far better to use such procedures than to insist on imposing a blanket prohibition to resolve the controversy. As in debates about nuclear power, arguments over abortion and eating meat are bound to be highly controversial, and the prospects of reaching agreement through reasoned discussion seem exceedingly small. Whichever group loses the debate will feel aggrieved by a ruling that subjects its members to an orthodoxy they do not share, especially on a delicate matter of individual conscience. If the ruling actually limits their opportunities to eat meat or seek an abortion, the outrage will be greater still. And if the university should impose a ban to prevent the showing of a film or the hearing of a lecture, it will find itself in the awkward position of trying to explain how it could resort to censorship in a community dedicated to the principles of free speech.

In light of these problems, what is to be gained by insisting on a uniform institutional policy in cases of this kind? Perhaps some committed students will feel strongly enough to insist that *their* university should refrain from practices that *they* believe to be immoral. Nevertheless, so long as these students need not participate themselves in the practices they oppose, their claim seems insubstantial and out of keeping with the nature of an academic institution. Universities must fix uniform rules to maintain the safety and privacy of individuals and to protect other tangible interests that should be respected in a civilized community. The administration may also take a firm position in controversial cases where only a single decision can be reached. After all, there can be only one academic calendar, only one choice of a commencement speaker, only one official position on a shareholder resolution. Finally, a faculty may establish rules in matters of educational policy by setting certain curricular requirements instead of allowing students to choose at will from a wholly elective curriculum. To this extent, faculties exercise a limited authority that reflects their greater experience in matters of education. But even in shaping the curriculum, most faculties give ample scope for individual choice and fix only a few minimum requirements. Moreover, faculty members do not manipulate the curriculum or use the classroom to force their opinions on students where matters of personal belief are concerned. Instead, universities are communities designed to encourage their members to pursue their own private search for appropriate values. It would be contrary to this essential spirit of freedom and tolerance for an administration to impinge upon the lives of its members by setting uniform rules in widely disputed questions of moral or political conviction.

This philosophy was put to a severe test during the Vietnam War when massive protests erupted on many campuses against the ROTC program. After repeated demonstrations, several universities agreed to drop ROTC altogether even though the program was obviously desired by a minority of students and did not inflict any demonstrable harm on the majority. Looking back, one can easily discern the motives of the protest leaders. Committed to help end the conflict, student activists searched for any issue that offered an occasion to demonstrate against Washington and dramatize the domestic opposition to the war. Much harder to explain, however, are the view of faculty members who voted to end ROTC, for many of the same professors were quite unwilling to support official university statements against the war.

Apparently, the point that ultimately told on many faculty members was the argument that ROTC programs utilized university facilities and received official administrative support. To this extent, sponsoring institutions could be said to help the military and even to support the Vietnam War itself. On reflection, however, such reasoning is not particularly convincing. In applying academic freedom to scientific research, the prevailing view in universities has been that an administration should not halt the work of a scientist on moral or ideological grounds merely because the institution has contributed essential and expensive facilities and services to support the research. Similar arguments could have been used in behalf of ROTC, especially since any support provided by the university was far outweighed by the benefits received by the institution from the scholarship aid that the government supplied to student participants. Nevertheless, the same argument did not prevail, perhaps because the professors involved did not engage in military drills and hence had less at stake in preserving that option.

In the case of ROTC, of course, one can argue that a lesser freedom was at issue—the freedom of students to participate in military training rather than the right of professors to pursue the truth. But it is still not clear why the majority was permitted to impose its views on the minority who wished to continue in the program. Once again, opponents of ROTC could argue that they had a right to see to it that *their* university did not support an immoral war. To accept this claim, however, would be to lay the groundwork for imposing orthodoxies in all sorts of analogous cases involving deep moral differences that divide the community. Moreover, the argument misrepresents what the institution is actually doing by maintaining an ROTC program. No sensible person would claim that the university is officially committed to smoking merely because it makes ashtrays available in student lounges. Nor should anyone insist that the institution endorses the killing of animals because it serves meat in its dining halls (or, conversely, that it supports vegetarianism because it goes to considerable lengths to provide added vegetable dishes). In these instances, the university seeks to maximize the freedom of its students to make their own choices in disputed matters of personal belief and avoids laying down a single mandatory rule. It is hard to perceive any valid reason why the same policy did not prevail in the case of ROTC.[2]

Bringing Pressure to Bear on Others

The situations just described do not often occur. More common are proposals asking universities to divest their stock or participate in boycotts to combat specific corporate practices that seem unjust. During the 1970s, for example, students urged their institutions to stop buying goods from Gallo Wines because of its refusal to bargain with the United Farm Workers' Union, to stop buying towels from J. P. Stevens because of its coercive antiunion tactics, to avoid purchasing Nestlé products because of the company's marketing practices in distributing infant formula in the Third World. Other campus groups mounted campaigns to force trustees to sell the stock of American companies manufacturing antipersonnel weapons for use in Vietnam. These efforts did not come about through a concern simply to avoid association with particular firms. Instead, activists favor boycotts and divestment chiefly as a means of applying pressure to change corporate behavior. Boycotts often exert such leverage by causing the companies involved to lose sales and profits. Selling stock will rarely inflict comparable losses, since universities do not hold enough shares in any firm to depress the market price. But public divestiture, like boycotts, may put pressure on a company by generating unfavorable publicity, especially if the action is taken by a large, visible organization such as a major university.

2. Of course, there is no compelling reason why a university should be obliged to commence an ROTC program in the first instance any more than it should be obliged to start any extracurricular program. The problem arises when a program already in existence is terminated on political grounds. I should also make clear that nothing said in the text should imply disagreement with the decision of several universities to deny *credit* for ROTC courses taught by military personnel. It was a mistake ever to offer credit in the first place, since the faculty should not delegate power to give approved courses to an outside agency that is not under its control or to instructors who are not selected in accordance with normal academic procedures. Still, denying credit is one thing and banishing ROTC altogether is quite another.

BURDENS ON THE UNIVERSITY   If a university engaged in campaigns of this kind, it would quickly encounter a number of serious practical problems. In order to proceed in a fair and principled manner, the administration would have to respond to each demand for boycott or divestiture by a careful investigation of the facts, allowing each company a decent opportunity to respond to the charges against it. This task would not be trivial. In the Nestlé case, for example, opponents claimed that corporate salespersons improperly urged mothers in Third World villages to use infant formula without sufficient warning of the health hazards involved. The company vigorously disagreed. Although many facts about this dispute have come to light in recent years, a university would have been hard pressed when the controversy first arose to determine what was actually taking place in these remote areas of the world. Moreover, a conscientious administration could not simply respond to activist demands to take action against particular firms. As I noted in considering efforts to initiate stockholder resolutions, a university would also have to monitor the actions of other suppliers and companies in its portfolio to ensure that its standards were applied in a consistent manner. The cumulative burdens of embarking on this policy could be extremely onerous.

Boycotts and divestiture can also expose a university to financial losses. These burdens may not amount to much in the case of a boycott, since the administration will usually be able to switch to an alternative product of roughly equivalent price and quality. In some instances, however, the costs will mount significantly and may even become prohibitive. What could a university do, for example, if it received an urgent demand to stop doing business with the telephone company or the local electric utility? Sales of stock can also impose costs, since a university must pay brokerage fees on such transactions and bear the opportunity costs of being kept from investing in particular firms. These burdens may be small if an institution merely liquidates its shares in a single company. But it is hard to imagine any principled standard for divestment that would not expose the university to the risk of selling stock in a number of corporations, thus creating a risk of substantial financial losses. For example, a decision to sell the shares of any firm doing business in South Africa would entail a total cost that has been estimated in the millions of dollars per year by each of several large private universities.

The prospect of significant losses does not merely create practical problems; it raises troublesome questions of principle as well. We can all agree that an educational institution should not inflict harm on others merely to fatten its coffers. But it is a very different matter for trustees to use institutional funds to help redress an injustice in the outside world for which the university is not directly responsible. As previously mentioned, the resources of the institution have been given in trust for educational purposes and not for political and social causes, however worthy they may be. An administration would surely violate that trust by giving university funds to black nationalist organizations to help them fight against apartheid. It is far from clear why the same would not be true of an attempt to accomplish a similar result indirectly by selling large amounts of corporate stock.

Beyond these legal inhibitions, universities could also endanger their independence by moving aggressively to boycott and divest in order to bring pressure to bear on corporate executives. It is one thing to vote one's stock in the manner expressly provided by law and quite another to search for novel ways to generate publicity and exert economic leverage in an effort to influence the behavior of others. As I have already observed, society respects the autonomy of academic institutions because it assumes that they will devote themselves to the academic tasks that they were established to pursue. This does not mean that universities should refrain from trying to influence the outside world. It does mean that they should exert an influence by fostering the reasoned expression of ideas and arguments put forward by their individual members and not by taking institutional steps to inflict sanctions on others. Universities that violate this social compact do so at their peril. They cannot expect to remain free from interference if they insist on using their economic leverage in an effort to impose their own standards on the behavior of other organizations.

THE PRACTICAL RESULTS OF DIVESTMENT   In the face of all these problems, one must ask what universities can hope to accomplish by resorting to such tactics. This question is particularly troublesome in the case of divesting stock. As previously mentioned, no institution can expect to place direct commercial pressure on a company by undertaking to sell its shares. At best, divestment may be unusual enough to attract temporary publicity that will call attention to the disputed practices of the firms involved. Like official political statements, however, the news value of divestment is a rapidly wasting asset. The first time that Harvard or Stanford sells its stock in General Motors or Texaco, the newspapers will take notice; the tenth or twentieth sale will not even appear on the back pages. And even on the first occasion, corporate executives will undoubtedly be resilient enough not to allow a few newspaper articles to push them into actions they consider harmful to their firms.

To be sure, if the financial stakes are small and the business practices under dispute seem questionable, publicity may goad executives into taking remedial action. But there are other ways of persuading a management to respond in this fashion. In particular, activist groups can readily take steps to place a resolution on the corporation ballot and have their views communicated to other stockholders at the company's expense. The use of shareholder resolutions has several advantages over selling stock. Divestment does not require the management to defend its position in a public forum. In addition, once the stock is sold, the shareholder loses all influence with the company. If every socially concerned investor proceeded in this fashion, all shares would soon be in the hands of those who care very little about the ethical standards of corporate behavior. It is hard to believe that this result would further the cause of social responsibility.

Despite these arguments, one still hears students or faculty members speaking as if divestment were the strongest available sanction to force corporations to change their ways. And yet, business executives seem to *prefer* that protesting shareholders sell their stock, rather than continue to present resolutions and force management to respond to their concerns. This sentiment is reflected in the so-called Wall Street Rule, which holds that dissenting shareholders should not try to reform the company but should simply get rid of their holdings. Even the more experienced proponents of corporate responsibility have questioned the effectiveness of selling stock. As one church representative declared in 1972, shareholders "may be able to create more pressure by running an on-going campaign . . . instead of selling stock. That has been the logic up to now. This creates much more pressure on a company than divestment."[3] Over the past decade, the record seems to support that conclusion. Shareholder resolutions have often led to changes in company policy. There is no evidence that divestment has had a comparable effect. In these circumstances, it is all the more difficult to expect universities to incur the burdens and costs of selling their stock in an effort to improve corporate behavior.

We can bring these observations into sharper focus by briefly reviewing the strong campaign that students have mounted on many campuses to persuade universities to sell their shares in American companies doing business in South Africa. Advocates of this policy hope that divestment will lead corporations to abandon their South African operations. Those who take this position presumably know that a university cannot exert much direct leverage on corporations by simply selling stock. Nevertheless, they believe that divestment will result in widespread publicity, lead to other acts of protest, and help create a climate of moral indignation that may eventually force such companies to withdraw. According to this argument, the departure of American firms will help overcome apartheid by forcing the government to change its policies, or by provoking massive unemployment and internal strife, or at least by removing economic interests that inhibit Washington from imposing effective sanctions on the Afrikaner regime. In this way, divestment may set in motion a chain of events that will ultimately help destroy a flagrant system of injustice and oppression.

A careful review of these arguments suggests that a strong case for divestment can be made only if *all* the following propositions are likely to be true.

1. The withdrawal of American companies will impose pressures on the South African government that will help materially to overcome apartheid.

2. Corporate withdrawal will contribute more to the defeat of

3. Testimony of Tom Smith before the House of Representatives Subcommittee on Africa of the Committee on Foreign Affairs, *U.S. Business Involvement in Southern Africa, Part I*, 92nd Cong., 1st sess., 1972, pp. 206–207.

apartheid than an effort on the part of American companies to improve the wages, employment opportunities, and social conditions of black workers.

3. Selling university stock is likely to succeed, directly or indirectly, in causing many companies to leave South Africa. (If this is not true, it will be difficult to justify the heavy costs and other disadvantages of divestiture.)

4. Divestment is a substantially more effective way of inducing companies to withdraw than voting on shareholder resolutions.

In reality, every one of these propositions is highly doubtful, and the possibility that *all* of them are valid seems extraordinarily slight. The hope that selling stock can set off a chain of events that will somehow force American companies out of South Africa seems highly remote, to say the least, and it is far from clear that the prospects of achieving this result are any better through divestiture than by voting corporate shares. Moreover, the departure of American corporations would probably have no effect on apartheid, because their operations would presumably be taken over by local businesses or foreign investors and because there are many factors other than American investments that affect our government's policy toward South Africa. In the unlikely event that withdrawal did result in large-scale unemployment and recession, the further question arises whether such privations would provoke a rebellion against the Afrikaner regime and what the consequences of such an uprising would be. Black South Africans, as well as knowledgeable persons in this country, are sharply divided on whether insurrections would occur and whether they would do more to overcome apartheid than the gradual improvement of employment and social conditions. Resolving these questions calls for predictions about the future course of events in South Africa that are all but impossible to make, especially by officials of an American university far removed from the daily flow of events.

However one may feel about the preceding issues, there is also a strong possibility that the decision to incur insignificant losses by selling stock would constitute an abuse of trust by university officials. In the end, therefore, a decision to divest would open the trustees to the risk of liability while costing the university substantial sums of money and exposing it to all the burdens and hazards of using investment decisions as a weapon to influence corporate behavior. In return, the chances of producing constructive results in South Africa seem extremely small. For these reasons, a policy of systematic divestment must be regarded as an extraordinary step that would hardly receive serious consideration were it not for the passions so understandably aroused by apartheid and all its attendant injustices.

THE EFFECTS OF BOYCOTTS Boycotts differ in several respects from divestiture. For one thing, they do not merely generate publicity; they can also bring pressure to bear by hurting the sales and profits of the companies involved. This point has sometimes led activists to claim that universities cannot pretend to be neutral when their suppliers are embroiled in ethical or political controversies. In contrast to merely holding corporate stock, the act of purchasing goods helps every firm that can sell its products at a profitable price. As a result, one can argue that the administration cannot avoid making a moral choice whenever it is confronted with a request to boycott a supplier. Either it will support the firm by continuing to buy its products or it can oppose its behavior by terminating the relationship.

This argument would be stronger if a university deliberately chose its suppliers to express support for their social and economic practices. But academic officials have no such intention when they make their purchases; they simply choose the company that can provide the needed goods and services at the best available price. Granted, such transactions have the effect of adding something to the supplier's profits. Still, the university's purchases normally make up only a tiny portion of the company's sales. Hence, the support provided by the institution is typically so small that it is clearly overshadowed by the risks to academic independence, the dangers of making arbitrary decisions, and the heavy expenditure of time and effort required to devise appropriate standards and apply them consistently to all suppliers.

Most activists who urge universities to join a boycott are not much moved in any event by intricate questions of neutrality. They are simply convinced that a company is harming innocent people and that the university should stop buying its products as a positive step to help put an end to injustice. Such persons will not be persuaded by arguments based on administrative burdens or risks to academic independence. They will argue that the need for social justice overrides these concerns and that the university should join in trying to reduce the sales and profits of the offending firm to the point that it will cease its objectionable practices. Although I am not persuaded that the burdens to the university can be brushed aside so easily, it may be useful nonetheless to push the matter further and consider the merits of commercial boycotts as a means of bringing about social reform.

Many readers will be inclined to look favorably on boycotts in appropriate circumstances. We are all aware that corporations sometimes engage in irresponsible acts—whether toward their employees, their customers, or some other hapless group. We also know that the government does not always act quickly to prevent such abuses; through inadvertence or the influence of determined lobbying, public officials may fail for years to pass needed legislation or even to enforce the laws already on the books. Beyond our borders, multinational corporations may continue indefinitely to perpetrate abuses in countries with corrupt or complacent governments. In all these cases, a well-organized boycott may provide the most effective way of bringing pressure to bear on irresponsible officials. Small wonder, therefore, that consumer movements have often gained a respected place in our history and traditions. One need only remember the boycotts to desegregate lunch counters in the South to appreciate what such tactics have meant to the cause of social justice.

Despite these examples, an unmistakable ambiguity surrounds the use of private boycotts in this country. It is always tempting to join with kindred spirits to impose one's own enlightened standards of behavior on erring organizations. But it is much less edifying to consider the effects of giving similar power to every other institution and group in the society. Unfortunately, we cannot have it both ways. If universities claim the right to pressure companies to do what is morally right, we must also expect that other groups will likewise feel free to turn the screw in behalf of standards that *they* consider important and correct. The results will not necessarily be to our liking. The movie companies that blacklisted employees suspected of Communist activities may have acted out of patriotic conviction, but few reasonable people would approve of the results, let alone be confident that scrupulous fairness was observed in finding the facts. Women's groups are rightly concerned with eradicating sex discrimination, but one can sympathize with their cause and still be troubled by the interests of innocent bystanders—such as the hotel owners who are boycotted by a professional association because they happen to do business in states that have not enacted the Equal Rights Amendment.

Faced with this dilemma, we are on firmest ground in supporting the right of private individuals to join a genuine consumer boycott. Such movements draw upon the basic freedom of each person to decide whether or not to buy a particular product. They are also hard enough to organize that they will generally succeed only in response to some real injustice that is widely felt in the community. Hence, the risk of abuse is minimized while the interests of individual liberty are clearly present.

Much greater dangers arise when large organizations and institutions decide not to deal with companies or individuals of whom they disapprove. Because large organizations enjoy more market leverage than individual consumers, the right to boycott can confer power on a relatively small group of influential people to supersede the government and impose standards of conduct on those too weak to resist. The prospects are not reassuring. Those who participate in such boycotts are not subject to the legal checks and balances normally imposed on public officials. Their conduct is not accountable to the public will, nor are they required to hold hearings, gather evidence, or observe any other procedural safeguards before deciding whether to bring their market power to bear on an offending party.

All sorts of troubling possibilities come to mind in thinking about a world where organizations were free to initiate boycotts. Enterprising civil rights leaders might persuade foundations to agree to withhold all grants from universities that failed to achieve specified goals in admitting minority students or hiring women professors. Libertarian groups might induce corporations not to purchase goods from firms located in states with particularly stringent environmental or consumer legislation. Fundamentalist leaders might refuse to purchase time from television stations carrying programs that allegedly promote violence, sex, or atheistic and immoral behavior. One may approve or disapprove of these objectives. But few of us would feel comfortable at the thought of encouraging private organizations to use their market power to impose such views on others.

These concerns apply to academic institutions just as they do to other private organizations. When political issues are involved, universities can be just as susceptible to passions, prejudices, and errors of judgment as many other kinds of institutions. Those who dispute this point should pause and consider where the logic of their position will lead them. Suppose we were to agree with the activists that universities help every company from which they purchase goods and thus cannot be neutral when their suppliers become embroiled in controversy. If universities accepted this responsibility and began to engage in boycotts, why should they not assume the same obligation to police the off-campus behavior of their professors, their employees, their students, and everyone else who is subsidized or supported in some fashion by the institution? If a university must sever its relationship with a firm that has treated its employees unfairly, why should it not suspend an assistant dean who has mistreated his wife or evicted his aged tenants? Such action might right some wrongs and forestall some indefensible behavior, just as a commercial boycott may sometimes support a worthy cause. Even so, few of us would want a university to assume such broad responsibilities over the private lives of its members; the consequences are too unsettling, the risks of error and injustice too severe. Yet similar dangers will arise whenever universities and other large organizations begin to use their economic leverage to influence the behavior of suppliers.

In short, boycotts present a troublesome dilemma. In some instances, they may provide a valuable force to correct injustices that would otherwise persist by virtue of the delays, the oversights, the inevitable mistakes and abuses that characterize even the most enlightened governments. In other cases, however, boycotts will cause injustices of their own through the errors and prejudices of strong-willed people who act without the normal restraints that society places on public officials. In these circumstances, is it wise to urge organizations to resort to boycotts whenever they believe that their cause is just? Or should we shrink from encouraging the exercise of private power that is not accountable to the public will?

One way out of this predicament might be to encourage organizations to join in boycotts for worthy ends and rely upon the courts to correct any errors and injustices that happened to result. But courts have not clearly accepted this responsibility nor are they particularly well equipped to resolve these issues. Such a task would require judges to pass on all manner of vexing political and moral questions with very little guidance from the legislature. Moreover, courts are a clumsy instrument to deal effectively with matters of this kind. Either they must act quickly and issue an injunction, with the inevitable risks of haste and error, or they must wait and assess damages years after the harm is done. Neither alternative is fully adequate to do justice.

These difficulties help to explain the ambivalence that the law has traditionally displayed toward boycotts aimed at social or political ends. At times, courts have suggested that such efforts are legitimate when the ends pursued are worthy. On other occasions, judges have condemned boycotts in terms so sweeping as to permit virtually no exception. Such inconsistencies reflect uncertainties that seem to be widely shared throughout our society.

In considering how the university should respond to this dilemma, one should remember that those who object to the actions of particular corporations have other ways of pressing their grievances. They may introduce shareholder resolutions by purchasing stock or by persuading another shareholder to act on their behalf. They may resort to various forms of publicity to bring their case to the attention of the public. They may petition Congress to hold hearings or consider appropriate legislation. They may challenge the company by initiating a lawsuit or by persuading some government agency to intervene. Students and faculty members are often adept at pressing their case in these various ways.

Within the campus community itself, individuals will usually have an opportunity to make their sentiments felt simply by refusing to eat, drink, or use the products sold by firms to which they take exception. Indeed, as noted earlier, a university should do its best to make alternatives available whenever significant numbers of students and faculty object to consuming particular goods or using specific services.[4] If sufficient numbers of people decide to refrain from using a controversial product, they may make a more eloquent statement than they could convey by pressing their university to join a boycott. At the same time, they will neither force their opinions on others nor require the institution to assume the burdens and risks of agreeing to boycott questionable companies.

These arguments ultimately seem decisive. Clearly, any policy that encourages the university to engage in boycotts (or sales of stock) will have grave disadvantages for the institution. There will be complex investigations, internal controversies, and the ever-present risk of compromising the university's critical stake in remaining free from outside interference. In view of all these drawbacks, universities have every reason not to engage in boycotts unless there is a compelling social need. As I have observed, however, it is hard to make a convincing argument on that ground. From the standpoint of society, institutional boycotts, if not actually undesirable, are at least of questionable virtue as an instrument of social change. For members of the community, there are alternative ways in which to press for social reform. In these circumstances, as in the issuing of political statements, the wiser course for universities would be to refuse to engage officially in such campaigns while leaving individuals free to pursue their objectives through other means.

4. There are thoughtful people who believe that students and other concerned individuals should not be offered alternatives because they should learn that they must pay some personal price for their convictions. But it is one thing to approve of such sacrifices and quite another to impose them on others. It seems especially awkward for a university to compel students to live in dormitories and eat in dining halls and then assure them that they are perfectly free not to use the sheets produced by J. P. Stevens or drink the beverages supplied by the Nestlé Corporation.

Conclusion

I END THIS INQUIRY by returning to a question asked at the very beginning. How valid is the concept of institutional neutrality in an era when universities have grown so deeply involved in the life and affairs of the society? In my opinion, the term does retain a limited value. It still helps remind us that official orthodoxies may inhibit free expression and that collective efforts to induce political change will invite retaliation from the outside world. On balance, however, the concept of neutrality has brought more confusion than clarity because it is so easily taken to mean that universities should seek to carry on with no institutional values or moral commitments. If this study accomplishes nothing else, it should at least disabuse the reader of that impression. In reality, universities must constantly address moral issues and ethical responsibilities in all their relations with the outside world.

To begin with, academic institutions must observe the basic obligations required of every participant in a civilized society. They must fulfill their contractual commitments. They must refrain from acts of deception. They must abide by the requirements of the law. More broadly still, they should endeavor not to inflict unjustified harm on others.

The last obligation does not mean that universities must avoid all actions that cause suffering or financial loss. On the contrary, certain forms of behavior in a university are generally considered important enough to justify the damage they inflict on others. For example, academic institutions bear no collective responsibility for the views expressed by their professors despite the harm that such opinions occasionally cause, for our society is committed to the belief that we will make greater progress in the long run by avoiding censorship and promoting a free exchange of ideas. In addition, as everyone knows, students receive failing grades, applicants are regularly refused admission, junior faculty are denied promotion and are forced to leave. All these decisions inflict pain. Even so, as long as the decisions are arrived at fairly and for valid academic reasons, they are considered proper and are accepted as such by those who enter into relationships with universities as faculty members, students, or applicants for admission.

And yet, however much importance one attaches to teaching and research, an academic institution is not justified in damaging the legally recognized interests of people who have not consented to assume such risks. A university does not have the right to allow experiments using methods that expose people to significant danger of physical harm without their consent, nor can it build new classrooms that destroy the recognized property interests of abutting homeowners. In such cases, the institution must either halt the activity in question or pay for any damage inflicted on others. Moreover, obligations to respect the rights of others may exist even in the absence of legal safeguards. Although an admissions committee may make a special effort to enroll significant numbers of black and Hispanic students, it must frame its policies in a manner that takes account of the legitimate interests of other applicants. Similarly, a university that engages in technical assistance projects abroad should do its best not to damage the welfare of others even though no statute exists to compensate such persons for any harm they suffer.

Within this framework of basic social obligations, universities also have obligations to uphold certain academic values that are widely considered essential to the progress of learning and discovery. These responsibilities include a commitment to maintain an atmosphere within the institution that leaves every member as free as possible to learn, to search for knowledge, and to express his own individual beliefs and opinions. In addition, they involve an obligation on the part of university leaders to do everything possible to protect the institution from outside pressures that would restrain the expression of individual views or interfere with decisions on academic issues such as the admission of students, the selection of faculty, and the shaping of the curriculum. No university can possibly be "neutral" about its commitments to academic freedom and autonomy. On the contrary, these values are so central to the mission of the institution that they must not be compromised save for the most compelling reasons.

Despite the importance of these principles, many of the moral questions that have troubled the university most deeply have not involved attacks upon its academic values or claims that it has inflicted unwarranted harm on others. In recent years, the sharpest conflicts have come when activists have urged the institution to respond in some collective fashion to social needs and problems that are not of its own making—problems such as war, apartheid, poverty, or other forms of social injustice.

When claims of this sort are made, the concept of neutrality is again of doubtful value, for virtually any academic program that responds to social needs requires some collective judgment of a normative kind. In theory, of course, one could escape such judgments by providing a completely unstructured curriculum under which professors could teach what they wished and students could choose a program of their own making. But a university constructed on these lines would be of little use to its students and would command scant support from the society on which it must depend for its existence. Academic institutions vary widely in the structure they impose on their curricula and programs. But if the university is to have any coherence, it must make at least *some* collective decisions concerning which programs to establish, which courses to prescribe, which students to admit. And in the end, the institution can hardly make such choices without taking account of the values and concerns of the society.

There is no reason for universities to feel uncomfortable in taking account of society's needs; in fact, they have a clear obligation to do so. After all, institutions of higher learning have a near monopoly of vital intellectual resources in the society. They give credentials that are essential for access to many desirable careers; they perform the bulk of basic research in the country; they command a large portion of the supply of certain forms of valued expertise. Moreover, much of the funding they require for their very existence comes directly or indirectly from the taxpaying public. In these circumstances, it is only fair that universities seek to use their resources in a manner that is reasonably responsive to social needs. The problem is to decide what kind of response is appropriate.

When universities confront this issue, their leaders must consider at least three questions. First of all, how important is the social need and how likely is it that the university will succeed in doing something about it? Obviously, no institution should feel obliged to commit its energies and resources to a problem that is trivial, or a cause that is hopeless, or a course of action that other agencies and organizations can pursue with greater skill. In addition, educators have to ask whether the action requested will interfere with the freedom of individual professors and students, and especially with their freedom to form their own beliefs and express their opinions as they choose. When conflicts of this kind occur, the university will surely wish to look for some other way of responding that will meet society's needs in a less intrusive fashion. If no such alternative is available, the project may even have to be abandoned unless the reasons for proceeding are compelling. The final issue to consider is the effect that the desired initiative will have on the operation of the university as a whole. Attempts to address a moral problem or a social need may burden the institution in several ways. They will often require expenditures of money that must be raised from outside sources or diverted from existing activities and programs. They may demand significant amounts of time from administrators and professors. They may expose the university to pressures from society that threaten its autonomy or hamper its existing activities. Since universities serve important public functions, all these burdens represent costs that must be carefully considered in deciding how the institution should define its social responsibilities.

As I have tried to point out, these considerations can apply to specific situations in so many different ways that the proper response will often depend upon the particular circumstances of each case. Nevertheless, one broad generalization does emerge from this study. Universities have an important responsibility to address social needs through their normal academic functions, such as teaching programs, research, or technical assistance. They should respond to racial inequality by taking special pains to enroll minority students; they should contribute to economic progress by helping to translate their discoveries into useful products; they should make their specialized knowledge available to assist the development of poorer nations. Under careful administration, all these initiatives are consistent with the proper activities of an academic institution. In contrast, however, it is much harder to justify the use of nonacademic methods such as divesting stock, boycotting suppliers, or issuing formal institutional statements on political issues.

Several reasons help to account for this general rule. For one thing, the university's social obligations are much stronger in employing its resources for teaching and research than they are in acting as a purchaser or investor. Society can legitimately ask that universities be responsive to social needs in return for the public support they receive. But what society has paid for and what it expects in return are educational programs and new discoveries rather than boycotts or political campaigns. Similarly, though universities have social responsibilities that flow from their near-monopoly of scarce and valuable resources in the society, these resources are intellectual and academic rather than economic or political in nature. Thus universities may control access to legal or medical careers, and this control may carry certain social responsibilities. But academic institutions have no comparable power or responsibility when it comes to owning stock or buying food for their dining halls.

Furthermore, when universities purchase goods, or sell their corporate stock, or issue political statements, they must take explicit institutional positions on matters that are usually controversial and highly political. Such actions may not merely prove divisive but actually inhibit freedom of expression on the part of at least the more vulnerable members of the community. In contrast, though efforts to mount new academic programs to respond to social needs may demand some form of collective action, the university's response will rarely entail explicit political commitments that impinge in obvious ways on the intellectual freedom of the community. A decision to found a business school may imply support for the free-enterprise system, but few critics would go so far as to suggest that professors with collectivist views will feel inhibited as a result.

Finally, universities that go beyond their normal educational functions in an effort to influence events are likely to jeopardize their autonomy in academic affairs. After decades of controversy, we have managed to achieve a wide understanding in society that professors should have great freedom to express their views and that faculties should enjoy broad discretion to make decisions about such vital matters as appointments, curricula, and admissions. Universities can hardly expect to retain this freedom from social pressure if they insist on exerting their leverage as purchasers or stockholders to influence the behavior of other institutions in society. Since autonomy in academic matters is vital to the life of the university and to the quality of teaching and research, it is only prudent to refrain from pressuring other institutions save in limited cases, such as voting stock, where the government has clearly invited shareholders to express their views.

This policy may seem excessively cautious and self-protective, exhibiting too little concern for the struggles and sufferings of others. In the long run, however, universities will doubtless accomplish more by concentrating on their traditional functions. As a practical matter, faculties are much more likely to do good work that has real value for others by expressing themselves through teaching and research. An academic institution has no special advantage in making collective political judgments on controversial issues, and its power as a shareholder, purchaser, or institutional critic is so slight that efforts to influence society by these means will usually have little chance of achieving any results whatsoever.

For all these reasons, universities are justifiably reluctant to employ nonacademic methods to address social problems. In some cases, to be sure, they will sell their stock or refuse a gift, or cease doing business with a firm whose behavior they find offensive. But they will normally take such action not to force a company or a government to change its ways but to avoid compromising their own integrity by profiting from the immoral practices of others or helping them to achieve unworthy ends.

The unwillingness to divest, to boycott, to issue pronouncements, or to take other forms of political action against injustice in the world has undoubtedly disappointed many students and professors who are deeply troubled by social evils. In a time of disillusion over the quality of government and the integrity of public officials, those most deeply committed to reform often turn to unorthodox methods of achieving social change. Students and professors of this persuasion understandably hope that universities will join these efforts and are keenly disappointed when they refuse to do so. To such individuals, universities seem distressingly complacent. Worse yet, they appear to be grossly hypocritical in professing humane ideals while refusing to risk their endowments or endanger their reputations even to fight the most obvious injustices.

Confronted with these frustrations, many educators are distressed in turn to see such anger directed at the university and its leaders. Why should presidents and deans be pilloried for refusing to act in ways that are likely to prove costly to the institution without accomplishing anything of practical value? After all, only a romantic could believe that divesting stock will force American companies out of South Africa or think that the departure of such firms will topple the apartheid system. Only a dreamer could suppose that initiating shareholder resolutions will cause a company to stop building nuclear plants. Why, then, have many students invested so much of their time trying to push their universities into taking such actions?

In pondering these questions, it will not do simply to dismiss these student activists as excited adolescents or as sinister radicals. Such descriptions hardly do justice to most of the individuals involved. For them, the moving forces lie much deeper. Students today have grown up in circumstances very different from those of earlier periods. They have enjoyed more security, greater opportunities, higher standards of living. But they have also never known the ready sense of optimism, the instinctive belief in continuing social progress, the end of legally sanctioned segregation, the triumph of World War II, the decline of anti-Semitism, and the other experiences that shaped the American dream for preceding generations. After all, today's students first began to notice the outside world at the height of the Vietnam War. Since then, they have watched a long succession of dispiriting events—Watergate, recession, economic stagnation, factional politics, and continuous charges of incompetence directed at the highest government officials. Unlike their predecessors, they have known no heroes in public life. Since the assassinations of John and Robert Kennedy and Martin Luther King, not a single figure has emerged in the United States who can challenge and inspire a younger generation.

Living in this environment, many students have grown inured to the problems of the world and have become preoccupied with their own careers, their friends, their personal needs and experiences. But others retain a strong concern about society with all its problems and injustices. To them, it is important to find a way of doing something tangible to alleviate suffering and overcome injustice. Yet this is no easy matter for students living in a university. In these unlikely surroundings, how can one justify one's privileged position by proving to others, and to oneself most of all, that one truly cares about the sufferings of others and has not succumbed to the selfish preoccupations of ambition and career?

Students who struggle with this dilemma are often impelled to transmute the evils of the world into problems that they *can* get their hands on even in the sheltered atmosphere of the modern university. Thus the issue of apartheid is transformed into the task of forcing the university to sell its stock; the specter of global poverty becomes a struggle to persuade the trustees to boycott firms that market infant formula in the Third World; the problem of migrant labor emerges as a contest to persuade the campus purchasing office to stop buying nonunion lettuce. These mental processes may seem strained and impractical. And yet, to those who anxiously search for *some* way of struggling against injustice and deprivation, it is small comfort to hear that divestiture and boycotts are not only inappropriate but ineffective as well. Such messages only heighten the sense of impotence and play upon the nagging fear that there is nothing that people of good will can do to lessen the urgent problems of the world. What these students crave are not declarations of neutrality or protestations of impotence but a signal from established institutions and the adults who guide them that they also care, and care enough to make some act of sacrifice, regardless of the risks and despite the meager chances of success.

Looked at in this light, universities face a much more serious dilemma than their leaders commonly suppose. The issue is not merely whether student activists can be turned back, outmaneuvered, co-opted, or pacified. The real challenge is to discover a way in which the university can keep its proper course without discouraging its students to the point of extinguishing their fragile concern for injustice and suffering. Universities may have learned to resist efforts to lead them into ill-advised political adventures. But as the cries of protest recede from the campus, one wonders whether these lessons have been purchased at the cost of strengthening attitudes of cynicism and indifference toward the problems and injustices of the world.

Critics may reply that the university has no responsibility for the social conscience of its members and that its proper concern is with the minds and not the hearts and feelings of its students. But this is a shriveled view of education that can hardly withstand examination. For better or worse, colleges and professional schools dominate the lives of young people during a critical time in their development. These institutions may not be competent to address every human need. But surely they should help wherever they can to strengthen the nobler sentiments of their students. At the very least, they must endeavor not to create an environment that reinforces a lack of concern for others or encourages a callous indifference toward every purposive effort at reform.

The issue facing the university, then, is not whether it should trouble itself with the social concerns of its students but how it can respond in ways that support their generous instincts while fully respecting the academic values and legitimate interests of the institution. This is not a simple problem, and I can hardly pretend to offer any strikingly effective solutions. Yet there are some useful steps that a conscientious administration can take.

At the very least, presidents and deans can find time to address the important moral issues affecting the campus by setting forth as best they can the policies of the institution and the reasons and arguments that support them. Since questions of this kind are inherently controversial, official explanations will never be convincing to everyone, nor will they satisfy those who seek to use the university as an engine of political reform. Nevertheless, the willingness to issue such statements and devote great care to their preparation may help to persuade some students that the institution does have a concern for ethical norms and a desire to act on the basis of reasoned, principled arguments. If nothing else, educators who take the trouble to present their views in detail will be less likely to find themselves caught up in awkward inconsistencies or labored rationalizations that can only damage their credibility and deepen the cynicism of their students and faculty.

Those who administer universities must also try to demonstrate their concern by seizing the initiative and identifying ethical issues *before* they emerge from the pages of the campus newspaper or the demands of some community group or student faction. Despite our distaste for the violence and conflict of the late sixties, we often forget how many of the demands from that time have since been accepted and incorporated into the daily life of the university. Most academic institutions now think carefully about voting their stock, make conscientious efforts to recruit minority students, and exhibit concern for the interests of tenants and neighbors in planning institutional expansion. Only rarely did these practices begin at the initiative of the administration; in most cases, they emerged only after bitter student protest. In contrast, it is hard to think of many important ethical reponsibilities in this period that were adopted spontaneously by the typical university administration. Such a record hardly adds to the moral credibility of academic leaders or convinces students that established institutions have a genuine concern for their social responsibilities.

Another useful initiative lies in encouraging the teaching of moral reasoning and applied ethics at both the college and professional school level. I will not repeat the reasons I have given to justify these courses or restate the need to develop faculty members who can teach them adequately. I would merely add that the mere existence of such instruction will help communicate to students a sense of the importance the institution attaches to problems of moral responsibility. In my experience, alas, especially in the professional schools, the interest in having these subjects taught has often seemed much greater among the alumni than within the faculty. The message conveyed by such neglect can hardly be lost upon the students.

A further step worth considering is a greater effort to encourage programs that enable students to offer their services to those in need of help. On every campus, one can find student activities to tutor underprivileged children, provide legal services to the poor, or assist the handicapped. All too often, however, particularly at the undergraduate level, these initiatives proceed with little involvement or support on the part of the administration. And only rarely can one find a serious program to identify jobs for students who wish to work in poor communities for a summer or a year, in this country or abroad. With a little effort, the university could expand these opportunities and help more students find a practical way of assisting those less fortunate than themselves. By taking more interest in these activities, an administration might also communicate a greater sense of concern for social service while helping students gain a more lasting appreciation of the human needs and privations that persist throughout the world.

Finally, while universities must limit the range of their activities and respect the academic purposes for which they are created, they can at least be imaginative in finding appropriate ways of addressing important problems in the society. If selling stock is a questionable means for combating apartheid, surely it is possible to offer scholarships to black South Africans who are blocked from entering universities in their own nation. If the quality of government in this country does not meet our expectations, there must be opportunities to make a contribution by discovering better ways of preparing able people to perform more effectively in public life. If millions starve and millions more are ridden by disease, then clearly there are possibilities for helping interested faculty members to search for hardier crops and more effective vaccines. The opportunities are legion and can be seized without slighting the importance of pure scholarship or displacing the more traditional modes of education. It is in these ways that the American university has traditionally rendered its greatest service to the nation. The need is no less great today. Education and research may not be the most visible or heroic means of striking at the evils of society. But taken as a whole, they represent the surest way by which academic institutions can resolve the moral dilemma of continuing to enjoy the quieter pursuits of learning in a world filled with suffering and injustice. If universities pursue this course with enough energy and determination, even their angriest critics may eventually come to appreciate the full weight of their social contributions.

Index

Abortion, 131, 284

Academic freedom, 5, 6, 7; as basic academic principle, 11–12, 35–36; case for, 18–20; opposition to, 20–26; practical problems, 26–35; related to research, 185, 189–190; in international assistance programs, 199–204

Academic science, 142–148; optimum conditions for, 143–144; career opportunities for, 143, 145; equipment and facilities, 143, 145, 185; working environment, 143, 145–146; freedom of choice, 143, 146–147; quality control, 144, 147–148; morale in, 144, 148, 163; threat of technology transfer, 149–151; and social responsibility, 185–194

Accreditation: self-study for, 56n; regulation of, 57

Activists: and the multiversity, 78–84; and moral education, 125; and research, 185–194

Admission of students, 51; government intervention in, 57–58; problem of racial inequality, 91–104; preferential, 93–94, 98–100; goals of admissions officers, 94–95; grades as criterion for, 95–98

Affirmative action, 7; government intervention for, 54; in choice of students, 99; in hiring faculty, 105, 109; for students vs. faculty, 110–112

Age discrimination, 50

Agency for International Development, 196

Alumni, 85

American Anthropological Association, 21n

American Association of University Professors, 5

American Indians: admission of, 91; and preferential admissions, 100, 102; in faculty posts, 104, 108

American Jewish Congress, 256

American Sociological Association, 173

Angoff, William H., 96n

Apartheid, 306; effect of divestiture of stock on, 289–293, 305

Applied ethics: courses in, 121–124, 134–135; issue of indoctrination, 126–128; limits of reason, 128–132; qualifications of instructors, 133

Applied research. See Research

Arms Export Control Act, 178

Arnold, Matthew, 62

Ashby, Sir Eric, 65

Asian-Americans, in faculty posts, 104

Assistance programs abroad. See Technical assistance abroad

Astin, Helen H., 108n

Atomic bomb, 172, 177

Authority, in the university, 84–85

Autonomy, as an academic value, 11

Bangladesh, 210

Barzun, Jacques, 67

Dalton, James, 221n
Data Resources, Inc., 141
David, Ed, 140
Deans, power of, in university, 85–86
Decentralization, in the multiversity, 70
Declaration of 1915, 5
Defense research, government restrictions on, 178–180
Department of Defense, 189
Department of Education, 48
Department of Health and Human Services: regulation of research by, 38; position on patents, 140
Department of Health, Education, and Welfare, 52, 176
Dewey, John, 4
Diversity, limited by government regulation, 42, 50–51, 56
Divestiture of stocks, 289–293, 304–305
DNA research, 141, 164; Harvard's role in, 136, 160; fears aroused by, 169
Donors: of gifts that endanger academic values, 266–270; of "tainted" funds, 270; of restricted gifts, 277–278
Dripps, Robert D., 138n
Dworkin, Gerald, 174n

Economic productivity, 137–138, 140, 220–221
Education: government regulation of quality of, 56; European models of, 61–62; American involvement in national needs, 62–63; development of multiversity, 63; threat to standards of, 69; moral, 117–121, 308; of local residents by university, 220, 224; mixture of public and private institutions, 227–228; midcareer, 242; lobbying for, 261–265
Eisenhower, Dwight D., 37
Eliot, Charles W., 118
Emerton, Ephraim, 118
England, education in, 61
Entrepreneurial ventures: university participation in, 100–106; safeguards for, 167–168

Ethical problems: in methods of research, 186–188; in effects of new knowledge, 188–189; university vs. government, 190–192; responsibility of university on, 192–194; statements on, 307–308; prompt identification of, 308; teaching related to, 308; service programs, 308–309. *See also* Moral development of students
Ethical standards: decline of, 11, 121; new awareness of, 122–123; new efforts at teaching, 123–124; 127–128, 134–135, 308
Ethics. *See* Applied ethics; Ethical problems; Ethical standards
Europe, education in, contrasted with U.S., 74–75
Euthanasia, 130–131
Evans, Franklin R., 101n
Extraterrestrial life, 183–184
Exxon Corporation, 140, 157

Factions, university: activists, 12–13; traditionalists, 13; administrators, 13–14
Faculty: responsibility of, toward university, 5; outside role of, 6; government regulations on choice of, 38, 51; federal requirements for minorities, 104–109; preferential treatment in hiring of, 110–115; character as basis of appointment, 117–118, 122; as teachers of applied ethics, 133; relations with industry, 140–141; commercial links and appointment of, 161–162; community services of, 236, 238, 240, 241, 243; political involvement of, 248; petitions by, 252–253. *See also* Professors
Federal regulation: significance of, 38–40; justifications for, 40–41; costs of, 41–44; strategies of, 44–52; proposals for avoiding inappropriate intervention, 52–54; proposals for promoting new services, 54–55; guidelines for preventing abuse, 55–60
Federal requirements, 109; for hiring minority faculty, 104; difficul-

Institute of International Development (Harvard), 195–196
Intervention, government: avoiding inappropriate, 52–54; for promotion of new services, 54–55; preventing abuse in, 55–60
Investments: problematical, 281–283; and boycotts, 288–289; divestiture of stocks, 289–293, 304–305
Investor Responsibility Research Center, 256, 257, 258
Iran, 195, 208–209

Jackson, William, 221n
Jensen, Arthur, 29
Jevons, William Stanley, 28
Johnson, Jerald, 81, 82
Judson, Horace Freeland, 146n

Kapitza, Pyotr, 147
Keniston, Kenneth, 67n
Kennedy, John F., 305
Kennedy, Robert, 305
Kerr, Clark, 1, 63–64
Kilson, Martin, 99n
King, Martin Luther, Jr., 305
Kissinger, Henry, 17, 33–35
Krupp Foundation, 274

Ladd, Everett Carl, Jr., 21n
Law schools: teaching and research in, 72; admission of minorities to, 101; and professional ethics, 123
Lazarsfeld, Paul F., 23n
Leadership, role of, in university, 84–88
Leibniz, Gottfried Wilhelm von, 28
Leone, Robert A., 235n
Libya, 267
Lilla, Mark T., 127n
Linn, Robert L., 102n
Lipset, Seymour Martin, 21n
Lobbying, 261–265
Lovejoy, Arthur, 4
Luria, S. E., 79
Luria, Zella, 79
Lyman, Richard W., 52n

McElheny, Victor K., 147n
McGill, William, 38n

Machlup, Fritz, 252
Market forces: strengthening of, as strategy of regulation, 45–46
Massachusetts: expenditure on public education, 220; financial benefits from private universities, 220–221
Massachusetts Institute of Technology, 157
Medical schools: Congressional intervention in, 54; incentives for enlarging, 63; need for research in, 72; and teaching hospitals, 77; and professional ethics, 123
Medicine, basic research in, 138
Metzger, Walter P., 4n
Meyer, John R., 235n
Midcareer education, 242
Milton, John, 204n
Minority groups: and the university, 7–8; admission of, 38; preferential admissions, 98, 261; as role models, 112–113. *See also* Blacks; Hispanics; Women
Monsanto Corporation, 141, 157, 159–160
Moral development of students, 116–135; early approaches to, 117–121; revival of moral education, 121–124; evaluating new approaches to, 124–135
Moral difficulties in international assistance programs. *See* Technical assistance abroad
Morale, in academic science, 144, 148, 163
Morrill Act, 62
Mucha, Zofia, 220n
Multiversity: emergence of, 61–65; criticism of, 65–66; issues embodied in, 66; traditionalist critique of, 67–78; activist view of, 78–84; role of leadership in, 84–88
Municipalities. *See* Cities and towns

National Institutes of Health, 184; regulation of research by, 38; on DNA research, 169
National Science Foundation, 140, 184, 193
Nearing, Scott, 4

Please remember that this is a library book,
and that it belongs only temporarily to each
person who uses it. Be considerate. Do
not write in this, or any, library book.